The Defining Years of the Dutch East Indies,
1942–1949

The Defining Years of the Dutch East Indies, 1942–1949

Survivors' Accounts of Japanese Invasion and Enslavement of Europeans and the Revolution That Created Free Indonesia

Edited by JAN A. KRANCHER

McFarland & Company, Inc., Publishers
Jefferson, North Carolina, and London

A caricature, by an unknown fellow prisoner, of the editor's late father-in-law, Cornelis Otto Rudolph Hauber, at age 31, fashioning clogs in a POW camp in late 1942, where he was interned apart from his pregnant wife and two children following the Japanese takeover of the Dutch East Indies in March 1942. He survived working as a slave laborer on the infamous Death Railroad in Burma and was reunited in late 1945 with his family, which now included the 3½-year-old Irene Joyce Hauber, whom he had never met. She is today the wife of Jan Krancher, editor of this book.

The present work is a reprint of the library bound edition of The Defining Years of the Dutch East Indies, 1942–1949 *first published in 1996.*

LIBRARY OF CONGRESS CATALOGUING-IN-PUBLICATION DATA

Krancher, Jan A., 1939–
    The defining years of the Dutch East Indies, 1942–1949 :
survivors' accounts of Japanese invasion and enslavement of
Europeans and the revolution that created free Indonesia / Edited by
Jan A. Krancher.
        p.   cm.
    Includes index.

    ISBN-13: 978-0-7864-1707-0 softcover: 50# alkaline paper)

    1. Indonesia—History—Japanese occupation, 1942–1945—
Personal narratives, Dutch.   2. Indonesia—History—Revolution,
1945–1949—Personal narratives, Dutch.   I. Title.
DS643.5.K73   2003   959.803'092—dc20   95-51307

British Library cataloguing data are available

Cover art: Original pen-and-ink drawing supplied by Andre (Andy) A.
van Dyk, Ashfield, New South Wales, Australia (used with permission);
background image ©2003 Clipart.com

Manufactured in the United States of America

McFarland & Company, Inc., Publishers
    Box 611, Jefferson, North Carolina 28640
        www.mcfarlandpub.com

This book is dedicated to those who did not survive
the Pacific War, to those who did, and to their offspring.
May the horrors of war and its consequences and the years
of infamy in the former Dutch East Indies never be forgotten.
And may a lesson be learned from all that carnage.

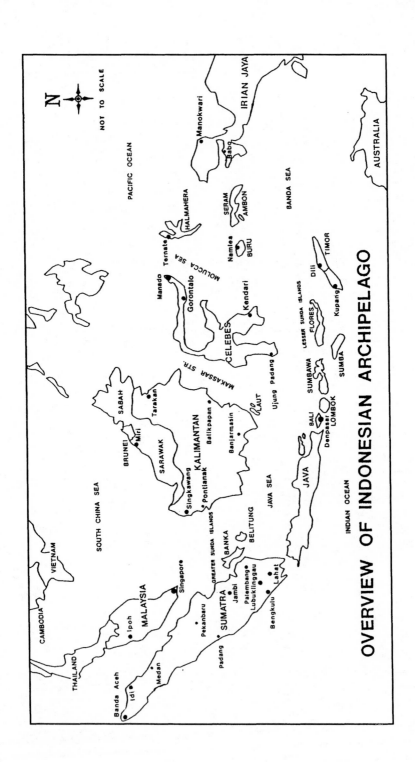

OVERVIEW OF INDONESIAN ARCHIPELAGO

CONTENTS

PREFACE

War stories rarely rise to the level of literature, but I believe the firsthand accounts collected herein make the grade. By recounting their personal experiences during this tumultuous period of history, the writers have lifted the veil ever so slightly for the reader to gain some appreciation of what took place during and after the war in this sometimes forgotten part of the world.

I was a child in Malang, East Java, during the Japanese occupation, so these accounts hold special interest for me. After the war, during the chaotic backlash against the Dutch which came to be known as the Bersiap period, I was placed in a "protection camp" with my mother and two older sisters, separated from my father who was interned in a men's camp. We all survived the war and the Indonesian independence movement, but as the stories collected herein reveal, many families were not so fortunate.

The compilation of this work was truly an international endeavor, with articles coming from Australia, Surinam, Canada, the Netherlands, England and the United States. The majority of the contributors responded to a written plea for true-to-life stories placed in two journals with worldwide distribution to Dutch and Dutch Indonesian readers. An Australian author also lent a hand by broadcasting my intentions in Australia. Some of the contributing writers found out about my call for stories by way of friends or relatives, and one story was acquired through serendipity. Its author happened to be corresponding directly with the British contributor who had earlier placed an ad in a Dutch magazine, indicating his desires to meet old war buddies in the Netherlands. His moving story reveals the hardship and deprivation experienced by the Dutch.

The contributors represent a tremendous diversity of backgrounds

1

and experiences, as the biographies at the ends of the chapters attest. They include homemakers, secretaries, medical doctors, engineers, authors in their own right, and several professors with Ph.D. degrees. Nevertheless, in their formative years they all shared the experience of a traumatic youth, adolescence or young adulthood under the Japanese yoke. Some paint a pleasant picture of their lives in the Indies before the war, but then the reader will descend with them into scenes of despair and gloom as their lives changed radically under Japanese occupation of their homeland.

The writers' parents belonged to each of the three main groups of Dutch and Dutch-Indonesian people in the Indies at that time: the plantation operators and employees; the urban business and professional classes; and the government workers, including administrative and military personnel and teachers. The latter two composed about 80 percent of the total Dutch population of the Dutch East Indies and lived principally in the larger communities. Here living conditions were excellent with fine houses, elegant clubs, a variety of entertainment facilities and an abundance of cheap and pleasant native servants. Life in the back country—on plantations, in mission centers, or at oil fields on government posts—was by contrast rather dull. The days were routine with little to do but work, and electricity, good roads, modern stores and other comforts of the cities were often lacking. Nearly all the whites in these rural areas lived in anticipation of their periodic furlough in Europe, usually triennial. They did not know then how good they had it. Their stories reveal how traumatic the transition from freedom to slavery can be.

A few words about modern Indonesia are in order here. During the formative period of the revolution in this colonial outpost, the youth of Indonesia played a decisive role. The nature of the Japanese occupation enabled them to condition themselves for the struggle for national independence and social change. Once the war ended they were faced with the problem of building national political power while at the same time pursuing a revolutionary policy. This difficulty resulted in divisiveness within both the political elite and the army.

All these events colored the whole intrarevolutionary struggle for power. In the context of the international power balance, could a successful national revolution permit a concurrent social revolution? Could a national revolution develop sufficient political thrust without a social revolution?

Several prominent leaders emerged during this period, but none was as persuasive as President Sukarno. From the day in August 1945 when he read a proclamation of independence to a small group assembled outside his Jakarta house to the day in March 1966 when he authorized General Suharto to act in his behalf, Sukarno occupied the center of the Indonesian stage. The 20 years of his preeminence were full of drama and increasing authoritarianism. But in the end, it must be acknowledged that he brought his nation into the fold of sovereign powers. His successor, Suharto, still holds sway at this writing.

I should comment briefly on the spellings of placenames and Indonesian words that appear in this book. The contributors generally wrote their accounts using the Dutch spellings that prevailed prior to Indonesian independence, but it was decided that modern spellings should be used instead in order to make the book more accessible to an audience unfamiliar with the old spellings. There was a further problem, however, in that two or more spellings may be found in current usage for some placenames (as, for example, in the case of Jogjakarta or Yogyakarta). I have made an earnest attempt, using authoritative sources, to identify and use the most accepted forms. All forms I encountered are included in the index with cross-references to the spelling used in the text.

Similarly, in the case of placenames that have changed altogether (e.g., Batavia is now Jakarta and the island known as Borneo at the time of the war is now Kalimantan), I have used the new forms, again with index cross-referencing. This approach seems more useful to future researchers who may consult these accounts as historical documents.

In this collection I have liberally imbibed from wells I did not dig. My thanks go to those who responded so graciously and unselfishly to my request for stories. The Dutch organization *Vereniging Kinderen uit de Japanse Bezetting en de Bersiap, 1941–1949*, of which I am a member, has been a particular inspiration for me to collect and publish these international stories in English. Their contribution, especially in providing the basic framework for the introductory chapter, is hereby gratefully acknowledged. The many who have assisted in proofreading and editing the manuscript also deserve a special thanks, including Greta Kwik and Donna Rengh.

And finally, my eternal gratitude goes to my beloved wife Joyce and my teenage daughter Corinne, who was still living at home when I was preparing the manuscript, for putting up with an absentee husband and father as I slaved on the book while being employed full-time.

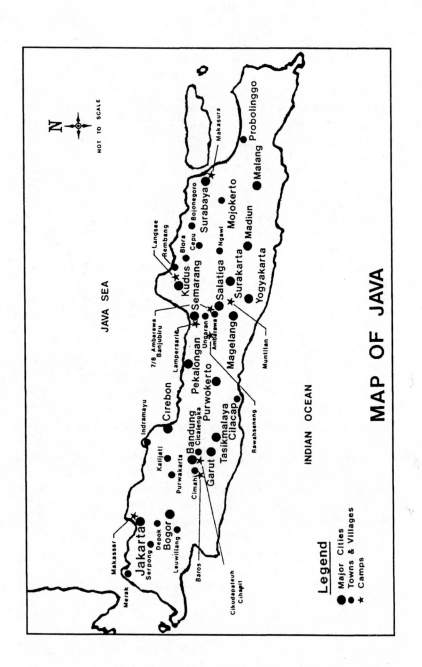

MAP OF JAVA

INTRODUCTION

In the years before the Japanese invasion of the Dutch East Indies (now Indonesia) during the Second World War, very few statesmen anticipated the earthshaking events that would soon occur. Perhaps more should have guessed what was to come. Those in power were well aware that Japan had a rapacious appetite for mineral resources, particularly oil, to fuel its war effort. And oil was abundant in the 575,893 square miles of the Dutch colonies consisting of 13,700 islands of which some 3,000 were inhabited. The territory stretched from Banda Aceh, Sumatra, to Merauke, Irian Jaya. If projected over a map of the United States, this archipelago would more than cover the entire nation. In the early 1940s, it was inhabited by 65 million people, of whom 250,000 were classed as Europeans. Dutch citizens composed the vast majority of the Europeans, totaling around 220,000. The Dutch colonial regime was propped up by a token force of approximately 65,000 European and indigenous military troops.

The Dutch leadership relied primarily on the protection of the Americans and the British in the event of a Japanese invasion. It was generally considered unlikely that an inferior, war-weary Japan would dare to challenge the Western Allied powers.

But Pearl Harbor was bombed on December 7, 1941 (Dec. 8 in the Indies), and the following spring America acknowledged defeat in the Philippines. Singapore fell on February 15, 1942, and Japanese forces invaded Sumatra and captured the Dutch naval base in Ambon. The battle of the Java Sea became an honorable but devastating defeat for the Dutch navy. And the enemy continued to advance. A disaster was definitely in the making.

The Japanese invasion of Java commenced on March 1, 1942. Then, for three and one-half years, Japan would control most of the archipelago. It was not until September 29, 1945, one and one-half months after the Japanese surrender of August 15, 1945, that British troops finally came to liberate the Dutch colony from its brutal oppressors.

The Dutch government was totally obliterated in the early stages of the invasion. Officials could count themselves lucky if they escaped with their lives. Many civilians did not. Soon, more than 100,000 Dutch citizens—men, women and children—disappeared into Japanese internment camps. They literally were driven from their homes and robbed of almost all of their possessions. At least 40,000 Dutch military men became prisoners of war. A majority of them were shipped to camps in Thailand and Burma to assist in building the infamous death railroad, and many others ended up in Japan where they worked in coal mines and on docks as "guests" of Emperor Hirohito.

One of the various ethnic groups which suffered from this decolonization conflict was the Dutch-Indonesians, or Indos, a sizable segment of the population. They were descendants from Dutch as well as native individuals. And it was this group which was afforded the choice to stay out of the internment camps if they cooperated with the Japanese. Very few took advantage of this option. The overwhelming majority joined their Dutch compatriots who were already interned. And those who stayed outside often suffered as miserably as those on the inside of the concentration camps.

The Japanese occupation had several significant consequences which have left their mark even to this day. The conquerors immediately started the process of "Japanization" of the society. Every remnant of Dutch rule was banned from daily life. Batavia, the capital of the Dutch East Indies, was renamed Jakarta. Japanese became a mandatory subject in schools, despite the shortage of instructors in that subject. The use of Dutch was strictly prohibited. Even the calendar was changed—1942 became 2602. Local time became Tokyo time, meaning that sunrise and sundown now occurred ninety minutes later.

The economy was subjected to complete revision and was reshaped for an all-out support of the war effort. For example, rice was confiscated to feed the Japanese troops. As a result, the indigenous people, particularly those of densely populated Java, had to endure tremendous hardship. There were shortages of almost everything, especially of food and clothing. Unbelievable suffering occurred in internment camps, and the native population suffered as well.

More than 4 million *remushas*, forced Indonesian laborers, were pressed into service for the Japanese war effort. In a territory extending from Burma all the way to New Caledonia, they were put to work under unbearable conditions and died in enormous numbers. The total death toll amounted to some 180,000, and their nameless graves dot a large portion of Southeast Asia. The number of dead among the Dutch and Allied prisoners of war, who also had to perform slave labor, was extremely high as well, estimated to be 27 percent in comparison to about 4 percent among the British and American POWs who perished in German and Italian camps.

The Japanese were instrumental in creating the current Republic of Indonesia by their strong support of Islam, among other factors. Prior to World War II, the Dutch colonial government always opposed giving political clout to Islamic leaders; they could freely practice their religion but were not allowed to be politically active. The Japanese, however, consolidated all Islamic factions and formed one major party which played a pivotal role in the eventual birth of an independent Indonesia.

The occupation stimulated the further development of Indonesian nationalistic or independence movements. Nationalist leaders, such as Sukarno, Hatta and Sjahrir, earlier imprisoned by the Dutch, were set free and subsequently offered their cooperation to the Japanese. This was particularly true of Sukarno, a longtime admirer of Japan. He firmly believed in the ultimate Japanese conquest. He also collaborated with the Japanese in recruiting the *remushas* and unabashedly made propaganda for the war effort. Although, in retrospect, he bet on the wrong horse, the Indonesians never blamed him for the cooperation he gave the Japanese. The majority believed in the sincerity of his wish to gain independence for their country. So Japanese promises ultimately set the *Merdeka* or freedom movement in motion.

Initially, the Japanese did not want to grant the Indonesians their independence; they preferred to keep the mineral rich archipelago for themselves. After 1944, however, that attitude started to change. The continual defeats at the hand of the Allies convinced Japanese leaders that they were about to lose the war. At long last, the Japanese leadership declared that the Indies could become independent. But it was not until May 1945—after Japan's ally Germany had already lost the war—that the Indonesians were allowed to fly their red and white flag and sing their brand new national anthem. Not long thereafter, Sukarno met with several prominent figures in Jakarta to prepare for independence. He gave his now famous *Pancasila* speech on June 1,

1945. The *Pancasila* is still the nation's five-pronged philosophy, embodying belief in God, humanitarianism, national unity, democracy and social justice.

On August 7, 1945, one day after the A-bomb was dropped on Hiroshima, the Japanese made a significant decision. They created a committee which was to prepare for real and true Indonesian independence. On August 15, 1945, Japan capitulated, and two days later, Sukarno and Hatta declared Indonesia's independence.

In the Netherlands, the new Indonesian republic was labeled as "made in Japan." To regard the creation of the republic as being masterminded solely by Japan does an injustice, however, to the sincere nationalistic fervor which numerous Indonesians had harbored for a long time. In hindsight, the breaking away of Indonesia from the Netherlands was inevitable. Before the war, the Dutch deliberately delayed such a development for three apparent reasons.

First, the Dutch government was convinced that its domestic economy could not survive the loss of its colonies. An old saying in Dutch goes, "*Indie verloren, rampspoed geboren*," which freely translates into, "The Indies lost, dire adversity born."

Second, the Dutch government was convinced that the Indies could not last long without their leadership. They reasoned that an independent Indies would quickly deteriorate and would become easy prey to stronger countries in the area.

Third, the vulnerability of the Dutch military base in the archipelago demanded caution in encouraging the processes towards independence. Nationalistic fervor could easily deteriorate into uncontrollable chaos.

The Japanese had no long-term experience in governing colonies, so when they took control of the Indies, they had no pattern to conform to and could therefore establish any type of government they wanted. They had no qualms experimenting with the nationalistic movements; after all, Sukarno was prepared, as a reciprocal favor, to support the war effort. The Japanese approach was made from a position of strength and opportunism, in contrast to that of the Netherlands which was based on colonial tradition and responsibility.

The Japanese mobilized the Indonesians into military and paramilitary movements which were to assist in repelling any Allied attack. It was the youth who were primarily recruited and indoctrinated. The Japanese sowed the wind of freedom and independence during the war. After the war, the movement grew into a whirlwind, sweeping away

Dutch attempts to regain control by military means. Ultimately, it proved impossible for the Dutch to return to prewar conditions, even by means of force.

Numerous incidents occurred during the so-called Bersiap period, the formative period of the Indonesian independence movement which lasted from September to December 1945. But thousands upon thousands of Dutch and Indos, together with other pro–Dutch individuals, were victims of a reign of terror perpetrated by uncontrollable and unruly Indonesian militia. Many were seriously injured or lost their lives.

Very little is known in the United States about what actually transpired in this particular part of the world during World War II and the period immediately thereafter. These were truly defining years for those who were either born there or spent a considerable time in the colonies. The personal accounts contained in this book, covering the period 1942 to 1949, may prove to be very informative and educational. One Dutch observer noted, "It is unconscionable to allow future generations to forget what happened in the Indies, just as it is folly to turn our backs on the holocaust in Europe." What happened during the Pacific War is fading fast from our collective memory. Many of the younger generations know little, if anything at all, of its consequences. The passage of time also tends to obscure the reality of war and its consequences, and that should not be.

In order for the Pacific War and its consequences to be understood, it is helpful to read the memoirs of civilians as well as military personnel who lived through those harsh realities. The majority of these people have experienced firsthand imprisonment, "liberation," reinternment, and ongoing hardship due to Indonesia's independence movement and eventual freedom, and their own ultimate expulsion from the land they loved.

These, then, are their stories, honestly and compassionately told— recounted, often with a heavy heart, for the world to read.

ANDREW A. VAN DYK

Overview of the Imprisonment Experience

After the Dutch East Indies government surrendered to the Japanese invasion forces on March 8, 1942, the Japanese High Command on Java "invited" the Dutch colonials and those holding the Dutch nationality, whether of foreign or of indigenous birth, to place themselves under Japanese jurisdiction. This act entailed their entering so-called "protection centers," so that they would be safeguarded from expected Indonesian aggression toward the former white masters.

Initially, only the members of the armed forces were placed in prisoner of war (POW) camps. All Dutch civilians, including those of mixed blood (primarily Dutch-Indonesians), were to be registered and issued identity cards, complete with photo, and subsequently they were placed under house detention or arrested.

Requests to enter the street for personal or business reasons had to be submitted to the Japanese administration, which scrutinized each plea with suspicion. Only those requests which were deemed legitimate and essential were considered for final approval by the commandant. When such a request was granted, the applicant was issued an arm band, with a rising sun emblem in the center, which had to be worn at all times when leaving the residence. This arm band also displayed in Japanese characters the reason why the wearer was out and about. To be caught without this arm band by those at the many checkpoints and the roving military police would mean severe punishment or even death by decapitation. Additionally, a curfew was imposed for Indonesians as well as for Dutch nationals. The latter group had even more restricted daylight hours during which they could venture away

11

from their homes. Again, to be found wandering around after curfew was often punishable by death.

A few months after the surrender, the great migration to the protection centers commenced. All over the Indies, "invited" persons were being transported in shuttered trains, buses, and trucks to these centers, carrying only what was allowed by the Japanese escorts, usually one suitcase and a mess kit. Many came on foot. Soon these "invitees" found out that most of these camps were far removed from safe areas. The Japanese guards herded the new arrivals through the front gate with well aimed kicks and thrusts of bamboo clubs, amid raucous shouting of obscenities.

These protection areas consisted of certain sections in cities and towns, separated from the city at large by a ten-foot-high bamboo wall and coils of barbed wire obstacles. Strategically placed elevated platforms were erected above the fence from where the Japanese guards and later Indonesian volunteers could observe any movement near the fence. All this was done to prevent unauthorized entry and exit. Similar segregated areas were simply erected in the middle of the jungle.

Where the camps formed part of the existing developed urban areas, the accommodations were much better in comparison with those in jungle camps. The latter were usually cleared patches, properly fenced off with barbed wire. Sleeping and living quarters consisted of structures with dried palm leaf roofs, supported by bamboo frames. These roofs constantly leaked during the tropical monsoon downpours.

At night the inmates would sleep on elevated bamboo platforms, about three feet above the muddy floor, crowded together like sardines and placed head-to-feet. They were constantly pestered by lice, leeches, flies, mosquitoes and fleas. These long huts, resembling the renowned long houses of the Kalimantan Dayaks, had an opening on either end. A number of squares were usually removed from the bamboo walls to provide some light and ventilation.

Soon after all the "invitees" were inside these camps, Japanese police squads ordered the official camp staffs to conduct special parades in each camp. During such occasions, all males above the age of thirteen or often as young as nine were removed and separated from their mother and other family members. They were transported either to concentration camps for males or to boys' camps.

The Japanese High Command on Java attempted to coerce the Indo-European members of the former Royal Netherlands-Indies Army, Navy and Air Force to enlist in the Japanese army. A goodly number of Indos who refused were summarily executed and many ended up in camps. Additionally, the Japanese tried to force the Indo-Europeans to renounce their allegiance to the Dutch queen and to become Indonesian citizens. Those who refused were thrown into the various camps.

By early April 1942, there were a variety of enslavement centers in operation throughout the Dutch East Indies, and they could be classified in eight types:

1. Prisoner of war (POW) camps These camps held members of the armed forces of Allied nations, including Dutch, British and other commonwealth forces, Australians and Americans in addition to other nationalities such as Africans, Canadians, South Africans, Chinese, Arabs, and Malays. These men were billeted by nation of origin and by service. Later on, many civilians were imported to maintain the numbers for organized work parties after the majority of POWs were sent overseas to work on the infamous Burma-Thailand railroad, to Formosa (now Taiwan), to Hainan and to Japan itself to perform labor on docks and in the coal mines.

Cimahi, a town high in the mountains of West Java formerly used as a military garrison, was the major staging area for POWs about to be sent overseas. Three large camps were created by transferring barracks previously housing units of the KNIL (Royal Netherlands-Indies Army). These were Camp 4 (which housed the 4th Battalion) and Camp 9 (which housed the 9th Battalion Infantry and the garrison depot of the former Mountain Artillery Depot).

In Jakarta on West Java's north coast, Camp 10 was created out of the former 10th Infantry Battalion barracks. These accommodations were without brick blocks but had decent roofs, cement floors and plenty of ventilation. However, the Japanese ordered the partitions knocked out in order to create a long hall. The inmates slept next to each other in an area approximately three by six feet in size, coinciding with the size of their sleeping mats.

Every POW had to perform manual labor, either inside camp or on the outside. It did not take long for clothing to deteriorate, and the majority of the prisoners soon wore only their military green shorts, Indonesian style clogs, and some kind of hat, often one formerly used by the military service. They made their own eating utensils.

2. VIP camps Several camps housed inmates who were holders of high office in the former colony's government, such as the governor-general, members of parliament, commissioners, residents, administrators, lawyers, doctors, professors, clergymen, industrialists, officers of the rank of general and other dignitaries. However, it was not long before they, too, were dispersed to other islands, such as Formosa, Hainan and Japan.

3. Boys' camps These held boys between the age of nine and thirteen. After they turned fourteen, they were usually moved to civilian internment camps. In Cimahi, there was Camp 6 for this purpose; the present author spent one year there.

4. Civilian internment camps Here males age fourteen and upwards were held. These inmates were continually transferred between camps throughout the three and one half years of captivity. Working parties were assembled each and every day, every month of every year.

Such working parties labored on construction projects at various distances away from camps. When the job was in close proximity, the group marched on foot to reach it, escorted by one or two Japanese soldiers for every 40 to 50 inmates. However, when the job was far away, the working group was transported by army truck, some 70 men packed standing up on the flat bed, escorted by two to three guards.

As the war turned to the Allies' favor, the Japanese needed all their able-bodied men for the fighting in the Pacific. As a consequence, the Japanese guards were replaced by so-called auxiliary troops, most of whom were Koreans and Formosans. There were also troops recruited by the Indonesian pro–Japanese provisional government under the leadership of Sukarno. The volunteers were organized in a great variety of corps and formations, such as the *heihos*, an organization which consisted of Indonesian volunteers who assisted the Japanese army in the defense of the Indonesian islands.

As compensation, the Dutch inmates who labored at the various working parties received an extra measure of food, consisting of one or two pieces of boiled sweet potato. Those who found excuses for not being part of the labor detail and remained at their sleeping quarters, resting on their palm leaf mats, did not qualify to receive this "extra ration." In fact, many of them were actually so sick and afflicted that they died where they lay.

5. Jahat camps These were camps for the "bad" enemy. They held captured guerrilla fighters, many of whom had been betrayed by the Indonesians for cash awards; escaped and recaptured POWs; members of certain Allied units which caused Japanese invasion forces much grief, such as demolition and special forces units; and captured civilians who were allegedly discovered as being spies. Eventually all of these people were eliminated, usually by means of decapitation, after interrogation by the infamous Japanese military police, the *Kempeitai*.

6. *Prisons and jails* These institutions held criminals already held by the Dutch before the surrender as well as persons suspected of running black market operations as go-betweens trafficking in medicines, food and cigarettes between Indonesians and inmates. Also incarcerated here were members of clandestine newspapers, resistance group members, and persons who hid or otherwise aided escaped Allied servicemen. These unfortunates would be tortured by the *Kempeitai* and later disposed of. Examples of these facilities were Struiswijk, Glodok and Sukamiskin.

7. *Protection camps* In these camps, billeted for their own safety and protection, were members of Axis countries—Germans, Italians, Hungarians, Rumanians, and others—as well as some citizens of neutral countries such as Switzerland and Sweden. These camps are not to be confused with camps by the same designation after the war, during the Bersiap period, which housed persons who were in need of protection from marauding Indonesian youth.

8. *Concentration camps* Here, all females except those held for interrogation in other institutions, boys under age 12 and, in some early cases, very old men were interned. These camps held inmate populations between 100 and 18,000 and were found on nearly every island all over the Indies, primarily Java and Sulawesi.

The most frequently discussed camps were the so-called Cihapit camps of Bandung, West Java, which took up most of the city and held nearly 18,000 persons. The other infamous camp was Cideng camp in Jakarta, capital of the Indies, located on the north coast of West Java. In this camp a brutal Japanese camp commandant, Capt. Kenichi Sonei, held sway during the last years of the war. After the war, he was executed as a war criminal for his actions while in charge of this camp.

All concentration camp inmates had to be part of working parties. Even women up to the age of 60 had to perform hard manual labor. Inmates were used as garbage and junk collectors, sewer and drain cleaners, kitchen workers, furniture removers, clerical workers, grass cutters, and laborers to perform other chores outside camp jobs.

Initially when families moved in, they took along their pets. But before long, the Japanese ordered them either destroyed or removed from the camp. The author's family came to the Cihapit camp with our dog Keesey, a black retriever we owned for years when we lived at a sugar plantation in Banjumas, Central Java. As soon as the order to eliminate pets was issued, we hastily approached the all-Dutch women's camp staff to plead our cause to retain him. We had difficulties keeping rats from infesting our overcrowded living quarters, and Keesey was an excellent rat catcher. The Japanese camp commandant had a Japanese doctor evaluate the petition, examine the dog, and advise him on the matter.

The end result was that we were permitted to keep Keesey, for a while at least. However, I was to show the camp leader, a Dutch woman, a weekly quota of rats caught.

A number of houses were grouped in certain blocks. A group of 20 to 30, for example, was called *tonari-kumi*. The prisoners in charge were called *kumichos* and were identified by an arm band, denoting such a position in Japanese characters.

Blocks grouped together were called *aza* and the leader an *aza-cho*. These areas linked together were called *hans* or districts, and the leader was the *hancho*.

During 1944, the Japanese attempted to entice female prisoners to serve in bordellos. In some cases force was used, but eventually this practice was discontinued. As was discovered after the war, however, the Japanese government condoned the mass recruitment of "women of pleasure" from their conquered territory. Several Dutch women recently also stepped forward and testified that they were coerced into prostitution.

The inmates' clothing soon deteriorated due to excessive wear and tear, and no replacement garments or uniforms were available. Male POWs and internees, because of their intense day-in, day-out labor, were forced to wear leftover shreds of uniforms and civilian tropical gear. The majority went to their assigned tasks in some form of head gear, ranging from service caps or hats to native-style sun hats. Their outfits consisted of service shirts or jackets, uniform-type shorts and trousers, and boots—for those lucky ones who still owned them—or Indonesian-style wooden clogs.

Dresses worn by the female prisoners also wore out eventually, forcing the women to go about their daily chores in native-style hats or scarfs with halter tops, brassieres, sleeveless blouses or uniform shirts. Additionally, they wore various kinds of shorts and trousers with a variety of shoes, boots and clogs. Their sleeping or living accommodations varied considerably, depending on the type of camp and its location, whether in a city or in a jungle setting.

When concentration camps had been erected as part of an existing residential area, such as a city, town, or village, the newcomers simply were moved into dwellings, in numbers to suit the size of the living quarters. The families already living in their own home had to accept this new arrangement. They were merely allotted a room for themselves and the remainder of the house was to be occupied by other families or individuals.

Each room, regardless of its size, whether a garage or hallway, a veranda or pantry, was to accommodate either a family or a single person. Sometimes an average sized house held as many as 40 people. Sleeping arrangements were, in most cases, simple bedding on the floor, on cots, or on mats. There were also a few beds, army-type field stretchers and hammocks.

The serving of the three meals a day was organized by the communal field kitchens operated by designated inmates, and was scheduled according to a roster. However, the less-than-substantial meals could not satisfy the inmates' hunger, so each family or *kongsi* (cartel) prepared its own additional food. This nourishment, which was either found or stolen, was most often prepared on bricks, using modified tin cans with twigs underneath to fuel the fire.

In some instances, arrangements were made for one inmate in a particular house to be allocated food in bulk for all residents. This assignment was rotated among the residents of the house. Upon receipt of the food, the appointed individual would redistribute the portions. Food was brought in on a simple tow car which carried all pots and pans from the field kitchen to the houses.

Since there was a dusk-to-dawn curfew in effect, none of the inmates were to be outside their homes or in the streets. Severe penalties were applied to violators.

Boys and POWs were also sometimes confined in camps in urban areas. These camps generally utilized barracks previously occupied by units of the KNIL (the Royal Netherlands-Indies Army). Living quarters were located in long halls or blocks which held a number of self-contained rooms or units where soldiers with their entire families were quartered. The Japanese had the partitioning walls between rooms removed to form a long block with entrances at each end. Inmates lay side by side, head to feet, in an area often not larger than three by six feet.

Sleeping accommodations were either bamboo-based cots and mats or bamboo platforms, constructed in tiers in order to warehouse the greatest possible number of inmates. They were arranged against the walls of the block building so as to leave the center strip clear.

No lightbulbs were allowed within blocks. The traffic to and from the latrines, located outside, was the most hectic during the night, so a device was invented to ensure that inmates could eventually find their way back to their mats. One or two ropes were suspended from the ceiling at head level, strung from entrance to entrance. When someone wished to answer the call of nature during the night, he would get up from his mat, grope for the rope above his head in the center aisle and, having located it, follow it towards the nearer of the two exits. However, on the way back the person would need to search for the proximity of his mat by waving hands around, on bended knees, while trying to avoid waking up other sleepers.

Meals were prepared and distributed from large central field kitchens. Each block sent a designated person from a roster to act as a meal collector; he would accept the rations for each block for later distribution by block leaders. This was done under supervision of the Japanese block commandant, usually a sadistic sergeant.

Curfew was again strictly adhered to and intensely policed by roving pickets and patrols. Each block had to have fire sentries. One inmate had to remain awake all night at each entrance and exit of each block or hut to ensure that all people within that block were accounted for. When a roving Japanese sentry would come by on his designated rounds, the fire sentry would come to attention. He would bow deeply from the waist and shout in simple Japanese, which he had mastered in the meantime, that all was well within the block. He also had to account for how many men were in the latrine. The sentry would then grunt something to mean "OK, carry on!" and would proceed on his appointed round.

Camps were sometimes constructed by clearing an area out of virgin jungle. Huts were erected and everything was made of bamboo—walls, frames, roofs, sleeping platforms, etc. The floors were the existing dirt ground which quickly turned into a quagmire each time it rained. The roofs invariably leaked. The walls were left open at certain select spots, or sometimes an entire square was removed, to allow sunlight in. While this practice improved ventilation, it also resulted in rain entering the huts.

Inmates slept on the long bamboo platforms next to each other, head to feet. Those who died remained there until the "burial detail" made its rounds the next morning, moving from hut to hut to remove the corpses.

As in urban camps, meals were issued from a central kitchen block and individual cooking was strictly forbidden. Curfews existed in the jungle camps as well. The entire area was stripped clean of every type of vegetation. Nowhere could an inmate disappear from the watchful eyes of the Japanese guards in their towers or roving the areas in pairs.

Prisons and jails were existing institutions in brick buildings with barred windows. An empty four-gallon tin can was often used as a latrine, and there were no lightbulbs, furniture or sleeping mats. Inmates in the small cells slept on the bare concrete floor in the clothes in which they arrived. Sometimes men were mixed in with women. In many instances they did not even have enough room to stretch out to sleep. They had to huddle in as small a bundle as possible, not only because of space limitations, but also to provide a bit of warmth in the cold cell.

Meals, sometimes provided only once a day, were pushed through the bars of the window or slid under the massive iron door. The strongest prisoners and those closest to the meal thus were able to get the most food at the expense of the feeble and old.

Interrogations were conducted at nighttime. When the clash and clank of boots and weapons was heard approaching the cell, everyone shuddered from fright in anticipation of what was to come. Sometimes an inmate taken away for these nocturnal sessions was not returned, and all wondered about his fate. Was he found not guilty and transported to another concentration camp, or had he been executed? The death rate was frightening in these institutions. Even when the Japanese occupational forces had surrendered, the executions continued unabated for weeks thereafter.

The author's aunt was kept in jail in Surabaya, East Java, for many months on charges of assisting underground resistance fighters. She endured nightly attention from the *Kempeitai* and was ultimately decapitated many days after the war had ended.

The guards for these camps seemed to be handpicked for the job. They engaged frequently in sadistic behavior, beating and kicking prisoners on a regular basis and even participating in the occasional execution.

Right after the Dutch surrendered, a decree went out throughout the Indies that the Dutch language was not to be seen in print nor spoken or taught in school. Only Japanese and Indonesian (Malay) were to be used when speaking, even in the camps. Obviously this edict was not always honored, but all commands and orders shouted by the camp leaders had to be in Japanese if any Japanese were present. Violations resulted in severe beatings.

All inmates also had to bow from the waist whenever a Japanese soldier was encountered. One had to stop when marching or step down when riding a truck or car, turn to face the Japanese, and after bowing a few seconds, one could proceed with whatever one was doing.

I remember one occasion, when I was on garbage detail with six other boys and my sister, Betty, who was in charge. We were approaching the main gate with a former army horse-drawn cart, filled to overflowing with garbage. We had to be at the dump station, located some distance from the camp, at an appointed time, but first we had to pick up our escort from the guard house at the front gate. The cart was being pulled by two boys gripping the shafts to which, under normal circumstances, a horse would have been harnessed. On the rear and side, four other boys were pushing, while I sat on top of the cart, trying to prevent the heap of garbage from spilling. Betty was marching alongside, representing the authority which was in the form of a certificate, signed by the camp commandant and prominently carried in hand. Each of us was also issued a cloth badge, shaped in the form of a garbage can and pinned to our shorts or shirts.

We stopped in front of the Japanese sentry and dutifully bowed. Betty stepped forward to show him our approval-to-exit certificate and to wait for the escort, another Japanese soldier. However, she stopped dead in her tracks when the sentry angrily rushed forward to the cart and with wild gesticulation ordered me to descend. As I stood in front of him, he continued his shouting of abuses and wildly waving his arms. Finally it dawned on me that I had committed the unpardonable sin: I had not come down from the cart to bow for him. As penalty I had to remain still in a bowing position for a minute or so. Suddenly I felt a severe whack on my back. The Japanese had hit me with the butt of his rifle to vent his wrath. I was in great pain for days and could barely straighten up.

A typical daily routine adopted in most camps proceeded as follows. At about four o'clock in the morning, those inmates detailed to work in the camp kitchens would rise from their mats and trot off towards the kitchen compound. This compound was usually fenced off with barbed wire and guarded by Japanese roving pickets and sentry posts. Inside the compound were the so-called camp warden and selected POWs who patrolled the kitchen complex to detect any unauthorized entry or exit.

These camp wardens and the permanent kitchen staff, those selected inmates who prepared, cooked and distributed the meals, had been issued official-looking arm bands or metal badges. These came in the shape of a star, upon which symbols or letters had been engraved to indicate what kind of work the wearer was entitled to perform or whether the person was permitted to leave the camp. Leaving the camp was always under escort and was primarily done to purchase commodities from Indonesian marketplaces in the vicinity of villages or towns. Sometimes they collected supplies from the former Dutch government storehouses.

Kitchen workers had to wear these badges or arm bands at all times while on duty. Loss of these items or failure to wear them would result in severe punishment, so in order to cope with any possible loss, the workers made duplicates just in case.

Sleepy-eyed inmates would show their badges to the guard at the gates to the kitchen compounds to gain entry. Then the many open fireplaces had to be brought to a roaring blaze. This was probably the most pleasant time for the workers since so many camps were located in the mountains where it could be miserably cold.

After the fires had come to a full blast, 44-gallon drums, which reached chest high for young boys in the boys' camps, were filled with water and lifted over and installed above the fireplace.

Four inmates, having pushed two long bamboo poles through two rings soldered onto the upper rims of these drums, placed their shoulders underneath the poles, lifted the drums and staggered towards the open, blazing fires.

After the water had come to a boil, either tapioca, rice, coffee, tea or vegetables would be introduced in strictly controlled measures and left to cook. In the meantime, around six o'clock, the remainder of the camp would have been awakened by the sound of trumpet blasts, sirens or harsh shouting, accompanied by the smacking of bamboo truncheons. The Japanese guards and block commandants also liberally used their army boots to kick the tardy inmates.

Not long after the harsh wake-up call, prisoners would assemble in front of their blocks in the streets, on parade grounds and in various open spaces. The public address systems would blare some Japanese martial music and under supervision of circling and prowling Japanese guards, all inmates would commence *taiso*, or compulsory calisthenics. This activity would last up to an hour. Then the weary people were dismissed for breakfast, which would take from half an hour to an hour. Immediately thereafter, trumpets would sound again, shouts could be heard, and drums would beat, heralding the start of another work parade, or *tenko*.

Tenko, or roll call, involved forming in groups of 50 prisoners in front of the various parade grounds, each group attended by escorting soldiers. Subsequently, the parade commandant, usually the Japanese camp commandant himself, would order the counting to commence. Immediately, Japanese block, section, and line commanders, usually sergeants and warrant officers, would begin their shouting and bellowing to proceed with the *bango* or counting. This caused the same bedlam each and every morning. The Japanese rarely tallied their figures correctly the first time to determine how many inmates were actually in their group.

The POW in charge of each group would shout "*bango!*" and then the front row of the rank and file, patiently standing at attention, would sound off in Japanese, "*Ichi, ni, san, shi, go, roku,*" and so forth up to ten. Then the counting would start all over again. The Japanese leader would approach the man who was about to sound off in the front rank and would follow the count down the line until the last man had bellowed out his number. He would then figure out the total on his clipboard and consult the more senior Japanese commander to check and compare his handiwork in math. Eventually, all the figures would seem to tally and then the division for work parties would commence. Depending on the priorities of the various projects, a certain number of men would be allocated. As soon as every slot was filled, the details left either on foot, if nearby, or by truck if farther away.

Those parties that marched away had as their escort one or two soldiers for the entire day. Each of the inmates carried only a mess kit, consisting of empty tins which were used for soup or porridge and tea. Additionally, they had with them a self-made spoon, fork, and knife, and either a real water bottle or a length of bamboo cut so that one end remained closed. They marched along in shreds of clothing, wearing diverse headgear and footwear. Most of them had native clogs or walked barefooted. On their shoulders they carried shovels, picks, mattocks, and other pieces of equipment to perform work on the roads, in the field, or in the hills.

At lunchtime, a Japanese truck would rumble along and stop near the particular party at work. The Japanese escort would yell, "*Jasmi!*" and the prisoners would drop their tools and gather near the truck. From the back of the truck the POWs would be issued a measure of either soup or gruel into their mess kits. This was augmented by one or two pieces of boiled sweet potato and finally a cup of tea was slopped into the inmate's drinking cup.

After distribution of the meal, the truck would depart and the inmates would be prodded back to work until dusk, at which time they would march back to camp. The same procedure was followed by those who were sent by truck to the scene of the project.

The last meal of the day was issued in darkness. Upon return to camp the weary prisoners fell asleep almost as soon as they dropped onto their sleeping mats. The only ones to remain awake were those who had been detailed for night duties such as camp warden or fire sentry as well as the hospital staff.

Medical care in the camps was nearly nonexistent. The hospitals in many camps were nothing but huts with sleeping arrangements and facilities similar to those of the other huts. The grim difference was that inmates were carried in alive and often left in a bamboo shroud for burial. Doctors and nurses were forced to carry out their tasks without the benefit of drugs, equipment, or medication. They treated all kinds of diseases and injuries, performed surgery (primarily amputations), and did admirably well under adverse conditions. They often functioned without candles, hot water, or clean rags.

The patients were laid in tiers on bamboo platforms, with the worst cases on the lower level. The nurses went from one patient to the next, changing soiled rags and offering cool water to feverish lips.

There were men with tropical ulcers. This condition is unstoppable, and it eats away at the flesh until the bones are exposed. Victims had open wounds, crawling with maggots, which had to be scraped out, washed, and bound with clean rags. That was just about the best care available for this disease, apart from amputations, which were done only as a last resort. Far more numerous were patients with beriberi, cholera, dysentery and many other tropical diseases, such as dengue fever and the like. Those with beriberi could only be treated by giving constant attention. The "wet" version of the disease, caused by poor nutrition, would release body fluid from the cells. Fluid would collect primarily in the legs, rising up the torso and towards the lungs. This would ultimately result in death through drowning.

There was also a "dry" variant of beriberi. This type had just the opposite symptoms. The patient would lose body fluid through body orifices. Should this person fall and hit his head on a hard object, it could split open like a dropped watermelon.

Typhoid fever was another dreadful killer of POWs. The author's brother John almost succumbed to this disease in 1944-45. He was lingering in a coma for weeks and all the medics could do was to turn his body from perspiration-soaked bed linen onto fresh, washed rags. They also gave him as much fluid as he could take and constantly kept him under observation.

After nearly three months in that dreary hut, he got over the sickness and began to take an interest in life again. I was very worried and looked him up each evening after my duties in the soup kitchen, where I was working at that time as helper in preparing vegetables and rice soup. I was able to smuggle some raw vegetables such as carrots and beans in the seams of my shorts to avoid Japanese scrutiny at the kitchen gate.

The "hospital" was indeed a hellish place to be, and I did not look forward each night to being there in the presence of those wretched prisoners who were suffering intense pain without any relief in sight.

ABOUT THE CONTRIBUTOR

Andre van Dyk was born on a sugar plantation on Java in 1929. In 1940 when Germany occupied the Netherlands, he joined a volunteer air raid warning service, and when Japan occupied Java, he and his family were transported to various concentration camps.

Liberated in November 1945, he moved to Jakarta and served in the "new" KNIL until evacuation to the Netherlands where he continued his education. He was called up for initial service in the Royal Dutch Marines but later transferred to the army. He attended Officer Cadet School and was commissioned in 1951.

Andre served in various units, including NATO contingents in Europe, until he emigrated to Australia. He held down numerous civilian jobs before enlisting in the Australian army, serving for 18 years. Then he was employed as a staff officer in army headquarters until his second retirement at the age of 60.

He and his wife live in Ashfield, a suburb of Sydney, New South Wales, Australia.

FRANS J. NICOLAAS PONDER

A Soldier in the
Royal Netherlands-Indies Army

This story is written as a bittersweet memory of my Japanese imprisonment which started on March 10, 1942, in the town of Muntilan, Central Java. It ended on August 20, 1945, before the Bersiap period, in the jungle woodcutting camp of Linson (km 202) in Thailand. It was here that the prisoners heard the sweet news that the war was over! Subsequently, I survived the Bersiap, the prelude to the Indonesian independence movement in the former Dutch East Indies.

The places I have been during my forced wandering were Muntilan, Magelang, Yogyakarta, Surabaya, Jakarta, and Tanjungpriok (all on Java), Singapore, Johore Bahru, Ipoh, Kuala Lumpur (Malaysia), Banpong (Thailand), various jungle camps in Burma, then back again via Bangkok, Thailand, to Singapore. I went by ship to Moji on the island of Kyushu, Japan, and was billeted in the navy camp of Tanagawa. We were transported by train via Osaka to the Kamo coal mines on the island of Hondo, then back to Osaka. I was a member of loading and unloading crews on board ship and sailed via Formosa (Taiwan), Haiphong (North Vietnam), and Saigon (South Vietnam) to Bangkok, Thailand, where I disembarked and subsequently joined a work detail to build the railroad via Kanchanaburi, Chungkai to Linson.

This forced wandering through half of Asia and the experiences during the Bersiap period are recorded briefly and chronologically outlined in the following:

On March 8, 1942, almost without firing a shot, the KNIL (Royal

This chapter was submitted in Dutch and translated by Jan Krancher.

25

Netherlands-Indies Army) surrendered unconditionally to the Japanese army. What shame and dishonor! All weapons and ammunition had to be collected and stacked along main roads. The POWs were then transported by truck to "Depot Mitrailleurs" camp, located on the Grote Postweg, outside Magelang. Short of a couple of Japanese guards, there was no enemy in sight. The first few weeks we were assigned to maintain law and order. Family visits were allowed in the afternoon.

On March 18, 1942, the main invading force rode into town in a long convoy. They were greeted with cheers from the natives. What we saw were well-disciplined, heavily armed, front-line soldiers. The very next day, the camp guard was doubled and visiting hours were drastically curtailed.

On March 24, 1942, during morning roll call, 500 men were selected to get ready for departure within an hour—destination unknown—and I was one of them. We marched, tightly guarded, to the freight railroad station, approximately four miles away. We boarded shuttered freight cars, in which we had to stand upright one next to the other, and the train departed as soon as the doors were shut. It was extremely hot in these galvanized zinc cars—the tropical sun kept beating down on them. The canteens with water were soon empty. The train stopped after three hours and the sliding doors opened. The fresh air was a real blessing.

We disembarked in Yogyakarta, where we were given a piece of bread and were allowed to refill our canteens with lukewarm sweet tea. Soon, we boarded an empty shuttered passenger train in which we had the luxury to sit down.

After a relatively quick trip we arrived at a suburb of Surabaya, East Java, at dawn. We marched about two kilometers and then boarded trucks which took us to a school. Hundreds of other prisoners were already there, among whom were Dutch as well as American and Australian navy personnel. Discipline was very strict. Starting the next day, we found out just how tough. During roll call, a Jap commanded us in Japanese. Nobody understood what he said. Attention! Right face! Count off! etc., all in Japanese. The first blows soon fell. It was advisable not to attempt to ward them off because they would be followed by numerous kicks and thrusts with the butt of a rifle. Blood of the first victim flowed freely and we learned the first Japanese cuss words, *bagero* and *kanero*.

In Surabaya, we had to clean up and restore the heavily damaged harbor; load iron ore and other material such as rice; repair and extend the airport runway; backfill trenches; get firewood from Gresik, a small town west of Surabaya; sweep streets; clean and oil weapons; and sort out ammunition. Some guards gave us permission during our lunch break to buy sweets or tobacco and cigarettes from the numerous Indonesian vendors in the neighborhood.

April 29 was the birthday of the emperor of Japan, or *Tenno Heika*. Families were allowed to visit the prisoners and bring all kinds of goodies. Since my entire family lived in Semarang, Central Java, I did not expect anybody to show up. I was therefore surprised when I met Willy Kouthoofd, the son of a family with whom I boarded for a number of years. Willy took along, among other items, a large bottle of soy sauce, a bag of sugar and several packs of Mars brand shag tobacco. These were very valuable commodities for a POW to possess.

We moved from School Camp to the Jaarmarkt Camp on May 3. This camp had greater potential to serve as a reception center for internees but had a similarly stringent regimen.

On May 29, after a "medical examination" whereby a Japanese doctor stuck a glass rod in the behind to determine if the person had dysentery, I ended up in a group which was preparing for departure. Where we were going, nobody knew. In trucks we were driven to the station, where a long, shuttered train was already waiting. We left for the 10th Battalion transit camp in Jakarta, West Java, where we arrived the next afternoon.

By truck we were then taken on June 4 to the harbor and were loaded into a Japanese cargo ship, staying in the cargo bay below deck. Most of us were literally packed into the hold by kicking and the use of rifle butts. I was lucky and found a place to sit down on the upper deck. It was rather stuffy there but not as bad as below deck. Soon we were on our way to Singapore.

This old freighter must have weighed about 3,000 tons, and it laboriously ambled out of the harbor. After a few hours we were in open waters and a fresh breeze blew. As the ship started to heave, severe trouble started. The toilets were located on deck and could only be reached by stairs. Those who became seasick and had to vomit could often not get upstairs fast enough, emptying their stomachs prematurely. This usually happened near or on the upper deck, and in no time there was an unbelievably smelly mess.

In addition to seasickness, there were numerous cases of diarrhea. A Japanese guard was posted to control the use of the toilets. Before we disembarked in Singapore on June 9, we were lined up on deck in small groups and washed down with fire hoses. A number of POWs had died due to dysentery and were buried at sea.

From the port we had to march almost one hour through town before we reached the trucks which took us to a tent camp in Changi. This camp belonged to the 11th British Indian Division. Our group was responsible for the cultivation of a vegetable garden. Several hectares of coconut trees had to be uprooted. Jan Paul, my cousin, was in my work party.

I was admitted to the military hospital with bacillary dysentery on June 19. I met my brother-in-law, police inspector Jan Onken, who was laid up with amoebic dysentery. The attending British doctors and nurses were friendly and helpful and the quality of food was reasonable. I was moved from this tent camp to the Southern Area on July 7 and assigned as orderly and guard for Capt. Wulf horst and 1st Lt. Vetter, both armor officers. Our task was to assist with washing and drying clothes, cleaning their room, fetching their food, washing the dishes and, in general, keeping them company. Fortunately they were not conceited, star-struck officers.

During morning roll call on October 23, I was designated as a worker in a mixed group of American and Australian POWs under Australian command. We were driven to the harbor and loaded on a freighter. Among other things, the ship transported railroad cross beams. Early in the morning, we left the harbor. The next morning, the convoy was being attacked by an Allied submarine. Ours was the only ship which was torpedoed and sunk. We were lucky. We clung to the floating cross beams and survived.

Together with an Aussie and two other KNIL soldiers, we were picked up by a tugboat, returned to Singapore and placed in the Harbor Jail. I celebrated Christmas 1942 and New Year's Eve here. As something extra we were granted a piece of mutton in our soup. The survivors of the sunken ship were transported to Rangoon, Burma.

On January 31, 1943, all POWs were transported by truck to the station and subdivided in groups of 30. Each group had to squeeze themselves into the freight cars. The next stop was Ipoh, Malaysia. After eating and some rest, we loaded up a Japanese freight truck convoy with bales of rice and firewood. At last we were now able to stretch our tired and weary legs for a while.

We arrived on the last station of Banpong, Thailand on February 8. It was about an hour's march to camp. Behind the camp stood a bare tree on whose branches we saw vultures, birds we would certainly encounter often later on. Banana vendors came to the fence and tried to hawk their goods. However, POWs did not have money and several of them exchanged whatever they could spare in order to lay their hands on the delicious, tempting tropical fruits.

Reveille came at three o'clock in the morning on February 10. After breakfast of rice porridge and filling the canteens with water, the march towards a jungle work station in northern Thailand started. The first day we still walked on hardened, sometimes even blacktop road. The heat, however, was unbearable and we were not allowed to take more water or tea than was in our canteen. And neither were there enough rest breaks. Late in the afternoon we arrived at the first transient camp, consisting of a number of wooden barracks with palm frond roofs. They measured approximately 100 meters long and 10 meters wide. In the center was a walkway and on either side, bamboo scaffolding on which the POWs were to bed down. Each was assigned about 50 centimeters of space. The camp was located some five kilometers from Kanchanaburi where the railroad terminated.

The march resumed on February 13. We followed the tracks across an uneven trail leading to a jungle path. It was very dusty and unbearably hot. Our backpacks were as heavy as lead. There was not enough water to drink. Stragglers were beaten by the guards so that they would keep up. After about ten kilometers, we reached our second transient camp. The Jap gave us rice, a piece of salted fish and water which we had to boil ourselves. Several of us took a bath in the nearby stream and some even took a drink, risking all kinds of diseases.

The next day we departed to the next camp some 15 kilometers away. Once again, it was a tiring march on the railroad bed. The berm was completed, but the tracks were not yet laid. We passed the "nail group" whose task it was to lay at least two kilometers of track each day. I had pity for those men. Lugging the rails and the sleepers in the hot sun without sufficient drinking water was bad enough, but there were also the ever-present guards who beat them. All this abuse really took its toll on the weakened POWs. Many developed cracked lips as a result of the heat and the dust. They were unable to chew the rice and hence had to rely on eating porridge, leading to further weakening.

Those whose boots had been completely worn out now had to walk on bare feet. It was a very pitiful sight to see British, Australian and American POWs stumble along this way. After all, they were not used to walking barefooted. In contrast, the Dutch-Indonesian POWs just kept trucking along.

I donated a relatively good pair of boots to a British corporal who absolutely could not continue. Because they were a bit too small, the leather at the toes was trimmed to size. Out of gratitude, he gave me his Royal Engineers insignia. Deadly tired, we arrived that afternoon in the rest camp. After passing two more camps, we ended up at the transient camp, Noh Barada.

Before arrival, several men stayed behind due to sheer exhaustion and simply lay down. They were severely beaten. When our commander protested against this treatment, he too was severely whipped. Japan was certainly in a hurry to complete the railroad.

On February 20 we left early once again. Because the path was getting narrower, we walked single file. The person at the end had to swallow the most dust. Upon arrival in Tarsao, we discovered that several men who stayed behind had to be retrieved. Due to over-exhaustion, they just lay in the shrubs without being noticed by the guards.

In this large base and transit camp we were granted a few days of rest and were regrouped into several work details. I was assigned as one of the 50 men under the command of 1st Lt. Bert Sanders.

We now were part of the Toku-Butai party and were responsible for the construction of a bridge on the road near Tardan. Our camp consisted of one POW barracks and another barracks for about 20 Japanese engineers. They were in charge of supplying tree trunks and other materials for the construction of the bridge. The material had to be procured from the forest. The Japanese would then shape the material and build the bridge with the assistance of the POWs. I got to know Rob Poublon, an enlisted Dutch Royal Navy man. He became my permanent co-worker as well as my bunkmate.

At the end of June 1943 we went back to base camp Tarsao. I met Jan Onken in the lazaretto, sporting a huge tropical sore on his right shin. Maggots were literally crawling in it. The British doctors tried to cure such sores with salt, after spooning the wound out.

On July 2 the work party at Toku Butai was given orders to work on the railroad at Kurang Krai about 120 kilometers farther along. Our task was to construct the railroad, located along the Mekong River. Huge rock formations had to be dynamited and the ground leveled off. The march took nine nights and ten days.

I arrived in Kiangkali deadly ill. The majority of time we had to sleep outdoors since the barracks were not finished yet. On the way up, I lost a great deal of baggage. Rob Poublon gave me half a horse blanket to protect me against the severe mountain cold.

We worked very hard in this camp. We witnessed a large rock formation tumble down on top of a group of Australian POWs during the rainy season. Several were killed instantly and others were severely injured. We also celebrated the completion of the railroad in this camp, though I cannot remember the exact date.

From this camp, located near the Burmese border, work parties were frequently sent out to assist the workers in other camps. The few times we were assigned to such groups, I met several acquaintances, including among others Uncle Edu. One such assignment took us to camp "Mud Fun." We often had to work up to our waist in dirty, muddy water. Uncle Edu was laid up in the sick bay. He suffered from malaria, and both legs were covered with sores and wounds as a result of bites by the numerous blood suckers and water lice. He was nothing but skin and bones.

Many suffered rheumatic joint pains from working in the water for hours on end. In comparison with camps in Thailand, I found the ones in Burma worse. In camp 62, I also met my brother-in-law Jan Onken again. Here the famously tough yet fair Lt. Col. Platte was in command.

Around October our Toku Butai group was transported by train to base camp near Tamoean. Those few days, while we were stationed near a Thai village, we managed to "misappropriate" some ripe jack fruit. Eating this fruit was a real luxury we had not enjoyed for a few weeks.

By the end of the month we were transported to Singapore and were billeted in a camp near the harbor. At the beginning of November we boarded a ship and convoyed off to Japan. In comparison with other ship transports from Java to Singapore, we had much more space here. The food too was somewhat improved; at least we could taste the bouillon in the soup. Our ship reached Japan in only 29 days. By way of Formosa, where we were even allowed to swim in the cold ocean, we arrived in Moji on the island of Kyushu in early December. We were billeted in a camp near the navy base at Tanagawa. The holidays were celebrated in Camp Tanagawa, and we were issued warm clothing and a blanket. It was the dead of winter in Japan.

By train, which in comparison to other transport was much more humane, we went to the coal mines at Kamo on January 3, 1944. I did not stay here very long, two months at the most. During a morning roll call the Japanese picked a work detail, primarily Aussies and British, but I was among them. We were to be responsible for the loading and unloading of ships in the harbor. It was only during the first few days that we had this task. Soon we were distributed over two ships and became dock-type laborers, given similar responsibilities on board.

In Japan, large quantities of munitions and other materials were loaded up. Some of this was unloaded in Saigon, and bales of rice were taken on. The harbor prior to Saigon was Haiphong, where bales of beans were loaded. After Saigon, we departed for Bangkok and upon unloading we were billeted in a huge zinc hangar in the harbor. It was extremely hot here and sanitary facilities were totally inadequate—only three toilets and two showers for 100 men. Fortunately, a few days later we were relieved by a much larger group of British soldiers. Our group from Japan was divided up and spread throughout various camps on the railroad. We were given the responsibility to cut firewood as fuel for the trains. These were now traveling over the tracks laid by slave labor and POWs, and war materiel and troops were being transported to the Burmese front. The railroad also transported sick and wounded front soldiers to military hospitals in Bangkok and other large cities.

Around May 1944 we were housed in transit camp Kanchanaburi, where I stayed for about two weeks. I was assigned to a work detail to take care of the truck transport route which ran parallel to the railroad. I ended up in Tampi.

In July I was admitted to the hospital with a severe case of malaria tropicana, also given the nickname of blackwater fever due to the dark coloration the urine takes on. Once I dreamt that my head became detached from my body and rolled across the camp ground. I chased after it and saw it disappear in a well. I jumped after it and landed gently on the muddy bottom. I barely could see it disappear in a tunnel. In my subconscious I knew that I had to retrieve my head in order to survive, so I pursued it down the dark tunnel. I could see daylight again. As I exited the tunnel and looked around, I observed not too far away a beautiful young lady. She had my head in her hands. She motioned me to come to her, pressed my head on my shoulders and said, "Frans, return to your camp, because they are looking for you." I woke up and sensed that I was being lifted off the ground by a navy nurse who placed me back on my cot. During my delirious state, I had fallen off my cot and crawled across the floor.

Around the beginning of September I was shipped off to the hospital camp Chungkai; then roughly the next month, we were transported by train on flatbed cars, commonly used for the transport of tree trunks, to the woodcutting camp of Linson. My brother-in-law was also assigned to this group. It was a work detail of about 300 men, consisting of Australians, Britons, and Dutchmen. Our primary task was to cut down trees, chop them into 50-centimeter sections and transport these pieces to the railroad. They were stacked up and used as fuel for the locomotives. In addition to woodcutting, we also had to repair many bridges and railway yards. These sites were increasingly being bombed by Allied airplanes.

Towards the end of November 1944, during the loading and unloading at the yard of Brangkasi a few miles from our camp, there was an early morning alert. The Allies were now lord and master over the skies. Together with some other co-workers, I found cover behind a load of sand and gravel. The entire train and the yard were completely demolished. During the bombardment a load of sand and gravel was thrown against the right side of my face, resulting in a nasty eye and ear infection. Years later this incident turned out to be the cause of my eventual status as an invalid. I lost the sight in my right eye and became totally deaf on the same side. For this injury I was awarded the Dutch Purple Heart.

For my eye infection, I had to go to the hospital in Chungkai around December in order to receive better treatment. However, there was still a lack of medicine. The infected eye was cleaned well daily with boracic water and sulpha preparations. We were still in Chungkai at Christmas and were served clean white rice, a relatively good soup, and a snack from the British kitchen.

At the beginning of January 1945 I was declared cured by the Japanese doctor and found to be fit enough to return to Linson. In spite of the fact that almost daily we heard Allied airplanes flying over, our camp was spared from attacks or bombardments.

In April I was transported with twenty POWs and five Japanese guards to Kanchanaburi to forage for the Japanese kitchen. I learned that my former commanding officer of Tardan camp, Reserve 1st Lt. Bert Sanders, had died during one of the bombardments. He belonged to a small group of good, especially humane officers whom I encountered during my time in POW camps. We also heard the most fantastic rumors of Allied conquests. It was remarkable that camp food was actually improving, now featuring more meat and vegetables. The "hurry up" commands at work, usually accompanied by strikes with the stick, diminished considerably. Often we were even allowed to cease work earlier and go back to camp.

On August 20, 1945, during evening roll call, the Japanese commander gave a short speech relaying the most important message for the POWs: *Senzo owari*—the war is over!

Surprisingly, the next morning, Linson was already being dismantled after a night when hardly anybody slept. Even the Jap guards entered our barracks, not out of duty but out of free will and choice. They shook our hands and congratulated us. So in a joyous mood we marched to *our* railroad at the station at Brangkasi we saw several flatbed cars and the reserve locomotive. The Japanese machinist was exceedingly friendly, as were other Japanese station personnel. What a welcome change that was!

In our tattered outfits—some had barely a loincloth—we sang such songs as "It's a Long Way to Tipperary" and "We Will Be Driving Our Own Train When Peace Comes." Despite the fact that the railroad bridges were built by POWs—or perhaps because of it—I was rather apprehensive every time the train would traverse one of the unfenced bridges. We drove throughout the night and arrived safely at Kanchanaburi the next morning. There we saw the Allied flags waving—those of the Americans, British and Australians, and, of course, the Dutch tricolor!

We did not notice any Japanese around, and the Thais greeted us as though we were the liberators. Right after breakfast where we ate real bread for the first time, our group was disbanded. The soldiers of the other nations continued their journey to Bangkok while the Dutch contingent was subdivided and distributed throughout various Dutch camps. I ended up in Tamocan. It was a base camp which was eventually converted into a training camp where the fittest among us were prepared for anticipated combat in Indonesia.

Upon arrival in Kanchanaburi we learned that President Sukarno had declared Indonesia's independence on August 17, 1945. Thus the fight for freedom from Dutch domination had officially started. The first victims of battles during the formative period, the so-called Bersiap period, were unfortunately the defenseless European and Indo-European women and children who were already weakened by years of captivity during the Japanese occupation.

That bad news cast a long shadow over our festive mood. While the other Allied POWs were quickly repatriated to their respective homelands, our boys, after a cursory physical examination, were sent back into combat again. In spite of the fact that I was scheduled to have an eye operation, I was declared fit for combat. I felt somewhat cheated. It was only after the physical for the formation of two combat battalions that the attending physician remarked, "You are scheduled to go to Java with the first group for your eye operation." That was great news.

What was most worrisome for us was the frightening news from Indonesia about the developments there. But it was only after the women evacuees from Semarang, Central Java, had landed in Thailand and recounted their horror stories to us that we realized how serious the situation actually was. They also told how some Japanese soldiers often heroically rescued Dutch women and children out of the hands of the Indonesian extremists.

At the beginning of 1946, the Red Elephant brigade, also known as the 5th BL Brigade Seaborne Division, to which I belonged, left Thailand. Initially, we were not allowed to disembark on Java but were destined for Bali, Lombok and Sumatra instead. About three weeks later our echelon departed on the MS *Klipfontein*, reaching Jakarta in three days. Upon request by the British authorities, our group left unarmed, a typical ostrich policy because within 48 hours we were outfitted with the most modern weapons.

After billeting for about one week in Menteng Pulo, Jakarta, I went to sickbay to inquire about the status of my promised eye operation. I was placed on a waiting list and told that I would eventually receive written confirmation. In the meantime, I had to report for field duty.

The next day I was already detailed to Sgt. Major Jacques van Asdonck, a career soldier from Cirebon, Central Java. Our primary function was the protection and escort of "B" Division commander Col. S. de Waal.

It must have been towards the end of April or the beginning of May 1946 that our platoon was ordered to escort Lt. G.G. van Mook, Army Commander Gen. Spoor and the division commander to recently conquered Tangerang and nearby Serpong. What we heard and saw there was atrocious!

The main victims were Chinese store owners and their families. These simple and humble people were murdered in cold blood by Indonesian extremists in a most cruel manner merely because they allowed Dutch reconnaissance troops to get water from their well. As soon as the troops withdrew, the extremists took revenge. And how! Children were nailed to the doors and stabbed with sharpened bamboo spears. Girls and women, after being raped, were pierced with the bamboo spears entering their vaginas and exiting at the mouth. The men, with hands tied behind their back, were thrown into the well.

Those savage acts certainly could not be attributed to the *Merdeka* (freedom) ideal. Nor could it be the work of a self-respecting, republican army! I was rather used to seeing mangled corpses while serving in the military, but I hoped I would never have to witness such horribly mutilated bodies again.

It must have been either October or November 1946 when the headquarters of "B" Division was transferred to Bandung. Staff officers, their dependents and the remainder of the troops drove by convoy to the final destination. We arrived without incident. Headquarters was located in the renowned Transport and Public Works building.

Our task was expanded to include food transport escort services to various military outposts in the countryside. Honor should be given where honor is due—the infamous *anjing* NICA battalion was able to pinch many Indonesian extremist activities in the bud.* Their members also gave confirmation about atrocities committed in Bandung during the Bersiap period.

At a rather slack period, one week without receiving orders, I approached the company medical officer. I asked for the umpteenth time why I had to be on a waiting list in the first place. I was thoroughly annoyed that this military doctor did not know anything about the affair, even though his colleagues in Jakarta solemnly promised me that they would forward my case. Fortunately, this quack did not refer me to the eye care section on Naripan Road, a notoriously bad hospital.

Two relatively young eye doctors, graduates of the Royal Army, thoroughly examined me at another hospital. Since I was not in pain, they only prescribed pilocarpine drops and advised me to return in one month. So I did not get an eye operation after all since this was deemed unnecessary. I returned only twice as a result of participating in the first police action carried out by our detachment on July 20, 1947, and I had to leave Bandung. In a one-kilometer-long convoy, we traveled, under air cover, over winding roads and across deep ravines to Semarang, Central Java, where we arrived safely towards the end of July.

In November 1947, after morning roll call, I was summoned by Capt. Franken together with three other career soldiers with the rank

---

*NICA stands for Netherlands Indies Civil Administration. Its troops were given the nickname anjing (dogs) by the extremists.

of sergeant first class. I was merely an enlisted man without much prospect for advancement. I wondered what this was all about since I was sure I had done nothing wrong. Or could it be in connection with my eye operation? Inside, the captain was flanked by a staff officer and an administrative captain. After saluting, I was invited to sit down. The administrative officer asked me to examine and identify some books which lay open on the desk.

"Those are tabular books, a supply book and a cash book," I replied.

When I responded positively to the question and gave additional information about the schooling I had enjoyed, the officer said, "Starting today, you are our mess sergeant. Sergeant Sodeike will not return. Are you able and willing to do this job."

"I will certainly try," was my reply.

When the gentleman asked if I wanted to become a career soldier, however, I politely declined because I did not go for all that military charade.

It took me a week to familiarize myself with the job requirements. Between officer Schmidlen and myself, we had at our disposal a Jeep and a delivery truck, including a driver. Soon I met the officers' wives who bought commodities from us. As a whole, they were real ladies, although it seemed to me that some of them were too quick to complain.

About 1948, I applied at the Department of Finance for training as tax examiner. After a two-day test, administered by three graduate tax examiners, I was judged to be qualified. The only matters remaining unresolved were my demobilization and the medical exam promised me in Thailand and subsequently in Jakarta and Bandung. When I visited the military eye doctor he commented after examining me, "You should have been operated on right after the incident took place."

Once again I had to explain that there was no doctor in the jungle camp, let alone an eye surgeon. However, this time I liked his decision when he said, "I will operate on you in ten days, but not in this military hospital because this one is overcrowded and the equipment is outmoded."

At headquarters, rumors were going around of an impending second police action. Strangely enough, I had no interest whatsoever in such activities. I felt as though I had been abandoned by the military service, particularly due to the poor attitude of some of the eye doctors, who did not take my injury seriously. In the meantime, I taught a career sergeant the ins and outs of the job just in case I had to be admitted for the operation and in the event of my demobilization.

On December 7 I had to report to the Salvation Army hospital. The doctor introduced me to a Dutch-educated Chinese physician, who said that there was a certain degree of urgency and that I definitely had to be examined by an eye doctor every three months thereafter. On December 9 around 9:00 A.M. I had my operation. I had to remain in the hospital for at least two more weeks. The operation was a success, but I had somewhat limited vision in that particular eye. On the 15th I heard that I would be demobilized on January 9, 1949. This was the greatest news I had heard in the last ten years.

On December 19, 1948, the second police action was conducted. Very early in the morning, airplanes came roaring over the hospital heading towards Yogyakarta. I was discharged from the hospital three days later, and on January 8, 1949, I said good-bye to the army after thanking all staff officers, including Gen. de Waal and officer Schotborch.

And that's the way that seven valuable years of my life came to an end with the bitter conclusion that, at least in my case, everything was for naught.

ABOUT THE CONTRIBUTOR

Frans John Nicolaas Ponder was born in 1921 in Ambarawa, Central Java. He attended elementary school and college in the Indies. After the war, he studied modern business administration and followed courses at an Indonesian judicial institute.

He voluntarily entered military service. A usual tour of duty would have been 18 months, but due to the outbreak of war, he was in the military for almost eight years, including imprisonment and post-military service. The Dutch government advised him to opt for Indonesian citizenship. He held various jobs under the new Indonesian administration, rising through the ranks.

Due to political unrest, he decided to reapply for Dutch citizenship in 1959. After emigration to the Netherlands, it was difficult to find a suitable job. Eventually he was declared unfit because of war injury and in 1986 he was granted private and government pensions.

He and his wife Matilde currently live in Amsterdam. Among other hobbies, he often contributes articles to various Dutch and Dutch-Indonesian magazines.

WILLEM WANROOY

*A Letter
to My Grandson*

Dear Gill,

In the fall of 1944, when General MacArthur's forces were threatening to retake the Philippines, the Japanese started to increase the transportation of prisoners of war from the island of Java to the islands of Sumatra. A railroad was being built to transport coal from the west coast of this island to the east coast and then to Singapore.

My hellship journey began at Jakarta on September 15, 1944. I was 19 years old then. The day we all had been dreading for months, the day 2,400 of us would be riding on a prison ship, filled me with apprehension.

Two long lines of men slowly moved up two gangways to an old, rusty freighter, the *Junyo Maru*. One line, going in the fore section of the ship, consisted of about 4,000 haggard looking Javanese natives. We moved into the stern. Some 2,200 filed down into the hold, and around 200 of us—including myself—wound up on deck.

On September 18, we were steaming some 10 to 15 miles off the west coast of Sumatra. For more than three days I had suffered from the blazing sun during the day, and from bone-chilling rains at night.

But it was more horrid below deck.

Without enough drinking water, food or medicine, or fresh air, the fetid, stifling hold was like a black stinking oven with more than 2,000 souls melting in their own sweat and gasping for every breath.

Around five in the afternoon, as I stood near the open deck hatch, a sudden jolt shook the ship. As I looked up, I saw human bodies and pieces of wood, metal and other debris blown high in the sky from somewhere midship.

"Be calm! Break down engines," a Japanese voice screeched through a loudspeaker.

Then there was a second jolt and a thundering blast deep beneath my feet, followed by a few moments of silence. Then, chaos. Howls and screams. "Torpedoes!" "Abandon ship!" Panic set in. Men jumped overboard. Others threw life rafts over the side.

I helped some men climb out of the hold. A mob of panic-stricken men crawled, trudged and wormed on the single iron ladder. Scratched, beaten and bloodied, some reached the deck. The bowels of the ship were belching up. It was horrible.

Numb and discouraged, I sat down and took off my boots, putties and outer clothing, and jumped into the ocean. I was an excellent swimmer and got as far away from the ship as I could in one effort, then stopped and looked back.

Oh my God, what an awful sight. The ship was slowly sinking deeper and deeper, stern first, bow high in the air. Hundreds and hundreds of bodies crawled and clung to the sides and decks. Others dropped off like ants from a sugar loaf. Howls, screams and cries filled the air.

The ship disappeared against a sunset sky burning with yellows and oranges. Foam and water bells churned madly in a maelstrom of death and destruction.

More than 5,000 souls perished before my eyes.

I looked at death and saw a friend. And I decided to fight him with all the strength left in me. After two-and-a-half years of prison camps I was skeletal in appearance and, as a prisoner of war, I had contempt for the Japanese. As a physical man I was not worth saving. But mentally, I was. I told myself that, if ever, this was the time I needed courage—courage to remain afloat, to remain alive.

I swam to a deck hatch and hung on to it. There were about ten others doing the same. As the night wore on, hunger, thirst—especially thirst—and misery in a cold dark ocean would make drowning seem a welcome relief.

Close by a man started to laugh. And laugh. High-pitched giggles that ended in a gurgling sound as he pushed himself under water to come up, moments later, as a floating corpse. Mumbling incoherently, a few others followed his example. I kept on floating, hanging on to that hatch. And the night passed by. Slowly. Hour after hour.

The interminable night came to an end as daylight broke through over the eastern horizon, where land was. Far, far away. There were only two other men left with me on the hatch.

"Ship! Ship!" someone shouted.

"What is it doing?"

"Nothing, damn it. It stays where it is."

My head buzzed. Tongue and throat raspy dry from thirst. Body aching. The sun rose. It got hotter and hotter.

I had reached the edge of madness when I heard a voice deep, deep inside me: "Choose your fate and seek your way, by your own light. God watches all the while and guides your steps unaware." It was the voice of my father when I was still a young boy.

A last surge of energy and strength shot through my exhausted body. "Swim, swim to the ship," my mind commanded. "Pull the hatch with you for safety when you get tired. Swim and swim until I cannot command your body any longer."

I swam for five long hours, pulling the hatch and the two men. Stopping and going. Slowly, pathetically slowly, the little ship became larger and larger. It was maddening. I kicked and kicked my feet. My shoulders and legs ached. Flashes of pain shot through my body. Water, sweat and tears ran down my face. And I swam and swam.

"Hurry up," a voice screamed.

I howled in desperation, kicked myself off against the hatch, and swam like a maniac, arms and legs grinding through the water. A race against death, death the ocean. I left the two men on the hatch behind.

As the ship gained speed I grabbed a dangling rope. Someone pulled me on board. I was the last one picked up that day. There were no other ships to be seen. Once on deck I dropped exhausted on my knees, and someone poured cool water down my throat. I had survived a watery hell.

I couldn't help but look back. A hatch with a head on either side bobbed in the ocean. There were no hysterics; no defiant oaths. No screams, "Coward! Murderer!"

Yes, my dear grandson, I had had the courage, strength and responsibility to pull the two men with me. To be sure, having the hatch with me during the swim was partially a matter of self-preservation, but I could have left those men where they were and taken a smaller piece of driftwood instead along. Somehow, though, the company of the two men reminded me of the reasons of living.

Yet at the decisive moment the importance of my own life took precedence over compassion. Although I made that decision in a flash of a second, it was a conscious one. I have to live with it for the rest of my life. I survived the nightmare on the ocean, but the ordeal of it all is engraved forever in my memory.

The two men were picked up the following day. I saw them in the camp where we were initially assembled, but never met them again.

I don't know if they survived the war.

ABOUT THE CONTRIBUTOR

Willem F. Wanrooy, who writes his books and articles under the pen name Van Waterford, was a corporate communications director until he retired in 1984. Writing and acting are his primary interests. Wanrooy has authored 18 nonfiction books and hundreds of articles and stories. One of his first books, a consumer-oriented home computer textbook, became a best seller in its series.

His most recent book, a reference work titled, *Prisoners of the Japanese in World War II: Statistical History, Personal Narratives and Memorials Concerning POWs in Camps and on Hellships, Civilian Internees, Asian Slave Laborers and Others Captured in the Pacific Theater*, was published by McFarland in 1994. He is presently working on a book that deals solely with the strategies of survival the camp prisoners of the Japanese have used in order to cope, endure and prevail during their incarceration.

ARTHUR STOCK

A British Prisoner of War

Prior to the war in the Pacific, I, a British national, lived in England. I entered the Royal Air Force (RAF) at the tender age of 15 and was stationed, among other posts, in Aston Down, Gloucestershire, where I served for a number of years. In 1941, I was aboard a troop transport ship to the Far East and arrived in Singapore towards the end of July. I was assigned to No. 81 Repair and Salvage Unit, but since there was no equipment, our unit of about 120 men was set to work making dummy airplanes out of wood and canvas.

After the equipment did arrive in September, I was transferred into the state of Johor (Malaysia) to maintain two squadrons of aircraft, Blenheim bombers and Australian fighter-trainer Wirraways. In quick succession several other assignments followed.

By early January 1942, the Japanese were invading the northern boundary of Johor so the unit was ordered to Sebawang, an airfield on Singapore Island, to support a newly arrived squadron of Hurricanes. The island was being shelled from the mainland, and it was quite unpleasant to be both shelled and bombed daily. On the morning of February 12, the Japanese had already landed and were advancing southward towards the city.

What remained of our RAF unit was eventually evacuated from Singapore to Java just two days before the bastion surrendered. We sailed without escort and arrived in Jakarta safely a few days later. Having no equipment, we were billeted in the Koning Willem III School in the suburb of Djatinegara. We were given beds and bedding, were paid up to date in Dutch guilders, and then nobody took any further interest in us Brits.

So we explored the city, bought souvenirs, watched the population enjoying themselves, much as had happened in Singapore, as if the enemy would just turn around and go back to Japan. At the same time we were hoping that the authorities would soon secure a passage for us to Ceylon (Sri Lanka) or on to Australia. But it was not to be! The Battle of the Java Sea was fought and the Allied navies were made impotent. It was not long thereafter that the enemy landed at several places on Java at once.

As soon as this message came through, the unit was ordered to a military airfield in West Java, where a squadron of Martin bombers was operating. But as the unit possessed only men and no equipment, it was soon made clear that we were of no use and should leave the next morning. Then came a message from the prime minister, Mr. Churchill himself. All members of the RAF were to arm themselves and to make for the hills. Here we were to fight as guerrillas in a force to be known as the Blue Army.

Our unit was driven to Garut and issued rifles of uncertain vintage. Some firing practice was organized, but maneuvers had hardly lasted 24 hours before a counter order arrived. The unit was to make its way to Cilacap, Central Java, and await evacuation.

This news was greeted with great joy, so once again the personnel embarked in their trucks, heading eastward, passing through Garut. Here other news was received that the Dutch Army had capitulated, and the unit was ordered to travel to Tasikmalaya and surrender to the enemy.

So the Brits moved to their first camp, a school in Yogyakarta, the ancient city in Central Java. Screens were erected to minimize contact with the local population, but no great restraint was placed on movement of prisoners. There were no guards stationed within the camp bounds, although there was a guardhouse 100 meters away.

Each day the bulk of the prisoners marched with a small escort to the railway station and placed on trains for Maguwo airfield three miles away. There was no objection to trading with the locals. On arrival, we marched to the airfield apron and then past the Japanese commander who acknowledged our salute.

Working parties were arranged mainly for repair of bomb craters and buildings. There was no harassment by the Japanese. Indeed, they went out of their way to be friendly. However, there was another officer who was not so affable. He was rather irritated when he discovered that we had "accidentally" punctured most of the gas cans when unloading them from cars unto planks which happened to have exposed nails. But we were not punished.

All prisoners had acquired some kind of bed, laid out in the classrooms. The Japanese provided adequate food, even allowing a cash sum for purchase of food in the market. They also gave us permission to employ a local woman to assist in the preparation of indigenous foods. Unfortunately, because of the abundance of other food, we scarcely ate any rice, and the Japanese were angry when they discovered several sacks of it going bad in the store. They then reduced the availability of other foods, but meals were certainly good in comparison with later on during imprisonment.

After a few weeks in Yogyakarta camp, our quarters were moved to Maguwo. There were at first no boundary fences either, but after inspection by a senior officer, a barbed wire fence one foot high was erected. We were informed that this would be crossed at our own peril. A number of men who did do this on a shopping expedition once were apprehended and badly beaten. Most of us could see no point in attempting to escape at this stage anyway. Why should we? The Javanese were overwhelmingly pro–Japanese. We had no doubt that even if we did escape the Japanese, the Javanese would have surrendered us to them.

In general, the relationship between ourselves and members of the Japanese Army Air Force was cordial. They intimated that we would soon be leaving Maguwo for a prison camp and they were very sorry for us!

That prison camp was Jaarmarkt, Surabaya. Once we reached the camp we no longer enjoyed our semi–European diet. The food consisted of a bowlful of watery, milkless rice porridge, called *pap*, twice daily. We also received a pint measure of boiled rice, with a third of a pint of thin vegetable stew, mainly composed of pumpkin with up to half a dozen centimeter cubes of meat. The work parties here depressed us. The Dutch who organized them saw to it that any new arrivals went to the worst places—either the docks or the oil refinery.

Work was extremely arduous in both these places, and our captors really went out of their way to be nasty. Beatings with fists and rifle butts were administered largely because of our failing to understand their requirements. Fortunately, after a few days the Japanese changed over two of the work parties and we found ourselves in a more comfortable setting—a city block with Dutch, Eurasian (Dutch-Indonesian) and Ambonese women and children. They were plying us with food and money. Presumably, the unlucky Dutchmen now found themselves at the docks, shoveling up burnt sugar into hoppers for dumping at sea.

In the course of time the unpleasant jobs were shared more evenly, and there were fewer work parties. As we were paid 10 cents a day, the price of 16 cigarettes, plus the chance of a gift when released, there was quite a demand to get on the work parties. And even the docks and refinery became more congenial in time. The standard of food gradually improved. We had a Vienna roll, sometimes spread with butter, for breakfast and there was unlimited rice and soup in the evening for the outside workers. At midday, the *pap* was gradually replaced by rice and soup or spicy Indonesian sauce. We became quite fit again. Accommodations at Jaarmarkt were never bad. We all had a meter of space on our split bamboo cots.

Our relations with the Japanese were poor, due mainly to a lack of understanding. In particular, anybody found out of quarters at night was likely to be intercepted. The magic password in all these cases, in Japanese, was *"Benjo e ikimasu,"* which meant, "I am going to the toilet." Once learned, this phrase saved a great deal of trouble.

Also one had to remember to obey Japanese custom and salute the guard, who felt badly insulted if ignored. We found that, when bareheaded, we were expected to bow, although many thought this to be enforced subservience. However, when wearing headgear, a simple salute was proper. Even if bareheaded, a smart incline of the torso, Prussian style, was acceptable.

There were reasonable opportunities for recreation. A football pitch was laid out on the camp's open field. Indoor games of many kinds were avidly played. There were also classes in many subjects. I found Dutch language classes very interesting. There was also a canteen, limited in scope at first to coffee at two cents a cup, but later selling all kinds of fruit at reasonable prices.

The sick were well taken care of. Most of the officers who received pay equivalent to their Japanese counterparts contributed a substantial part of it to the "Health Service." Under this program, nutritious foods and drugs were purchased and donated to those who deserved it and, I am sure, to others who did not.

Most of the inhabitants of the camp were Dutch or Dutch-Indonesians. Under Dutch law, the offspring of mixed marriages were entitled to Dutch citizenship, but also became subject to military service. The men had been called up only a few weeks before the Japanese

There must have been 1,500 men on our 8,000-ton cargo ship. We did not think that we could survive the 14-day journey, but we all did, although we were weakened after being fed the extremely poor food. Happily, we were allowed to spend much time on deck, and sometimes the crew or Japanese passengers would pass unwanted food to us. Kasayama was also on board, and many of us had long conversations with him in English.

We arrived first at the port of Ambon, where we unloaded some supplies. Then we sailed north across the strait to Amahai on the island of Seram. The second ship unloaded all Dutch prisoners and supplies, while some of the supplies were unloaded from our ship. We then sailed back across the strait to Haruku, which is only approximately six kilometers square and which was our final destination.

We were taken to the quarters that would house us all. They were dreadfully built bamboo huts with palm roofs, set in a nutmeg plantation. In contrast, between the huts were beautifully built latrines with individual cubicles, set over trenches only half a meter deep. There was also a partly built cook house by the river half a kilometer away, but there was no firewood—and it was the wet monsoon!

There was plenty of rice, but no vegetables or meat. These commodities were still on the ship left at Amahai while all the cigarettes were still on our ship. The cooks slaved in the pouring rain to cut down bamboo and timber for the fires while we were unloading the ship. Eventually, we had some half-cooked, smokey rice and nutmeg water, ready just after sunset. What a treat that was.

Everybody was utterly miserable. We had no groundsheets, and the water ran right through the huts, soaking our straw bed-mats. The next day we were marched three kilometers up a grassy slope towards two hills. We had to scrape the tops of these hills and fill in the valley between to build a three kilometer airstrip. And this was using only manual labor, without wheelbarrows! We dug with hoes for two days. Then dysentery struck and all except 200 men got the disease. The latrines were overflowing, the rain kept pouring down, and the POWs were starting to die.

Those able to do light work dug the latrines deeper. All the cubicles were removed. I cannot recall how I was able to survive; I only remember drifting my way to the "intensive care" hut, going blind, and then, as if by a miracle, finding myself able to walk again. Finally, I was placed in a "convalescent" hut.

All this time, the fitter men were laboring on the airstrip for up to 12 hours a day with no respite. The daily death rate sometimes reached 30. It was, of course, impossible to build coffins, so the bodies were buried as they died in a common trench. By December 1942, 500 men had died. The medical officers kept a record of the cause of death, and, in their opinion, the greatest single cause was malnutrition. It is difficult, if not impossible, to understand how a civilized nation like Japan would allow such things to happen.

As the monsoon rains faded away, at long last, things started to get better. First the British officers persuaded the Japanese to allow a latrine to be built over the sea. The dysentery just about vanished. Then the leader of the guard arranged to build a new cook house next to the river. (Incidentally, this man was found guilty of cruelty and hanged after the war in front of the huts.) One by one the prisoners demolished the original huts and built new ones after working all day on the airstrip. A well was dug and a firm sandy square was laid out in front of the huts.

A hospital ship appeared and took the 500 sick men back to Java. Work on the airstrip continued, and by about February 1943, the first Japanese single- and twin-engine aircraft landed.

One day, a twin-engine plane crashed into the rock face at the side of the airstrip. The Japanese quickly set up a bucket brigade, using the POWs. Fire was averted, and the crew was rescued. The next day the Japanese asked for the names of the rescuers. At first they refused to identify themselves, but on being assured that they were to be rewarded, they responded. Each was given a beautifully worded document, praising them for their "gallantry," and a present of sweet rice cakes.

Later on we heard the sound of different aircraft. We ran like the wind away from the runway, which was then blasted by American B-17s. None of us was hurt, and the Japs soon had us filling in the holes. Down in the village, however, many huts, including the quarters of the Korean "comfort girls," were badly damaged. Some of us were detailed to help clean up the women's quarters. We were appalled to witness their living conditions. Out of gratitude, the women offered us food and drink. We felt very sorry for these conscripted prostitutes. The Japanese had treated Koreans like slaves from the time of the conquest of Korea in 1909.

Because of this bombing incident, the Japanese were determined to widen the airstrip. Now those of us who had been in the "hospital" when the strip was first built got our turn working on the coral rock face. We had to cut holes in the rock, using hammers and chisels, so that 100-kilogram dynamite charges could be placed and detonated. Then all the debris had to be carted from the tops of the hills to the bottom. By this time the Japanese had acquired enough material to make a crude railway on which hopper cars ran. A number of nasty accidents occurred on this railway.

Eventually the runway was completed, but it became obvious that the Allies had control of the skies and sea. The POWs were therefore moved to the next island of Ambon. There they were ordered to help finish the airstrip being built by other POWs at the town of Liang. The morale of these men was dreadful. They had never recovered from the dysentery, and the camp was in the same condition as ours was when we first arrived.

After a few weeks the airstrip was deemed complete, but by then very few serviceable Japanese aircraft remained. It was evident that we were about to be moved again, and we ended up being billeted in the Dutch Reformed Church in the city of Ambon.

That day, during a light air raid, leaflets were dropped advising everyone to leave the city, because it was about to be destroyed. The Japanese responded by moving us across the bay to a former leper camp in Lahat. Indeed, the next day the bombers arrived and completely wiped out the city. I was sent with two others the day after to find the body of a POW who was killed, and we buried him.

The leper camp was low lying and infested with mosquitoes. Fortunately we were soon taken to the docks, and about 500 of us boarded an 800-ton coaster. Well over half of us were stretcher cases. Since the holds were laden with empty 50-gallon drums, the stretchers were laid on top of these. The fitter men each acquired two drums to sleep on. It was not easy to find a comfortable position.

The Japanese imposed a rule that in general we should all stay below deck. Those who could walk were allowed above to use the toilets which were set over the ship's side; the sick men all needed makeshift bedpans. I was enlisted as a temporary male nurse, wearing a Red Cross arm band. This gave me the advantage of having access to the open deck at all times and raised my morale significantly.

We sailed westward from Ambon, reaching the southwest coast of Sulawesi after a few days. Here we were greeted enthusiastically by the inhabitants, who seemed to have a surplus of eggs, meat, and vegetables. While our ship was tied up, we were ordered to camouflage it with tree branches. We ate better than we had for years. Unfortunately, the price of everything inflated as the locals caught on. But we benefited immensely from the short stay.

After the Japanese had presumably been told that the area was cleared of Allied submarines, we sailed westward again towards Ujung Padang. Here we docked and loaded the ship with food. We left for the next stop which was the island of Laut on the southeast coast. We tied up for several days, receiving food again from the locals, before setting out southward towards Surabaya.

The journey had taken four weeks, but thanks to our enforced anchoring, we received plenty of fresh food. No more than 25 people had died. This was in contrast to a later ship which left Ambon for Java. They were not allowed ashore, and had to anchor in Makasar Bay for four weeks. Blackwater fever* killed half of those who had embarked.

Back in Surabaya, we were quickly transferred to a passenger train in which we traveled in comfort to Jakarta. We were accommodated in Kampong Makasar on the outskirts of the city. Camp conditions were better than those at Haruku when we left it, and work parties were employed almost exclusively at a market garden called Tanjung Oost. We had to march the six kilometers from camp, starting just before dawn at six. In camp we were each issued a 100-milligram loaf of yeast bread which was carried with us to the garden. We would arrive at about 8:30. An infusion of tea was provided while we ate and rested until nine.

We worked here quite leisurely with hoe, spade, and hands until one in the afternoon, when we assembled again for the return march. Back in camp we were given a rich stew of spinach and meat with rice. Unfortunately, I could not digest this food, possibly due to the long walk barefoot in the sun. I was unable to keep it down, but must have derived some nourishment from it, because I gained weight. And apart from the daily vomiting, I remained relatively fit.

Our next move arrived far too soon. Our destination was Singapore in Malaysia. For this journey we were accommodated in the steerage section of a small ferry. We were not allowed on deck, but the journey was over in three days. We were fed with good quality, indigenous food, but in quantity sufficient only to hold body and soul together.

---

*Also called malarial hemoglobinuria, this disease is an exaggerated form of suburban malaria wherein blood is liberated in the urine. In severe cases it results in death.

In Singapore we lived in the River Valley Road Camp, where we met people who had worked on the infamous railway between Thailand and Burma. Their conditions had been similar to ours but they had also been attacked by cholera, resulting in an extremely high death rate in certain areas.

Soon after, some of us were transferred to a camp within the dock area of Tanjungpagar. Here we were employed largely as dockers, and there were often useful pickings of tinned food and cigarettes from damaged cases. Unfortunately, by this time I had contracted chronic dysentery, which prevented me from joining the outside work parties. So I took to collecting unwanted scraps of woolen goods, unraveling them, spinning the thread into yarn, and knitting this material, using needles of either bamboo (for body items) or barbed wire (for socks). In this manner I was able to obtain food and cheroots by trading with those who were working outside.

The food ration by this time was extremely sparse. The military officer estimated that our daily issue provided about 400 calories. It was fortunate that in April 1945, we acquired Red Cross parcels, one to be split between each two of us. Our captors next decided that we should go to Changi Prison, the largest and most comfortable camp in Singapore. It was run in the recommended Red Cross style, administered entirely by the British army. Japanese guards were not allowed within the confines of the jail. It was highly organized. Red Cross parcels had been received, but were not distributed directly to the prisoners. Instead, the food was sent to the cook house to augment considerably the normal diet. This resulted in extremely tasty soup and rice dishes, supplemented by attractive extras. Red Cross clothing was received and sent to a tailoring department where one pair of American slacks was converted into two pairs of shorts.

By this time our personal clothing had dwindled to two G-strings and one pair of shorts. My own shorts were originally my RAF tropical trousers, which had been turned into shorts and patched 32 times. The issue of clothing at Changi Prison was a most welcome gift.

Life at Changi was far from arduous and intensely boring, except at meal times. We were glad when we were asked if we would like to move to a camp just outside the wall.

There were daily work parties, and we were given an issue of oatmeal porridge made with powdered milk, plus five cigarettes per day. The work took place mainly at the Chinese High School on Bukit Timah Road, which had been turned into an officers' hostel. It was intended that this would be the place of the Japanese last stand in response to the expected Allied invasion. We dug tunnels and trenches under and around the school. Sometimes we were made to work all night but were rewarded by ample food. Most of the enemy officers could speak English. We all did our best to convince them that it would be so much better for all if they were to surrender rather than fight to the last!

One day started differently from the others. This time I was not working at the school, but near a barracks. The soldiers were harassing us, and we were feeling quite uncomfortable when all of a sudden the guard said, "Work stop! All men go home!"

So back to camp we were driven and were told that the war was over. Since the Japanese had been ordered to keep all of the prisoners together, we moved back into the prison. The occupants of the cells were British Royal Navy, and we received a warm welcome from them. Outside, food started pouring into camp from Singapore cold storage, which was stocked almost as high as it had been at the surrender. Also interminable flights of U.S. B-24 Liberators were dropping food by parachute. Most of this ended up in the cook house. The HMS *Sussex* sailed into harbor and from then on provided us with a first class, three course dinner every evening. In spite of all this excitement, I was bored by the lack of work parties, so I eventually volunteered to help clear out the drains running under the prison, on a daily basis. It was a filthy job, but it was interesting to tour the catacombs. At least we got a hot bath with real soap after our four-hour stint.

After nearly a month of quasi freedom, the Dutch troop ship *Tegelberg* arrived to take us home. Once aboard, I gained weight at the rate of a pound a day. By the time I disembarked at Liverpool, my weight had increased from seven stone ten pound (108 U.S. pounds) at the time of Japanese surrender to over fourteen stone (196 U.S. pounds). When I arrived in my home village, my brother, emaciated after serving in the Middle East for three years, was thought to have been the prisoner of war, while I was taken for a war profiteer! How ironic.

ABOUT THE CONTRIBUTOR

Arthur Stock was born on March 13, 1922, in England where he attended school. At 15 he joined the Royal Air Force, and after assignment in the U.K. he found himself on the way to Southeast Asia. He survived the war years as a POW.

He returned to England in 1945 and became a military technical instructor at the RAF. He decided to continue to teach as a civilian and eventually worked for BOAC for a number of years.

He earned an electrical engineering degree and ended up working in Belfast, Northern Ireland, as a test engineer.

Stock retired in 1987 and is actively pursuing his numerous hobbies, among which is that of watch and clock repair. He still lives in Northern Ireland.

ANTON ACHERMAN

Glimpses of Camp Life

When the Japanese occupied the island of Java, they decided to eliminate the Dutch people from society in an attempt to make Java Asiatic. In Batavia, later called Jakarta, it all started with the rounding up and imprisonment of prominent Dutchmen. The Jakarta telephone book was used since it listed the positions people held, such as judge, policeman, engineer or director of a company. That first group ended up in Struiswijk prison.

The trade school, called Adek, was converted into a POW camp. Every week, selected areas in town were sealed off and men were flushed out of their homes and transported in open trucks to these camps. Most of them were prepared and had their luggage ready to go. After most men were picked up, the women's camp, called Cideng, was opened. Women and younger children were forcefully or sometimes voluntarily interned. In 1944, men from Struiswijk and Adek were relocated by train to Bandung, West Java, and placed in the 15th Battalion Cavalry, Camp Cikudapateuh. This camp consisted of barracks and many houses.

In the former Dutch East Indies, now called Indonesia, an archipelago the size of the United States, there were only some 220,000 Dutch or people of Dutch descent in the early forties. It would not have been very difficult to eventually lock all of them up, which was the grandiose plan of the Japanese.

In Bandung's 15th Battalion Camp, as the war progressed, one of the first things internees would do after they arrived was to scan the bulletin board for the names of those who had died. Next to the name, the person's age and occupation were noted. As it turned out later, age was a very important determinant of the survival rate. It revealed that 90 percent of those who died were in the 52–58 age range. This seemed to be the most vulnerable age group.

Acquiring accurate news was also important to all concerned. Of course, there were plenty of rumors going around, but there was also solid news that was obtained by monitoring three clandestine radios in camp. The Japanese were aware of their existence but never managed to find them. One was located in the kitchen, hidden underneath the seat of a small bench. Every time a search was conducted in this area, the commander was invited to sit on it. That bench was never turned over for inspection, so this was an excellent hiding place.

Food preparation was interesting and challenging. It started out with big cooking pots the size of oil drums, given to us by the Dutch army. These drums were placed on top of train rails. Underneath them, a wood fire was stoked, a very uneconomical way of using a limited supply of fuel. In the morning tapioca porridge was prepared, and since the pots were not covered, the smoke spoiled the taste of the porridge. Every time we took a bite, it was as if we were slapped in the face. But since we were hungry we had no choice but to eat it.

The supply of wood was gradually diminishing, so we had to find a way to work more efficiently. We had plenty of craftsmen in camp, so we built fireplaces with bricks salvaged from broken-down walls. Four pots could now be heated by one fire, so we managed to use the limited wood supply to our best advantage.

The type of fuel also changed. At first we used wood from regular trees, but eventually we used tea shrubs. This fuel burned hotter and was excellent for heating ovens to bake bread. We were fortunate to be able to do this baking in dome-shaped brick ovens. These domes were preheated on the inside until the bricks were hot. Then the fire was pulled out and the dough was inserted.

Thanks to the great skill of Dutch bakers, the camp was able to produce a top rate product. Instead of wheat, a mixture of corn, rice meal, tapioca and other ingredients was used. The proper mixture was critical to make a good-tasting bread. We each got one slice per day.

One of the usable byproducts of bread making was yeast, which was fed to the sick since it was high in vitamin B. There was also a lively trade being conducted in the camp. The main items for sale to the Indonesian guards and the Japanese, if one dared to approach them, were gold rings, watches, and articles of clothing. Foodstuffs, such as bread and rice were also traded.

The manufacturing of writing paper was another active enterprise. Since we did not have the right machinery, we went back to basics. We started recycling. Using a rock, we smashed, ripped and eventually boiled used paper. The mixture of water and paper was then allowed to stand in a tub. With a ladle, the mixture was poured out in thin layers, and after additional processing, paper sheets were the end result. These sheets, in turn, were transferred onto a sink plate and left to dry in the sun. The paper had an off gray color but was suitable for writing notes and letters.

There was also a great need for welding. Welding machines and rods were not available, and the Japanese were either unwilling or unable to provide them. But the problem was soon resolved. Rods were fashioned from barbed wires and cut into 12-inch pieces. The coating consisted of a mixture of crushed glass, fine coal and some sugar, using tapioca as a binder. The mixture had a consistency of heavy syrup and the rods were dipped into it and dried in the sun.

Two car batteries, a car generator and a one-third horsepower motor were somehow obtained to provide a power supply. The batteries for DC current and the generator, coupled to the electric motor, recharged the batteries. Now that we had the capacity to weld, we manufactured many items, such as cooking pots and buckets. The raw material consisted of zinc coated plates salvaged from the sheets covering the walkways between buildings.

Lighting a fire was always a big challenge since matches were unavailable. So again, we had to go back to basics. But there were plenty of flint stones in camp, so we used a pocket knife blade and clock springs as a metal striker to generate a spark. Moss, used as fuel, was smuggled in with wood deliveries.

Some enterprising souls were even able to get hold of some tubing. One end was sealed off, and a piston was inserted on the other end. A leather seal was made out of an old shoe, and a piece of moss was placed inside the piston. When air into the tube was quickly compressed, the heat which was generated was sufficient to ignite the moss.

There was also a hand-operated sawmill in the camp. The Japs provided the trees and we cut the planks for them. We were allowed to use the wood scraps for fuel. Another byproduct was sawdust, but this was difficult to burn and it smoked. But we found a novel solution and a smokeless burner was invented. A large can, about eight inches in diameter and ten inches high, was used to burn the sawdust into a gas fire. In the bottom of the lid, a round hole just the size of a broomstick was cut. The stick was then inserted into the partially filled can, and in this manner the dust was compacted. The stick was then removed and the sawdust was covered with the lid. If there was no lid available, sand or clay served equally well.

Subsequently, the can was placed on two rocks and the ring ignited with a small fire underneath the can. The hole started to glow as incomplete combustion took place. Eventually, out of the top, a hot blue smokeless gas flame would appear. This heat source was capable of bringing water to a boil and keeping it boiling for about three hours. For another two, it would keep things warm. We cooked such foods as sweet potatoes and jams this way. The best sawdust came from hardwood.

Safe drinking water was essential. Several potential well sites were identified, using a divining rod. Eventually wells were drilled at the most promising spots, and they indeed produced water. As a drill rig we used steel electrical poles, fastened on a tripod. After the well was drilled, a hand pump, manufactured from water pipe with a piston on the bottom, was inserted. Shoe leather was used as a seal, and concrete reinforcement rods were used as the pump handle. The pump was then sealed with clay and put to good use. The water was potable without being boiled.

There was entertainment in camp as well, and for exercise we went on daily walks on the soccer field. And of course we had to contend with the daily lineup for roll call.

Right from the start, there was a shortage of sugar and salt. The food rations became gradually smaller and smaller. As people became hungrier, the talk about food increased. So an intensive exchange of food recipes ensued. Storytelling was another popular pastime; people told stories about their occupation and various other subjects. Even some church services were allowed in Bandung camps.

Once the Japanese allowed the American Red Cross to send food parcels. This turned out to be a great blessing for us. The contents of a cubic foot box came to be merely one snack per individual. Each person received a small cube of Spam, twenty-five raisins, a small scoop of sugar, some candy, and two cigarettes. The main benefit of this handout was that some of the boxes contained sulfa tablets. This medication saved many lives and worked wonders for treating infections and for curing dysentery patients. We were most grateful to the American Red Cross.

The camp hospital was a special place. Most people working there were Dutch Roman Catholic brothers and the majority of them were teachers. The main reason they were employed in this capacity was because they were honest, very dedicated human beings. As a Protestant, I was working with a group of 12 brothers and a priest. The two years spent here proved to be one of the most memorable experiences of my life.

The leader of the group was Brother Antonius, who belonged to the Order of the Congregation of the Holy Heart in Holland. Prior to the war, he was a missionary on the small island of Bangka, off Sumatra's east coast. Besides being a teacher, he was also a manager of a pepper plantation.

There were some 80 patients in the hospital. The first year several cases of dysentery occurred, but during the last year beriberi was more prevalent, primarily due to malnutrition. In beriberi patients, fluid would accumulate, first in the feet and forearms, slowly progressing to the legs and upper arms, and finally engulfing the entire body. If the fluid reached the upper body, the heart eventually failed and the patient inevitably died. In a number of cases, the skin would actually rupture, usually in the legs, causing an infection. This would necessitate an operation, performed without any painkillers. Most patients did not utter a sound. I could never understand how they were able to stand the pain.

Brother Antonius was a man with many abilities and gifts. He was able to talk to patients, put them at ease and give them courage and the will to survive.

I personally believe that a human being goes through three stages before dying. In the first stage the person realizes that he or she is not going to make it but is mentally strong enough to fight it. Stage two sets in when the person accepts that he or she is going to die. The person is open for a religious talk but is incapable of giving himself or herself over to the Lord. The final stage is reached when the person is fully aware that the end is near but does not understand the religious significance.

Brother Antonius had the ability to recognize the second stage. As soon as this stage was reached, he called in a clergyman to talk to the person. This was also the time when members of the Roman Catholic Church would receive their last rites, a wonderful way to take the fear out of dying and to give them peace of mind.

In the two years I served at the camp hospital I saw over 150 men die. Very often I could read on the faces whether they died in peace or in fear. The Japanese required that a lock of hair and a nail clipping be obtained from each corpse, and these were forwarded to their family.

Three years after the war I saw Brother Antonius again. I was on the locks of the city of IJmuiden in North Holland to witness the MS *Oranje* pass through. My father was on board; he was on his way back to Indonesia. It was raining and another man was also observing the ship while waiting in the shed. We started a conversation and he turned out to be Brother Antonius' biological brother. He recounted his brother's experiences while serving in the hospital in the Indies. It turned out to be the same hospital where we served together. He mentioned that there was a sole Protestant among all those Catholics. I finally revealed to him that I was that Protestant boy. He was very surprised. As the ship passed, I could see both Brother Antonious and my father on board.

The camp had two foot-operated dental machines. The only filling available was wax, which lasted only a few months. A horse pharmacy and horse medicine were used to treat the sick. Later, more sulfa tablets arrived with the Red Cross packages, and they were literally a lifesaver. Several ointments were prepared from this drug to cure various ailments and infections.

A 1939 edition of *Reader's Digest* featured a study by the U.S. Navy that dealt with what to do in the event of war with Japan. These plans were followed almost to the letter, and news from clandestine radio broadcasts confirmed this fact. Obviously, the biggest surprise for everybody was the dropping of the A-bomb which ended the war.

When the war was over, the camp leadership was assumed by a Dutch medical team. The food supply gradually improved and the serving size increased accordingly. A group of men decided to organize a festival, but this activity was quickly canceled when the first postcards from the women's camps arrived. Reverend Van Duinen pointed out that the news could prove to be disappointing. He reminded everyone that, regardless of what would happen, life had to go on. This message was well-timed because most of the cards indeed contained bad news. An example read, "Dear Papa. I am here with Mrs. Jansen. Mama died last year. Hope to see you soon."

My father and I received such news. The postcard stated in a few brief sentences that my mother had died of malnutrition, primarily beri-beri, three weeks before the war ended. She was only 46. The minister's sermon was of great comfort to us and helped to eventually overcome our grief. My mother is buried in the Honor Cemetery at Menteng Pulo, Jakarta.

After the war, many of the Dutch families were gradually reunited. Approximately 95 percent lost one or more members. New families were subsequently formed as someone who lost a spouse would marry another survivor without a spouse. These people were usually good friends before the war and thus they usually provided the surviving children with a stable home.

Surviving patients with beriberi were placed on strict salt-free diets since salt tended to cause water retention and poison the body. Nevertheless, it was difficult to keep the sufferers from taking any salt.

During the war, the former Dutch consul to Japan acted as an interpreter. If we had certain problems with the Japanese, he would assist. He was familiar with the Japanese mentality and was wholly on our side. He would often tip us off in numerous ways so that we would give the right answer to guards' questions. He helped us to stay out of trouble.

After the war it was revealed that the Japanese intended to transport the Dutch to the island of Kalimantan. They planned to unload them on the beach and just sail away. With several hundred miles of coastline and no population to speak of, the consequences would have been disastrous. Thanks to the American submarine fleet in the Pacific Ocean, it was impossible for the Japanese to carry out this plan.

This account of concentration camp life was written some 50 years after the war. It has been a factual account as recounted to the best of my ability. I consider myself a successful survivor of the war, and in my opinion, survival is a combination of the following factors: strong religious values, faith that the war would end soon, an optimistic outlook on life, staying actively involved, and a will to live and survive.

The main thoughts that always occupied our minds during captivity were the welfare of our families and the question of when the war would end.

ABOUT THE CONTRIBUTOR

Anton Acherman was born on May 10, 1925, in Silowok-Selangan in Central Java, of Dutch parents. They later lived in a small town in South Sumatra. Educated at home at first, he later transferred to the Dutch-Chinese mission school in Bengkulu. His father was transferred to Lubuklinggau, but the Japanese forced them to evacuate to Jakarta in 1942. There he attended a technical school and stayed in a boarding house for boys.

When the war broke out, he joined the aircraft warning system in Jakarta, but he and his father ended up in Adek Camp. After 42 months they were liberated, and in early May 1946, Anton went to the Netherlands. He attended a technical college in Haarlem and in 1951, he graduated as a mechanical engineer.

He worked for a large electronics company, and after marrying his sweetheart in 1954, he emigrated to Canada. After four years, he came to the United States, settling in the San Diego and Los Angeles areas. He had a successful career in the aerospace industry as an engineer. He has been retired since 1989 and now lives in Los Angeles, California.

JOHANNES VANDENBROEK

A Teacher Turned Soldier and Imprisoned by the Japanese

The day Pearl Harbor was bombed remains the most unforgettable day in my life. I remember everything about that day well. Before going to school I always listened to the news on the radio. That day I could barely believe my ears. At school my colleagues had heard the news too and were busily discussing the consequences it would have for us.

One of us was director of the air raid defenses; another was a member of the team charged with the destruction of the vital services. I, being the youngest at the age of 26, would have to serve in the army. But the others had their functions too, except those older than 45. They had to try to keep the school operating.

We were surprised to hear that particular evening that the Dutch government in exile in London—the Netherlands was occupied by Germany then—had declared war on Japan.

A Dutch submarine on patrol in the South China Sea had surfaced that fateful night to find itself in the middle of a fleet of Japanese troop transports. The intentions of the Japanese were clear, but the submarine was helpless, because there was no state of war between the Netherlands and Japan. The captain radioed to London for instructions, ultimately resulting in the declaration of war by the Netherlands. Every torpedo the submarine fired was a direct hit, and the captain reluctantly turned back to Surabaya, East Java, the navy base in the Indies, to take in more torpedoes.

The Indies had been preparing for war for years but were not really ready. The Netherlands Eastern Forces Intelligence Service, comparable to the American CIA, was well informed; its agents knew just about everything that was going on. But because there was no state of war, they could do no better than keep a watchful eye on the many Japanese living in the country. Japanese merchants, photographers, tailors, dry cleaners and other tradespeople tended to be the best in whatever trade they were in. They were polite and did not overcharge for their services. After the attack on Pearl Harbor, these people disappeared, only to resurface as high-ranking officers after the Dutch surrendered. All those years they had been spying on us.

A couple of months earlier, General Berenschot, commander of the Dutch East Indies Defense Forces and a brilliant military man, had been killed in an airplane crash. It was widely assumed that the plane was sabotaged. General Berenschot, of mixed Dutch and Indonesian descent, had inspected the defenses in Singapore and Malaya and let his arrogant white British colleagues know in no uncertain terms that they were grossly deficient in their preparation for war. He tried to explain to them how serious the Japanese threat was, but the British seemed unimpressed. Churchill did send the battleships *Prince of Wales* and *Repulse*, but without their customary escorts of cruisers, destroyers, etc. These ships were both sunk off Malaysia in the first days of the Pacific War by Japanese torpedo planes and bombers.

The Japanese landed their troops in northern Malaysia. On bicycles they pedaled southward to Singapore, meeting little or no resistance. So Singapore soon fell. The amazing fact was that eventually almost 60,000 troops surrendered to only some 10,000 Japanese.

On March 1, 1942, again a Sunday, the Japanese forces landed on the north coast of West Java. By that time our small air force was already spent in battles over the Java Sea, bombing ships and Japanese installations including, among others, those in Serawak, Kalimantan. Our navy had suffered heavy losses in battles in the Java Sea and the Strait of Makassar.

On paper our army was an impressive 100,000 troops strong. Of these, half were native Indonesians. The remaining Dutch were 90 percent civilians, recently mobilized into military service. They were reasonably well trained, but were in reality still civilians. I was one of them. We handled ourselves well and inflicted heavy losses on the Japanese.

Neither the Indonesian nor the Dutch troops were used to modern warfare. So when the airplanes started bombing and firing, most of the Indonesian troops just disappeared among the native population.

Now the top military brass had to make an important decision. They realized that the Dutch civilians were the backbone of the administration, of commerce, of industry and of cultural life. It did not make any sense to make them fight a losing battle against an enemy which was supported by aircraft and other superior weapons. So ultimately the order was given to avoid contact with the enemy and to retreat as much as possible. This order was not received everywhere, though. Some outlying military units did engage the enemy but with few survivors on our side.

My company was stationed at a small village near the river Citarum, 30 miles west of Bandung, West Java, to defend a bridge in case of Japanese attack. Both men and materiel were hurriedly put into trucks, and we were driven to where the action was. Without a Dutch air force, the Japanese could land virtually unopposed and march on to Kalijati, the military air base outside Bandung. There was heavy fighting with many casualties.

In the daytime we moved forward, along the road to Kalijati, with rice paddies on both sides. In the late afternoon we retreated more than we advanced. As we were a mortar company we were stationed behind the machine gun soldiers who, in turn, had to assist the infantry. These front line soldiers had to bear the brunt of the fighting and took many casualties.

On March 6, we found ourselves in the mountains, in the Ciater Pass, waiting for the advancing Japanese. At around noon I was half buried by soft dirt thrown up by a 50-pound bomb dropped by a Japanese plane about 15 yards from where I was sleeping. I was lucky. Otherwise, nothing significant was happening so around five o'clock we were preparing to return to Bandung some twenty miles away.

Suddenly we received orders to move forward; Japanese were spotted approaching the defenses of the pass. "Follow me!" was the command and we followed the colonel and the major. No sooner did we move about 100 yards up the slope of the mountain then machine gun fire suddenly erupted. We dove into holes that had been dug for planting cinchona trees and saw the tracer bullets streaking like glowing nails over our heads. These tracer bullets were high enough that I thought I would take a chance. I ran back to activate a mortar we had stored in a shed by the roadside. I got help from two guys from my company but I could not establish the proper distance.

Almost all the troops that were passing by ignored my request for assistance, or else they did not know the exact distance either. Finally a captain gave me a range of 800 meters and I fired about 20 projectiles in the direction of the tracer bullets. I doubt if they actually accomplished anything, but at least I had the satisfaction of having done something constructive.

It became dark fast. A couple of officers prevented more people from running away. They stationed guards to look out for Japanese, and our group of about 100 gradually increased to about 200 as people returned from the mountains. It was pitch dark by then and we could hear in the distance cries for help. But the lieutenant refused to give permission to go out to give assistance. "It is too dangerous," he said; the place was crawling with Japanese.

At around ten, when the moon came up, he finally relented. Several of us went out in the surrounding hills, guided by the cries for help. I found one man who was wounded in the hip. He was heavy, but we got him down to the truck and with other wounded, he was driven to the hospital in Bandung.

At around midnight we received orders to disable all the equipment we could not carry along and then march the 20 miles to Lembang where we found the others fast asleep. They were the troops who had left us some six hours earlier. We later learned that both the colonel and the major who had commanded us had died in battle.

The Japanese had their headquarters in Kalijati, the former Dutch military air force base, 60 miles north of Bandung. But before our governor general and his entourage drove up there, the Japanese had dragged all the dead bodies they could find and placed them along the road they had to pass. And there were a lot of them!

Imagine the feelings of these officials seeing all these men who had given their lives for their country. Nonetheless the governor's conduct during the surrender negotiations—as if there was something to negotiate—was such that it forced the grudging respect of the Japanese generals. The governor had already earned the love and respect of his people.

The next day they asked for volunteers to go into the mountains to look for bodies and bury them. I declined, unable to stomach it. Most of the bodies, after removal of their dog tags, were buried in the same ready-made planting holes for those cinchona trees. Others were buried the conventional way.

During this expedition, the volunteers made a grisly discovery. They found a group of about 35 bodies of our "Jannen" company, so called because this company consisted of Dutch troops—Jan being a popular Dutch name—while the other companies were made up primarily of Indonesian troops.

These men were tied with their own puttees to rubber trees and summarily shot. There was one who had stayed alive, although wounded, for five days and cold nights without food or drink. This soldier recounted how the company had run out of ammo and had surrendered. However, when the Japanese had to retreat from approaching Dutch forces, they shot their prisoners. Although I was not proud of myself I was glad I had not come along. It would have been too much for me.

The time came that all of us became prisoners of war. We were sent everywhere the Japanese had active projects. In groups of a couple of hundred we were ferried to such places as the Lesser Sunda Islands to build airstrips; to Japan to work in the coal mines or on docks; and to Burma-Thailand to assist in building the infamous death railroad. I spent the final three months of the war on Singapore Island working at various sites.

Then the atom bomb was dropped, and with it came bigger food rations. For me, the bomb came just in time, because I was in bad physical shape. And I was not the only one.

Subsequently, we were "liberated" by the British. A few months earlier, Southeast Asia was transferred from the American to the British theater of war. Our men in Singapore, Saigon and Bangkok, instead of going home to Java, had to sit and wait despite the fact that the Netherlands had sufficient ships at its disposal to transport us.

Let the truth be known that these ships had been placed in a "shipping pool" headed by an Englishman. He used the ships to repatriate his own countrymen first; no ships were available for the Dutch. The Americans did not bother with this shipping pool; they flew their countrymen home instead.

The British who became the occupying force in Jakarta forbade the Dutch civilians to leave their internment camps to go home! During the war, Japanese officers who returned to Japan took all kinds of things they found in the houses formerly owned by the Dutch. Now it was the turn of the British, and the Gurkhas and Sikhs. Refrigerators, radios, record players, and furniture were loaded on ships bringing back the British troops.

When the Dutch military were finally able to return to Java, the Indonesian rebellion was in full swing, especially in the interior of the country. Even nine months after the Japanese surrender, in many areas,

Japanese soldiers were still armed and fighting side by side with the Indonesians against the Dutch. The Dutch pacification process progressed slowly but steadily.

Most of us, fresh out of POW camps, had to fight again to restore order. Our women and children in the interior of the country were placed in so-called protection camps, most of which were guarded by Indonesians and some even by Japanese. Prior to such an arrangement, many of these civilians died cruel deaths. It has been reported that in the early days, many atrocities were committed by the Indonesians against Dutch and Chinese women and children under the eyes of British troops. They did not interfere because they had "no orders"!

Then came the "good offices" of the newly created United Nations to mediate the conflict between the Dutch and the Indonesians. The "impartial" commission consisted of an Englishman, an Australian and an American. The Brit was openly against the Dutch and so was the Australian. Dutch shipping was boycotted in Australia, for example, and relief supplies, most of them intended for the Indonesian civilian population, remained on the Australian docks.

And what about the Americans? Naïve, inexperienced in Far East colonial affairs, idealistic and probably influenced by prospects of huge profits to be made with the Dutch out of the way, America was also on the side of the Indonesians. The conference was a sham; the results were predetermined. Negotiation time was primarily spent feasting; the Indonesians provided beautiful young women and good food.

The Dutch managed to restore a semblance of order and to placed many Indonesians in top administrative positions in preparation for the inevitable Indonesian independence. For one, the Dutch government's opinion was that Indonesia was not ready for independence; there were simply not enough qualified people to take over the reins. However, pressure from our "allies" was tremendous, especially from America which had the biggest stick—the Marshall Plan. If the Dutch did not knuckle under, U.S. aid would be withheld.

It was Queen Juliana of the Netherlands who had the unpleasant task of handing over the sovereignty of the Indonesian Archipelago to Sukarno, the new head of state, in December 1949. Sukarno was the collaborator who delivered 2 million of his countrymen to Japan to work in slavery. They were known as *remushas*, or forced laborers who worked all over Asia and died by the thousands. It was Sukarno who, through his hate campaign and speeches, can be held responsible for the death of hundreds of Dutch women and children.

Yes, it is true that the Dutch have not been without blame in the way they have administered their colonies. But the fact remains that in the early forties, prior to the war, some 220,000 Dutch ruled over 60 million native people in peace and prosperity.

ABOUT THE CONTRIBUTOR

Johannes Vandenbroek was born in 1915 in Surabaya, East Java to a Dutch father and Indonesian mother. Through a dispute between father and mother, the government took Johannes away at age five and placed him in an orphanage. He went to school in the Indies, finishing with a master's degree in education. After one year of compulsory military service, he started his career in technical school, attaining a lower degree in physical education. The war interrupted his career as a teacher which he resumed in 1947.

In 1958 he and his family went to the Netherlands where he worked as a substitute teacher at various schools.

In 1960 they emigrated to the United States, where he found employment in Longmont, Colorado. In 1963 he moved to California, where he worked as a die-cast machine operator until his retirement in 1981. He enrolled in adult education classes, among which was a "Creative Writing for Seniors" class. He currently lives in Oceanside, California.

WILLEM H. MAASKAMP

*A Dutch Youth Tortured and
Imprisoned by the Japanese,
Then Pressed into Service
Against Indonesian
Freedom Fighters*

It was December 1941 when my young life was drastically changed
and since that fateful day, December 8, 1941 (December 7 in the United
States), the memories of what happened can never be erased. The Japanese had bombed Pearl Harbor and the Dutch East Indies government
declared war on Japan. Our KNIL (Royal Netherlands Indies Army)
was immediately mobilized. Every Dutch citizen, young and old alike,
was called up for military duty.

I remember that I was still in school. I was 17 years old then, and
all my Dutch teachers were recruited into the military service; as a
consequence, the schools were closed. Every healthy Dutch citizen 18
and over was also inducted into the navy, army or air force. They had
to undergo a physical. They received their uniform, underwent an
accelerated military training of approximately 30 days, were issued a
rifle and ordered to go "fight the Japs for Queen and fatherland."

The 17-year-old Dutch youngsters were requested to "volunteer"
for certain civilian defense entities, such as the air defense services and
fire departments, in addition to serving as radio and telephone operators and assisting in loading and unloading government supplies at
harbors and airports. Every day you could read ads in the newspaper
requesting such volunteers.

71

I ended up at the air defense services department, sector XI, located at the Simpang Hotel in the city of Surabaya, the large seaport on the eastern part of the island of Java. I was trained to be a firefighter, and soon thereafter I was appointed as the assistant leader of the firefighting unit.

It was around Christmas 1941 that we noticed Allied forces in the city. There were several Australian and British soldiers and a goodly number of U.S. Navy personnel. I later learned that a flotilla of the U.S. Navy had arrived in the Indies to augment the Royal Dutch Navy, and I even remember some of the ships' names. There was a heavy cruiser, the *Houston*; the *Marblehead*; and several U.S. destroyers and submarines. I also remember seeing several Catalina flying boats and B-17s belonging to the U.S. Army Air Corps. At that time, I could not have foreseen that I would spend considerable time with some of these Americans in a Japanese concentration camp. I will recount these experiences later.

Surabaya had always been a strong Dutch navy base, and the KNIL was also well represented on the outskirts of the city, such as the city of Wonokromo where the Royal Dutch Shell oil fields were located. Because of the strong naval base and the rich oil fields surrounding the city, it was no wonder that toward the end of January 1942, Surabaya was bombed repeatedly by the Japs—not only the military bases and harbor, but the city itself.

As a consequence of all these military activities, many European families living in Surabaya moved to the interior of eastern Java. And the B-17s belonging to the U.S. Army Air Corps were also relocated and settled in the vicinity of the city of Malang, approximately 75 miles inland.

During the bombardment of Surabaya, we raced all over the city and harbor area extinguishing fires, pulling victims out of destroyed buildings, bandaging them up and loading them into ambulances for transport to local hospitals.

I was only 17 then, and what I saw at that time I can still remember vividly even now, more than half a century later. I cannot easily put all this war history behind me—I just cannot forget the mangled bodies I saw, some literally torn apart. I still see in my mind's eye those young children lying there, and all that blood. All that carnage made an everlasting impression on me.

The Royal Dutch Navy was defeated in the battle of the Java Sea on February 27, 1942. Some U.S. warships were also sunk in this fierce battle. The way to conquer the main island of Java then became accessible to the overwhelming Japanese invading forces. Only one week later, on March 8, the Royal Dutch East Indies government surrendered. The Japanese occupation which lasted until the end of August 1945 had begun. Three and one-half years of torture, famine, disease and concentration camps became an unfortunate part of our life.

I had two brothers who were mobilized. The eldest was called up by the Royal Dutch Navy, and after several attacks on his ship during the first three months of war, his destroyer was hit by a Japanese torpedo. We did not know what had happened to him, whether he was alive or had died for his country, until he came home after the war had ended.

As it turned out, he had been taken prisoner of war and, having survived the infamous Changi Prison in Singapore, had been transported to Burma and Thailand and made to work on the Death Railroad in the jungles. Finally he was shipped to Japan to work in the coal mines. Liberated by U.S. forces in Japan in August 1945, he was evacuated by the U.S. Navy on board an aircraft carrier to Manila, the Philippines, and later flown to Australia. He had to be admitted to an Australian army hospital in order to recuperate from the three and a half years of Japanese captivity and cruel treatment.

My other brother served in the Netherlands East Indies Air Force. He was highly decorated for having shot down four Japanese aircraft in the early stages of the war. He was flying a Glenn Martin bomber over the oil-rich island of Tarakan at that time. On February 28, 1942, this brother received the third highest royal decoration in front of the troops at the military airfield of Andir in Bandung, West Java.

Afterwards he was ordered to fly to Australia since the Allied forces needed experienced airmen as instructors. Two days later my mother received an unfortunate telegram from the Air Force, stating that he was declared "missing in action." We never heard from him since, and after the war he was declared killed in action. Fred was 24 years old when he died for Queen and fatherland.

It did not take long for us to have no job, no food and no schooling. There was nothing left to do. The Japanese army started to round up all their enemies. All persons of Dutch, American, British and French nationality—including the young, the old, women, and children—were herded into concentration camps.

The Allied military were already interned in POW camps throughout the Indies and elsewhere. Many of us civilians tried to hide and did all we could to stay out of the concentration camps. It became more and more difficult to stay out of the enemy's hands, and every foreigner had to register with the Japanese authorities. They were issued an identification card.

During this period I moved several times trying to evade capture. I finally found shelter in a home where the lady of the house was the wife of a Dutch naval officer. The Japanese *Kempeitai*, the military police, broke into the house one day in search of her husband. All the occupants were arrested, including me, and we were taken to their headquarters.

We were first frisked and later interrogated concerning the whereabouts of the naval officer, since he was not listed as a POW in any of the camps. Nobody knew where he was. His wife was severely beaten, not once but many, many times, day after day, night after night, and finally she was thrown back into her cell. The rest of us were treated no better. They extinguished burning cigarettes on our bodies. They beat us with whips, military belts, fists, and every other item at their disposal. We were to confess where Capt. S. was hiding.

On the way back to my cell where other Dutchmen were already locked up, we had to pass by other cells. We heard some of the inmates whisper, "*Oranje boven*" (Orange on top), meaning that the Dutch Royal House of Orange would always be on top. Just that saying alone kept our spirit up. I remember the next day, after a cruel beating, the *Kempeitai* officer in the interrogation room tied my wrists, made me kneel in front of him, pulled out his revolver and held it against my forehead. He yelled, "You better tell me where I can find your navy captain friend, or I will shoot you!"

I told him that I did not know.

"Did you see the navy captain come home in the night?"

And in this vein the interrogation went on and on. The Japanese officer called me all kinds of names—I was a dirty Dutch spy, a dirty S.O.B., and on and on he went, interrupting his tirades with blows and kicks to my body and face.

At one point, I felt blood streaming down my nose and my mouth was also bleeding profusely. While I was still in the same kneeling position, he stuck a piece of bamboo behind my knees and started to jump on it. What happened then I cannot fully recollect. I must have passed out because when I came to a few days later, I heard a voice saying,

"*Oranje boven*. Don't give up, don't give in. You shall overcome. God is with you. We will win the war!"

After a few days, Indonesian guards entered my cell and ordered me to get up and follow them. I could barely stand up, let alone move around or walk. So two Indonesian police officers picked me up and carried me to a Jap army truck. I was taken to Japanese-Indonesian Political Information Headquarters in downtown Surabaya. There I was locked up in a cell and given drinking water and a bowl of red rice with some kind of vegetable soup.

The next day I was interrogated by a couple of Indonesian police officers instead. I was hit again and again in my face with a wooden stick. I was asked if I knew of other Dutch enemy citizens who were in hiding in and around the city. After having been questioned with the inevitable beating, kicks and slaps in my face, I was taken back to my cell. They kept me there for about three days. I was then transported to the Werffstraat prison downtown and locked up in a tiny cell with other Dutch citizens.

One night, the sirens went off. I will never forget that particular night. Allied planes started bombing the harbor and the downtown area. Bombs exploded near the prison. The Indonesian prison guards let us out of our cells so that we could roam the prison yard to search for bomb shells. We did not find any. We saw the Japanese army search lights, attempting to spot Allied planes. We heard anti-aircraft guns, explosives, and the sound of aircraft engines, but then, a short while later, everything turned quiet again.

The guards returned and ordered us back into our tiny cells. When daylight broke, we found pamphlets everywhere on the prison grounds. One of the guards brought us one. It had a Dutch text which read "Soon we will come to liberate you and we will bring you food, medicines and freedom." The message was signed by the commander-in-chief of all Dutch forces, Admiral Helfrich.

Two months later, in January 1943, we were transported in Japanese army trucks to the major railroad station downtown. All Dutch and other Allied personnel were loaded in cattle cars, about 40 prisoners per wagon, the doors were chained down, and Japanese guards were posted on the platform. After a full day in the hot tropical sun, the train finally pulled out at night. We did not know our destination or how long it would take to get there, but by observing the sun, we knew we were going west.

The way the Japanese army handled the transport was very cruel, to say the least. We were almost all sick with malaria and dysentery. No food at all was served. At a couple of stations we were given a 20-gallon drum filled with water, although this was insufficient for all of us. We were also all suffering from the aftereffects of the tropical sun, beating down on the cattle cars. Several people were unconscious, and a number of the elderly even died during this transport.

After 44 hours locked up in these hot cattle cars, we arrived in our new camp in Bandung, West Java. We had traveled approximately 600 miles, averaging about 15 miles a night. As a precaution, we never traveled during daylight hours. The Japs parked the loaded cars on a side track in the hot sun, again during the day. The transport moved only when there was a locomotive engine available.

The Bandung concentration camp, in comparison to previous experiences in the cattle cars, appeared like heaven to us. It was a large camp, totaling approximately 10,000 inmates from all over the island of Java.

I was very, very sick when I arrived. I had suffered from bacillary dysentery in the Werffstraat prison in Surabaya. I had been transferred to the contagious ward of the local hospital where I was attended to by Dr. Nawir.

Dr. Nawir was a well-known personality in Surabaya before the war. He was a renowned soccer player and was married to a Dutch woman. When the guard called him to examine me, he entered my cell and spoke in Dutch to me. He told me not to worry. He would transfer me to the local hospital and treat me in the prison ward with an Indonesian police officer as my guard. As a matter of fact, I was still hospitalized when I was ordered back to the Werffstraat prison for transport to Bandung.

A few days after my arrival in this large camp, I was lying down on the bare floor because we did not have any possessions. A man entered the barracks and asked the barracks leader if there was someone there by the name of Maaskamp. As I heard him mention the name, I answered, while still lying on the floor, "I am Maaskamp."

He replied that he had expected an older fellow. In fact he had expected to see my father, whom he knew very well. He looked me over, we talked a little while and he said that he would be back. Indeed, the next day he returned to visit with me and he brought a piece of bread. He told me that he worked in the camp kitchen and that he would bring me extra food every day. He wanted me to get better and strong again so that I could assist him in the kitchen.

And so it happened that this man, a total stranger, a friend of my dad who passed away a few years before the war, helped me to recuperate. Also through this connection, I ended up working in the camp kitchen. Subsequently, I was able to help another friend, suffering from malnutrition, to survive.

After about a year in the Bandung camp, my Surabaya group was split up. The camp commandant ordered men in a certain section of the camp to pack up. We were transported again, this time by truck, to an even larger camp in the city of Cimahi. It housed approximately 15,000 people, and there were more nationalities here. I noticed Chinese, Filipino, Australian, British and American sections.

The Cimahi camp was not only larger but also stricter, more disciplined and worse than the previous camp. The Japanese army sentries were tough. They enjoyed beating the prisoners for no apparent reason. We had to work in the fields from 6 A.M. to 6 P.M. in the hot tropical sun. We had no shirts to wear, only hats we made ourselves from native bamboo or straw. We had no shoes, so we went everywhere barefoot. For lunch we were given a piece of cooked cassava. If we did not bow deeply enough, we were severely beaten.

A small contingent, of which I was a part, was ordered to assist in building a railroad in the jungles of Cicalengka, a small village in the mountains. We had no breakfast, only a hot cup of corn coffee. For dinner we were given a thin slice of tapioca bread and a small bowl of watery vegetable soup without any meat.

Most of the prisoners were very thin, and all suffered from malnutrition. The elderly had beriberi. There was no medicine, and about eight to ten prisoners died daily. As the war progressed, we also suffered more and more. I myself had an infected tooth pulled without benefit of any anaesthesia; a male nurse held me down by my shoulders and a dentist, using camp-made instruments, performed the extraction. Camp doctors in general could no longer perform any operations on inmates because there was nothing useful available.

In the meantime, all of us were merely trying to survive our ordeal of imprisonment. Only once did the Japanese camp commandant request U.S. Red Cross packages for distribution. We were given one box to be divided among 16 prisoners. We suspected that something fishy was happening. Six months earlier, we had been unloading railroad cars when we noticed that Japanese soldiers were smoking Camel and Lucky Strike cigarettes and eating Hershey bars. Where would they get these things? Now we knew for sure where those bastards got it.

Inevitably I contracted bacillary dysentery again and again I lost weight. I cannot count how many trips I made to the toilet. One day, my block commander announced that there was one vacancy in the camp bakery. Our block had won some kind of "lottery" from among all the block commanders. We were to send a strong, healthy young man to work in the bakery. The commander had an old deck of cards and announced that the fairest way was for those who were eligible to draw a card. We were called up alphabetically, and I drew the ace of spades.

My *hancho* in the bakery was an Australian. He told us that he used to operate his own bakery in Melbourne. He was an excellent cake maker and his fame had even reached the Japanese top command. Many times a Japanese would come into the bakery at night—we worked the evening hours from 6 P.M. to 6 A.M.—and ask him to bake a birthday cake or wedding cake for an Indonesian "girlfriend." The Aussie would then reply, "But I need good import quality flour, four dozen eggs, a big bag of sugar, ten pounds of butter..." and the list would go on and on, to include cigarettes as payment. And he got what he requested! Obviously, there was enough of these ingredients left over to share with the other inmates.

In the bakery, we also baked corn flour bread for the Japanese army commandant. Often about 40 to 50 loaves somehow ended up in the bakery's rain gutters. After the shift and upon departure, we would "clean out" the gutters to find to our surprise that there was extra food. This extra food came in handy for our sick friends and relatives and was even used to buy the latest news from American inmates in order to learn about the progress the Allies were making in the Pacific.

Some of us were aware that the Americans had a clandestine radio hidden somewhere in one of the many huge trees in camp. The street-smart Yanks exchanged this news for food since they were also hungry and suffered as much as we did. So, in general, we were pretty well up to date as to the progress the U.S. Marines were making under the leadership of the great General Douglas MacArthur.

It was the Americans who informed the Allied camp commandant regarding the Japanese surrender on August 16, 1945. Many of us did not believe our ears at first. The Yanks told us about two atom bombs which were dropped on Japan. We had no idea what an atom bomb was at that time. A few days later, the American contingent dared to come to the camp kitchen with their hand-pulled terrain carts, displaying a tiny American flag.

By then we also noticed that the Japanese sentries had ceased harassing us. The beatings had stopped, and we were receiving more food. As a matter of fact, a few days later, the Japanese commander of all Allied camps pulled into camp on his motorcycle with buggy and saluted our camp commandant. He made a deep bow and announced that the Emperor of Japan had ordered a cease-fire.

"Baloney! You are a bunch of fucking liars!" shouted the Americans. "You bastards surrendered unconditionally!"

The Jap colonel just stood there at attention and replied, "Japanese Imperial army will issue paint and brushes, for the prisoners to paint on the roofs of the barracks the letters POW." By doing so, we would enable the American planes to locate our camp so they could fly over in order to drop goodies, medicines, food, cigarettes and clothing. We were informed that "the day after tomorrow" the planes would come around 2 P.M. to make the scheduled drop. And they certainly showed up, but not before our patience was severely tested.

On the appointed day, we were all outside our barracks as soon as the sun came up. During the announcement the Japanese colonel had neglected to mention what time he was talking about—our (Pacific) time, Australian time, or U.S. time. So we just made a guess that it would be local time. Besides, there were so many rumors going around that we did not know whom or what to believe anyway.

We waited, and waited, and waited—noon, one o'clock, then two o'clock came around and still nothing happened. By 2:45 we heard airplane sounds, heavy engine noises which were getting louder and louder. The American POWs remarked that they were "four jobbers." We did not know what that meant so we asked them for an explanation. They replied that they were heavy four-engine bombers comparable to those of the U.S. Flying Fortresses.

As we stared into the blue sky, we finally detected a formation of planes. But they looked tiny—they flew so high! What good could they do from that height? Many of us had tears in our eyes, and some were openly crying. We said to each other, "They'll never spot us from that height. If they drop their loads now, the dirty Japs will get them."

And then, all of a sudden, the formation of the four jobbers started to dive. They turned around, flew over our camp, and turned around again and again, every time flying lower and lower. After about 30 minutes of this manoeuvering they had made their final approach and appeared right above our camp. We could now spot the U.S. Army Air Force markings on the wings and tail of these giant bombers. They tipped their wings as a greeting.

It was a sight to behold and never to be forgotten. The pilots opened the bellies of the planes—we could see the gaping holes in the fuselage—and big drums, attached to parachutes, came tumbling down. Some fell right through the roofs of our barracks, but we did not care and it was obvious that the bomber crew did not either. A few of the drums cracked open upon impact and, oh boy, did we have a treat! We later learned that these planes were B-24s, also called the Liberators, originating in western Australia.

We had been forewarned by the camp doctor not to overindulge and to be careful of what we were eating. Some of the food was too rich for our weakened tummies to digest. I distinctly remember that concentrated milk made a friend of mine very, very ill. All the goodies were supposed to be gathered up on orders of the Allied camp commandant for fair distribution among all POWs, and in fact they did a good job doling out the "manna from heaven."

By the end of August 1945, it was announced that Allied officers were going to inspect our camp. The team consisted of a Dutch captain, a British captain, an Australian major, a Nationalist Chinese officer of unknown rank and a U.S. navy commander. The Japanese guards stood at attention and presented arms, and when these Allied officers entered the main gate, we yelled, "*Kiotske! Kere! Norre!*" which translated to mean, "Attention! Bow deep! At ease!"

We noticed that each of these five Allied officers had a revolver hanging from his belt. We vicariously felt like victors ourselves as we saw the Japs standing at attention, presenting their arms. But this was particularly so when the Jap colonel handed his Samurai sword over to the Allied officers.

Our Allied camp commandant was asked who the war criminals were. We shouted in unison, "All of them. Hang all of them!" The Chinese officer wrote down some names.

What impressed me the most was when the U.S. navy commander ordered all American citizens to line up. There they stood, hungry, sick, dirty, mere skeletons with bandages on their feet, some on homemade crutches, some crying. I still remember vividly that one of the American prisoners tossed the one crutch he was leaning on away, dropped to the ground, clung onto the U.S. commander's leg and begged him, "Take me home, sir!"

I also remember the U.S. commander talking to the Chinese officer. He was grim-faced and appeared stunned; it seemed as if he could not believe what he saw. It was an undeniable fact that all POWs had lost a great deal of weight due to malnutrition, dysentery, and other tropical diseases, such as malaria, and black water fever to name a few.

The U.S. commander ordered the Japanese colonel to have transportation ready within 24 hours. Two days later, all Americans had left the camp in ambulances and Jap army trucks for the Bandung airport where United States planes waited to take them back to the United States via Australia and the Philippines.

Soon the Aussies also departed and so did the British and other nationalities. But the Dutch stayed behind, all by themselves—we had nowhere to go, no homes, no families, no transportation, nothing! That really was a shame.

In the meantime, the Indonesian population was about to fight for their independence from the Dutch who had ruled them for more than 300 years. Armed Indonesian youth groups started to roam through the street, shouting "*Merdeka*" (freedom) while terrorizing neighborhoods, villages and entire cities. It did not take long for it to become unsafe to be on the outside of the former POW camps. The women's and children's camps in particular were terrorized and attacked by these young Indonesian freedom fighters. During this period of time, know as the Bersiap period, numerous Dutch citizens were murdered, including women and children.

It was almost worse than being in a Japanese POW camp, if that was possible. A majority of our Dutch military men were still recuperating in Thailand, Burma and elsewhere. The British command in Southeast Asia ordered the Dutch to stay in the camps while the Allied troops were preparing themselves to liberate us. The Indonesian revolution was quickly gaining momentum and the populace was getting bolder.

In the interior of Java, the Indonesians started rounding up all Dutch citizens and throwing them into prisons or internment camps where men, women and children were locked up again. People were beaten and many were literally hacked to pieces. The Indonesian freedom fighters—terrorists—were out of control.

I myself with a few friends had sneaked out of our camp in Cimahi. We went to the railroad station and jumped onto a moving night train to Surabaya. I wanted to see my girlfriend again after all these years. In the city of Yogyakarta, we were met by representatives of the International Red Cross. We were asked many questions and told to stay in town so that we could give them the names of all the people we knew in our camps. This turned out to be one of the first lists which was compiled, a survivors list of those who were in the many Japanese concentration camps.

The next day we continued our train trip to Surabaya. The Red Cross had paid for our ticket and for our overnight stay in a hotel. My mother, sisters and young brother, who were in Magelang, Central Java, where we stopped off, were very surprised to see me. A few days after my arrival my 13-year-old brother was picked up by the Indonesian freedom fighters and sentenced to death. Having been declared an enemy of the state, he was facing a firing squad. His hands were tied behind his back. Can you imagine, a 13-year-old being the enemy of the state?

When we received word of this verdict, I immediately went to see the British RAPWI (Recovery of Allied Prisoners of War and Internees) commander and pleaded for his intervention. Fortunately, a Lt. Trigg responded, jumped in his car and was eventually able to negotiate my brother's release.

Later on, the British command asked me to come to work for them as an interpreter as I spoke Dutch, English and Malay fluently. The Brits housed me, fed me and took good care of me. Then one day the Indonesian freedom fighters started to attack our housing project. So we were all moved to a former military camp. The Indonesians demanded the surrender of all Dutch citizens. At last the three British officers had to give in to the Indonesians' ultimatum.

We were loaded on open trucks and transported to the local prison and locked up in cells. What a fate we were facing! We lived in cells before under the Japs and now after the Japanese surrender, the Indonesians arrested us and we were locked up again. After approximately ten days, however, Lt. Trigg arrived at the prison gate with about thirty Gurkha troops and demanded that I be released.

I was called up by the Indonesian prison commander and set free. What a blessing that was! Lt. Trigg assured the rest of the inmates that a battalion of Gurkha soldiers would be arriving in town soon. All remaining Dutch prisoners would be freed within a week.

We were in this new British camp for only a couple of weeks when the Gurkhas, who were guarding us, were suddenly attacked by screaming and yelling Indonesian freedom fighters. The attack lasted several hours, and the next day an even heavier assault took place. The fight lasted all day. It got so bad that the British commander called up fighter planes to repel the thousands of Indonesian rebels who had surrounded our camp. Two fighter planes raked the vicinity with machine gun fire, and within 45 minutes it became quiet as could be. The Gurkhas, in the meantime, had also taken a stand with rifle in one hand and a special sword in the other. However, they did not have much ammunition left. Fortunately, early the next morning Royal Air Force (RAF) transports dropped ammo, mortars, food and other necessary supplies for their ground troops.

We observed about forty parachutists descend from the sky, about six of whom landed outside the perimeter of our heavily fortified camp. Lt. Trigg and the British Gurkha commanding officer asked me if I could possibly assist in retrieving these men. They each had a heavy load of mortar shells, hand grenades and other ammunition with them.

I in turn asked several of my friends to volunteer. We sneaked out of camp and ran towards the six chutes. The Gurkha soldiers were previously alerted about our mission and had ceased firing on the Indonesians who were holed up around the camp.

We were busily retrieving the last chute when all of a sudden the Gurkhas opened fire on one of our boys who turned a corner of the fence. In the confusion one of my friends, Benny A., was hit in the lower body and fell to the ground. We yelled to the Gurkhas to stop their fire.

A British officer shouted to forget about trying to get the last chute with ammo and to return to camp with our fallen comrade as soon as possible. We carried Benny on our shoulders and ran back as fast as we could. Unfortunately, it was too late to save our friend. He died in our arms as we carried him into the camp. The next day, Benny was buried in camp with full British military honors. Every British soldier stood along his grave and saluted this brave young man.

A couple of days later I was ordered by Lt. Trigg to board a British military convoy to Semarang on the north coast of central Java. After a few days of rest at the British-American Tobacco Building, the British commander called me into his office. He thanked me for what I had done and informed me that my services were no longer needed. Everything was under control, and I was to board an RAF transport plane the next day for evacuation to Bandung.

This city was divided into two sectors, a northern sector where the European community lived and a southern sector where the Indonesian freedom fighters held sway. The border was the railroad track. Marauding youth crossed this line every night and raised havoc upon the European community close to the tracks. Europeans were kidnapped and never found again. The British military contingent in Bandung consisted of Sikhs and Pakistanis.

The Pakistanis who were Muslims and the Sikhs were very sympathetic toward the Indonesian cause, and it did not take long for the Europeans to lose faith in these British troops' ability to protect us. Therefore, young Dutch males were called up by the returned Dutch army officers to join a newly formed Dutch army battalion. Almost all of us had had some unpleasant experiences with the Indonesian freedom fighters and many, like myself, still had family in their territory.

This NICA (Netherlands Indies Civil Administration) battalion was trained and fully equipped within about eight weeks of intense training in, among other skills, hand to hand combat. We were even given the nickname of "*anjing NICA,*" Indonesian for "the dogs of the Dutch." Troops from the NICA were soon deployed to guard the POW camps in Bandung and the city of Cimahi.

Later, when the Dutch troops, fresh from the Netherlands and elsewhere, arrived to fight the Indonesians, the battalion was deployed in almost all critical areas, not only in West Java, but also in the central areas of Java. They were the special forces or corps d'élite for General Spoor, the supreme commander of all Dutch armed forces in the former Dutch East Indies.

In the end, however, the Dutch government, under pressure of world opinion among other factors, finally gave up the fight and granted the Indonesians their sovereignty on December 29, 1949. This was undoubtedly one of the defining moments in the history of the Dutch East Indies, and a turning point for its citizens.

ABOUT THE CONTRIBUTOR

Willem H. Maaskamp was born on November 7, 1924, in the former Dutch East Indies, where he lived and attended the Dutch school system until the outbreak of World War II. He spent considerable time in several prisons and internment camps.

After the war he was called up by the Royal Netherlands Indies Army to serve until 1948. He found employment in the city of Bandung, West Java, and eventually his employer sent him to West Germany to learn more about textile dyes and chemicals.

He returned to Indonesia at the end of 1956 as head of the Import Department. In 1958 he was forced by the Indonesian government to leave Indonesia, and he repatriated to the Netherlands.

In 1959 Maaskamp emigrated to the United States and lived in Massachusetts, where he worked for a large East Coast lithographic printing corporation. Eventually he decided to move to southern California, where he was employed by several large printing companies. In 1987 he was forced to retire due to failing health.

DENIS DUTRIEUX

"They Can't Be Human Beings!"

"Dark clouds above the Pacific, the Netherlands declare war on Japan." "It is better to die while standing upright than to live in a kneeling position."

These were some of the headlines in the local Dutch newspapers heralding the grim reality that World War II hovered like a giant bird of prey over the beautiful islands in the Pacific affectionately called "The Belt of Emeralds." The Indies was suddenly and unwillingly transformed into a battlefield.

My twin brother Dick and I were drafted in the Dutch conscript army on December 12, 1941, and were both stationed in Cilincing, a coastal village north of Jakarta in West Java. We were 18 years old and were scheduled to serve nine months in an anti-aircraft battalion.

These nine months extended into seven and a half years. Judging from the military buildup, I could not help but think that Cilincing was earmarked by the Japanese for an invasion. As it turned out, however, the Japanese 16th Army, under command of Lieutenant General Hitoshi Imamura, landed with an estimated 60,000 troops at the following sites on Java on March 1, 1942: in the vicinity of Merak, Bay of Banten, West Java; at Eretan Wetan, West Java; and in the vicinity of Kragan, East Java.

As a consequence, our battalion fell back and settled inland in the town of Bandung, where we made a final stand in the vicinity of the *Lembang stelling* (Lembang fortification). The capitulation of all Dutch forces came on March 8, 1942.

The most trying years of my life now began as I became a prisoner of war. For three and a half years, I migrated from one POW camp to another in Indonesia, Singapore, Vietnam (then known as French-Indo China), and Cambodia. This list gives the locations of the POW camps where I spent the most horrible years of my life: Camp Bandung, Java; Camp Cimahi, Java; Industries Fair Camp, Surabaya, Java; Camp Maumere, Flores; Camp Talibura, Flores; Adek Camp, Jakarta, Java; Camp Makassar, Jakarta, Java; River Valley Camp, Singapore; Dock Camp, Saigon, Vietnam; Lien Khang Camp, Vietnam; Rubber Plantation Camp, Dallath, Vietnam; and Camp Phnom Penh, Cambodia.

My twin brother, who was wounded in the battle near Bandung, joined me in Camp Cimahi. We were subsequently separated from each other for the remainder of the war while in Camp Makassar.

There was a contingent of British, Australian, American and Dutch military personnel in most of the camps. We were entirely at the mercy of the Japanese and Korean camp guards. Savage beatings and harassment were the order of the day.

In order to warn our fellow prisoners that a Japanese patrol was inside the camp, ready to strike and hurt us, we would yell "*rood voor*," Dutch for "red ahead." The color red obviously is the color for danger, and in this case it also refers to the color of the ball on the Japanese flag.

"*Rood voor*" was a terrifying, panic inducing warning, an emphatic but futile attempt to somehow strike back against injustice, against a flagrant violation of human dignity and pride. It was a dangerous time to insist on one's *point d'honneur*. The warning initiated a scramble to execute the correct Japanese commands, to make the right moves at the right time.

For example, if someone yelled "*kiotske*," you had to stand at attention. When he shouted "*kere*," when inside the barracks, you had to take off your hat and bow your head. However, when you were outside, you had to salute if your wore a hat. If you did not wear one, you had to yell "*norre*," and after the Japanese guard saluted or bowed his head in return, you had to stand at ease!

If you made just one mistake, disaster would strike. Even the dogs in Camp Cimahi—all of which the Japs killed eventually—sensed the anxiety. They seemed aware of the evil and destruction those little bow-legged characters in ill-fitting uniforms, wearing inverted flowerpot caps and split-toed sneakers, could unleash. One animal would always run for cover the moment he heard the call "*rood voor*." The Japs finally caught him too, and nobody could stop the ruthless killing that followed.

One detested Japanese prankster took great pleasure in unexpectedly inspecting the barracks in Camp Cimahi while chanting the Japanese version of *"rood voor."* It sounded something like "loo vool, loo vool," and woe be the man who dared to laugh, smile, sneer or forget the correct command and the right moves. The yellow imp would strike again and again.

Soon, more and more Japs grasped the meaning of the warning, and it became downright dangerous to use it within hearing distance of the sons of Nippon. Muffled voices passed on *"rood voor"* from barracks to barracks in Camp Maumere on the island of Flores, or the warning was dispersed by swift-footed, soft-stepping Dutch equivalents of Paul Revere.

One of our barracks-building groups in Camp Maumere came up with what seemed like a brilliant solution. They decided to use the word *"hamer,"* the Dutch word for hammer, instead of *"rood voor."* This idea backfired, however; there was one guard who somehow knew what the word meant. He told the group that hammers were not needed, because the bamboo poles were supposed to be connected and spliced with ropes made of bamboo skin. In addition, he reminded the group that hammers were not allowed in camp anyway because they could be used as weapons. One of the prisoners was then beaten savagely to underscore his statements. So much for that brilliant idea! In general, however, the warning *"rood voor"* served us well. It prevented numerous beatings and kept the brutal guards more or less at bay.

It was at *"luchtdoel kamp Bandung"* (air target Camp Bandung) where hell broke loose. The advance of the Japanese forces was fast and furious. Their landing forces met weak resistance at Merak, and there were no Dutch troops at the other landing sites either. Moreover, the air force had been completely annihilated at the time of the landing or in battles elsewhere.

Those Japanese troops that landed at Eretan quickly secured the airport of Kalijati, where British troops were stationed. Kalijati was taken by surprise. Attempts to recapture the airport with motorized and mechanized units were successful at the outset, but the lack of infantry gave this operation the death blow. The motorized units then fell back behind the *Lembang stelling*. This particular fortification had to endure continuous heavy bombardments.

Our troops had no air support whatsoever, and the thin line of defense in the form of anti-aircraft guns, hastily placed in position, were silenced during the first bombing raid. The capitulation of the

Dutch forces was subsequently negotiated on March 8, 1942, after the Japanese threatened to wipe out the city of Bandung. There was an enormous concentration of women and children in that city at the time.

About 10,000 POWs were assembled in the anti-aircraft barracks in Bandung, where in December 1941 my twin brother and I started military training. It was a sort of boot camp, which was a rude awakening from a relatively easy school routine.

The second awakening was worse than rude—it left indelible scars on our young minds. There were very few Japanese guards the first two weeks and it was relatively easy to sneak out of camp. I received word that Dick had been wounded in a battle near Bandung. A witness told me that he was covered with blood and had been taken to the military hospital at the outskirts of town.

I slipped out of camp that night. There were Japanese patrols, so I had to hide several times. When I finally arrived, it turned out to be a bustling place. The air was laden with the smell of medicines and blood. Moaning, sobbing, crying, screaming was all I could hear. I asked every nurse I ran into if she had seen a wounded soldier who looked exactly like me. One of them had, thank God!

Dick was very weak, and the pain was written all over his face. But when he saw me, he smiled and said that he was OK. The doctor told me that he was hit in the hands, arms and chest by bomb shrapnel, including a wound only two inches above the heart. He assured me that no vital organs were affected and advised me to return to camp immediately. I left with a heavy heart but made it back to camp before daybreak.

A week later, we were allowed to send a radio message to friends and relatives. My message was short and juicy: *"Kick gezond. Dick gewond.* [Kick healthy, Dick wounded]" Kick was my nickname, known only to family members and close friends. The message hit home! My escapade to the military hospital was timed well.

Several weeks later, three military POWs tried to escape and were caught. With their hands tied behind their backs, they were strapped to the fenceposts along the roadside. They were blindfolded, but one of the prisoners told the Japs to uncover his eyes. He then spat in the face of the Japanese commander and yelled, "Long live the Queen!" His last words were for the Queen of the Netherlands, Koningin Wilhelmina van Oranje. The prisoners were then barbarically bayoneted to death while the entire camp population was summoned to look on.

Disbelief then turned into intense hatred. After the cowardly bayoneting, accompanied by the most revolting, blood chilling, beastly screams I have ever heard, the moaning of somebody in great pain was still audible. The commanding officer drew his gun and finished the job his underling had failed to accomplish.

"Bastards. They can't be human beings!" I heard others saying all around me. Surprisingly, one of the officers fainted—he could not take it anymore. The bodies were left tied to the poles for quite some time, a grim warning and grisly reminder for us all, with compliments of *Dai Nippon*.

This execution is still riveted in my mind and I will never forget it. The Japs did not bother us too much after that horrible scene, though. They even allowed cabaret performances, boxing matches, and several great musical presentations and jam sessions. There were also a host of entertainers with excellent material who had an unquenchable desire to poke fun at the sons of the Land of the Rising Sun. Fighting Mick and Jimmy K., for example, were the prime pugilists and top performers, although it was often difficult to determine whether Jimmy was actually boxing or just waltzing in the ring. (I had him timed more than once to the beat of Johann Strauss' beautiful "Blue Danube.") He was a real crowd pleaser, that Jimmy.

It was nevertheless a lonely time for me in spite of all the attractions and distractions. The fear, the anxiety—there was so much to share, but hardly anybody trustworthy to share it with. I really missed Dick, especially since it was the first time we were on our own.

Rumors were rampant that a prisoner transport with unknown destiny was about to take place. It turned out to be a transfer to Camp Cimahi, some 30 kilometers northwest of Bandung. We had to march the entire distance.

This infamous march to Camp Cimahi reminded me somewhat of the slave roundups two centuries earlier. The participants, however, were not cast in the same molds. The white man was the slave now, a pariah who could be disposed of without further ado. A herd of screaming, yelling, kicking, hitting *hanchos*, *samurai*, and *donos* were masters pro tempore.

The Cimahi march may have been a far cry from the death march of Bataan in the Philippines, but it had many of the same horrible ingredients—cruelty, high-handedness and a total disregard for human life and well-being. Many of the marchers took all their belongings along, and for some it was just too much to carry.

Those who suffered the most were members of the Land Stormers, the last army reserve units, consisting of men in their thirties and forties. During marches the natives were held at a safe distance from the main road. We were not allowed to talk to them. However, I heard sneers and howls whenever we passed through a *kampong* or native village or went by a group of Indonesians.

It was quite obvious that the booing was directed at us because nobody in his right mind would have dared to trigger Nippon's wrath. After an exhausting trek we finally reached the outskirts of Cimahi. Groups of people, not all Indonesians, were lined up along the road.

Suddenly, a voice rang out: "Kick, we heard your message. Be strong!"

I stopped dead in my tracks and tried desperately to catch a glimpse of the individual who spoke up, only to be reprimanded by a push of a rifle butt, a guttural "*kura, bager!*" and another shove. I guess I got off easy that day. I wanted to thank the invisible morale booster but could not.

Upon arrival in Camp Cimahi, we saw a cage made of barbed wire which adorned the front yard. Its purpose was all too clear: "disobedient" prisoners could wind up in it, where they would be continuously exposed to the elements. Even the terrifying appearance of this cage was comforting compared to the bullet-ridden wall, where, we were told, the executions of nine prisoners had taken place only a month earlier. Some of the bullet holes were at gut level and below.

Eyewitnesses gave the following accounts. Five Menadonese (inhabitants of the northern tip of Celebes, now called Sulawesi), two Ambonese (inhabitants of Ambon, a small group of islands northeast of Java) and two Dutch prisoners were caught by the Japs during an escape attempt. First the Menadonese were shot, while the other four prisoners were forced to witness the execution. Then it was the two Ambonese's turn, as the Dutch prisoners looked on. One of the Ambonese prisoners just would not die until the seventeenth shot finally put him out of his misery. In the meantime, what the two Dutch prisoners had to go through before it was their turn to be shot defies all description. Only barbarians could devise such atrocities.

In another Cimahi camp, two Dutch corporals were apprehended. This eyewitness account was given about the execution, combined with some observations, as recorded in the Dutch military memorial book *Gedenkboek KNIL, 1961.*

On May 5, 1942, the inmates were startled by piercing screams which seemed to come from all directions. Everybody was summoned to assemble at the large square in the center of the camp. There they saw two handcuffed Dutch prisoners, Corporal Braams and Corporal Peetoms, and an armed Japanese escort. Japanese machine guns were placed on the corners of the camp.

Japanese officers and the Dutch camp commander stood in the center of the square. Approximately 2,600 Dutch prisoners were assembled on three sides of the square. The two Dutchmen and the Japanese escort lined up on the fourth corner. An interpreter gave the Dutch camp commander a briefing of things to come. The prisoners were blindfolded.

Then a Japanese soldier held up a large blackboard on which was written the message that the two prisoners were to be shot because they tried to escape. Screams of rage filled the air. Some prisoners had to be restrained from attacking the Japs. Suddenly, raucous noise came from the Japanese escorts. Guns were cocked and aimed.

Corporal Peetooms, standing tall, shouted with a clear voice, "*Leve de Koningin! Weg met de Japanese honden!* [Long live the Queen! Down with the Japanese dogs!]." Eight shots rang out and it was all over.

Camp Cimahi was the garrison of the former Dutch 4th and 9th battalion infantry. It was a huge emplacement, and I spent the first week trying to locate friends and relatives. One of the scouting expeditions yielded a pleasant surprise when I saw a familiar face in a sea of people. It was Guus, my eldest brother. I was overjoyed to find him in good health. I knew that his howitzer battalion had been involved in the battle of Kalijati. His first question after a tumultuous greeting was, "Where is Dick?" I told him everything I knew, and he interrupted me several times with such exclamations as, "But he was not hit in the stomach? Are you sure?"

That was typical of good old Guus. He had always shown his concern as our big brother. His presence lifted the gloom and somberness which had been my constant companion for quite some time, providing a ray of hope and a determination to be strong and stay healthy.

Yet another pleasant surprise came my way. I was selected to perform yard work at the military hospital, located some ten miles away. Making contact with the patients was not allowed, but while repairing a section of a fence, I heard the call of a Tabongo morning bird, a distinctive three-tone call. To my knowledge, this bird call is only heard in Tabongo, a hamlet near my birthplace of Gorontalo in north Sulawesi.

My father owned a modest coconut plantation, called "*Mon desire*," near the hamlet at the rim of a dense tropical jungle. Actually it was more a family retreat than a business enterprise. Dick and I could mimic this bird call, a feat which was never duplicated by other members of the family. It was our special call. There was no doubt in my mind when I heard the call. Dick was there—pale, thin, weak, but smiling. I yelled, much to the aggravation of the Japanese guard, "*Nari, kura, kanero, bagero!*" I could care less! There stood Dick.

"Thank you Lord, thank you!" was all that I could utter. That night, upon my return, Guus and I celebrated the good news that Dick was OK with an extra cup of coffee and a "*Weduwe van Nelle shag tabak*" cigarette, a typical Indies brand.

At one point, an order was given to crop our hair to such a length that it could not be pulled or grabbed. The Japs enforced this rule with more than ordinary gusto, as many longer-haired men soon found out to their grief. Severe beatings were the penalty and there were instances in which the Japs used their bayonets to trim the excess hair of recalcitrant prisoners.

Most of the men obeyed this order promptly. It was a strange sensation to have short hair. Somehow, it provided a sense of cleanliness and a certain degree of hygiene. Some went so far as to shave themselves bald, and others carved out the initials "K.K.K." for "*kale koppen kamp*" (camp of bald-headed ones).

From then on, everyone jumped on the K.K.K. bandwagon. Some enterprising souls even sold K.K.K. coffee and called themselves "*kale koffee boeren*" (bald-headed coffee farmers.) Their clientele became very extensive. Payment was made in cash using the camp cent, a small bamboo disk with the letter K.K.K. burned onto it on one side and the number "1" on the flip side. Other prisoners sold K.K.K. *bandrek*, a hot and spicy extract of ginger root mixed with other appropriate ingredients. Once you had survived the initial onslaught on your taste buds and the subsequent jolt to your digestive tract, *bandrek* tended to soothe your nerves and promote the urge to socialize. Or did we just imagine these things? Some gave high praise to the brew's healing properties. For a sore throat, cough, stomach ache, or virtually any other ailment, they encouraged its use. As one enthusiast put it, "*Bandrek* kills the bugs before the bugs kill you!"

A most peculiar gathering place was the IVI market. The abbreviation stood for "*Indo verneukt Indo*," or "Indo fools Indo." Indo is the nickname given to Dutch of mixed racial extraction, originating in the former Dutch East Indies. All kinds of refreshments and spicy tidbits former Dutch East Indies. All kinds of refreshments and spicy tidbits were on sale here.

I have often wondered how the ingredients of those delicacies found their way into camp. Some prisoners claimed the camp kitchen was the main distribution point. Others assured me that most of the stuff was smuggled into camp by daring members of out-of-camp work details. Daring is indeed the correct adjective to use, when one considers the intensive body searches these workers were subjected to upon re-entry. They would be savagely beaten if they were caught red-handed with contraband in their possession.

One fateful day the infamous cage had an unfortunate occupant. The rationale was that the particular individual must have been caught smuggling. Nobody knew who he was because a black cloth sack was pulled over his head. Yet some of his movements were telling—the bobbing and weaving of his head, the side stepping. It did not take long before I had it figured out. The captive was none other than the shadow boxing—or, rather, shadow waltzing—Jimmy K., our eminent pugilist. I hoped the Japs would let Jimmy go without further punishment, and fortunately they did. Some time later Jimmy appeared in a scheduled boxing match, and he again waltzed to his heart's content.

We were still in pretty good physical shape in Camp Cimahi, a fact to which the excellent soccer and boxing matches attested. It was during one of those games that somebody stepped up to me and nonchalantly said, "My, you are certainly fast. I saw you and other new arrivals march into camp just a minute or so ago."

This could only mean one thing—Dick had arrived in camp. And so he had! It was a day of joy and celebration. We finally heard firsthand from him what he had gone through. He showed us his smashed right hand with two stiff fingers. Then he pointed out the spot on his chest near the heart where a piece of shrapnel hit him. The doctors left the piece of metal in his body because it was lodged in an artery leading away from and not toward his heart. As a consequence, Dick developed numerous pimples all over his body. When squeezed, they would release minute steel fragments. This prompted his buddies to call him "Dick the steel mill."

Happy days followed, only to be clouded by persistent rumors of yet another pending transport with the usual unknown destination. Fear was always our companion, as persistent as a cancerous tumor. We just had to learn to live with it.

Two significant topics under discussion in Camp Cimahi kept the

the Javanese prophet Joyo Boyo. The series of Geneva Conventions were well-known, and several experts were only too willing to expound on the four international agreements, especially Convention III, which addressed the treatment of war prisoners and reparations for their imprisonment, an issue which came to the fore during World War I.

However, Convention III responded to past occurrences rather than looking toward the future. Some of the experts warned us therefore not to expect much in terms of protection, since "the value of the Geneva Convention is its humanitarian spirit which is ageless and is not letter-bound." We soon found out though that there was not a trace of humanitarian spirit in those Japs, let alone a subserviency to the letter of the conventions. Thus the intent of the Geneva Convention fizzled out in the wake of a brutal attack on humanity by an unscrupulous, barbaric enemy.

And then there was Joyo Boyo, which was quite a different matter altogether. Some prisoners dreamed of the prophecy and even had their hair not millimetered, expecting to be liberated in 100 days.

Why 100 days? According to the Joyo Boyo specialists, we would be imprisoned only for the duration which would be equal to the flowering time of the corn stalk, or approximately 100 days. This concept was referred to as "*jagungan*," a term meaning facts pertaining to the corn plant.

Joyo Boyo was a prophet born in Java many centuries ago. He claimed to be in direct communication with God. Since people could neither read or write in those days, he made his predictions in the form of a collection of passages. Some of his predictions follow:

- There would be a time that a large snake would crawl overland, spitting fire and smoke while making loud hissing sounds.
- Yellow bow-legged monkeys would occupy this land for a time equivalent to the flowering time of a corn plant, approximately 100 days.
- The land of the yellow monkeys would be visited by steel dragonflies and the sun would be darkened.
- When the yellow monkeys left this land, the white buffaloes would return to their stables.
- A big strong fighting bird would take many souls under his mighty wings.

The interpretation of the first prediction was well received and accepted as plausible by most prisoners. The fire and smoke spitting snake had to be the train, which became operational in 1873 on the snake had to be the train, which became operational in 1873 on the island of Java. Its locomotive spit fire and smoke and produced hissing sounds.

We had some problems, however, interpreting the second prediction. The yellow bow-legged monkeys were, according to the these specialists, the members of the Japanese occupying forces. Everybody agreed with that too. But the matter of the 100 days was rather controversial. Apparently, the true meaning of *jagungan* somehow got lost in the translation.

As was reinterpreted years later, Joyo Boyo was apparently referring to the germination potential of the corn seed which was considerably longer than the flowering time. But in camp, we clung to the 100 days interpretation and the count was on. As time went by and nothing happened, hope changed into doubt and even sometimes into ridicule.

So the ever clever entrepreneurs once again muscled their way in, and one day the *Joyo Boyo bal* made its entry. This "ball" was made of grated sweet potatoes with brown sugar in the center. This delicacy was Dick's favorite.

The specialists obviously could not be more specific regarding the other predictions. The outcome was locked up in the future.

So life went on with or without Joyo Boyo. It was not an easy life. The secret was to stay away from the Japs, avoid them at all costs, keep them at a distance if at all possible. Nevertheless, this sound plan was an impossibility for one of our fellow prisoners who was an excellent artist and accomplished caricaturist. He owned an impressive collection of drawings, some in color, of camp scenes and of very handsome prisoners.

His talent especially impressed a certain Japanese prison guard who was endowed with slant eyes, high cheekbones, protruding gold teeth with spaces between them like a bicycle rack, and an upper lip adornment resembling a discarded toothbrush. This guard decided to commission the artist to make a portrait of him, similar to the nice ones in his collection.

So what was the artist to do? His solution was simple. The guard got his portrait, as ordered—a grinning beau sabreur, complete with an Errol Flynn mustache, soft, rounded cheekbones, eyes visible as he was grinning, and inconspicuous ivory-colored teeth and molars. The guard was predictably delighted with this representation.

Queen Wilhelmina's birthday was not to be commemorated. We

were informed to ignore this important event. Yet we were reminded of it in a unique way by the Dutch kitchen staff. They wrote the menu of the day on a blackboard and it read like this: Red chili—White rice—Blue soup. These colors represented the Dutch tricolor. The flag was complemented by an orange pennant, an old custom.

Apparently the kitchen staff could not whip up an orange colored dish, so they hung a bunch of carrots on the blackboard. The announcement remained there the entire day, but the carrots not surprisingly disappeared in no time. And the soup had indeed a blue-grayish color to it. It was even edible!

Song and dance shows with inmates dressed as women were very popular and valued highly by the Japs. They probably noticed a similarity between our shows and their own kabuki performances back home. "Remember My Forgotten Man" was the top hit in camp. I could even hear the echo of the song on the other side of the barbed wire fence, underneath the streetlamp at the barracks gate. It surely was a far cry from Marlene Dietrich's rendition.

Another song which made the camp hit parade was Carmen Miranda's "Argentine Nights." The man imitating Carmen, swinging his hips and flashing his eyes, deserved an Oscar for his performance. It was wonderful.

It was obvious that this artificial, carnival-like bubble in which we lived was bound to burst someday. Something was brewing, and many of us felt that we better be prepared for a big and ugly event to occur.

This eerie feeling never left me, so I volunteered several times to perform outside camp duties. I did this just to enjoy another glimpse of the Indonesian countryside, a sight that I loved so much. In the meantime, the once friendly and lovely natives somehow had turned against the Dutch. Yet I knew someday this all would change. I silently said my good-bye, "*Selamat tinggal*, until we meet again, God willing."

The day of departure came sooner than we expected. The eve of that day was spent in fear and trembling. Some of the prisoners remained cheerful outwardly; others merely sported a mask of joyfulness—but that nagging fear remained.

Sleep at last gained the upper hand, if only for fitful periods. Then there was a far-off whisper and a soft pleading voice, singing the words of a Dutch Reformed Church hymn:

En leid Uw kind
  (And lead thy child)
Tot ik aan d'eeuwige stranden
  (Till I find rest)
De ruste vind...
  (At the eternal shores...)

It was the morning of April 18, 1943, a day never to be forgotten by me and my fellow POWs. We were off to face more hardship and more trauma. However, let the above stories about Japanese internment suffice in conveying the feeling of gloom and doom of imprisonment. After three and a half years, we indeed survived and had gone through a harsh dawn, with *"red ahead"* still.

ABOUT THE CONTRIBUTOR

Denis Dutrieux was born on May 18, 1923, in Gorontalo, Sulawesi and attended school in the Indies for 15 years. He was drafted in the Dutch conscript army in 1941 and fought to defend the colony against the Japanese invading forces during World War II.

He became a POW on March 8, 1942, living in various POW camps for the next three and one-half years. After liberation he was required to serve in the military again until his honorable discharge in 1949.

Denis worked in electrical sales and engineering for nine years and repatriated to the Netherlands in 1958. After four years of employment in Amsterdam, he decided to emigrate to the United States, settling first in Missouri and then in southern California.

He continued his college education, earning an A.A. degree and a B.S. degree. He worked for 24 years in the telecommunications industry and retired in 1986. Dutrieux and his wife now reside in Los Angeles.

In 1990, forty-five years after his liberation, Denis in his capacity of chairman of *Comite 15 Augustus 1945* finally could realize a long cherished dream of publicly commemorating and honoring the members of the Dutch armed forces and civilians who perished during World War II in the former Dutch colony and other parts of Southeast Asia. The annual ceremony takes place around August 15 in Los Angeles.

MATHILDE PONDER-VAN KEMPEN

A Wartime Girlhood

Dusk fell for me and many other children during the Dutch Saint Nicolas festivities on December 5, 1941, in Kudus, Central Java. My sisters, Dorothy, age ten, and Engeline, age eight, and several of our schoolmates were celebrating this feast on the weekend of December 6 and 7. How we enjoyed our newly acquired toys; we were happy and considered ourselves fortunate. As an 11-year-old I was not particularly interested in world affairs. What did we, as children of that generation, living in a peaceful country like the Dutch East Indies, know about the ravages of war and similar issues anyway?

On December 8, 1941, as I sat down at the evening meal with my parents, two brothers and two sisters, Dad told us that war had erupted. We were about to face a difficult time. My sisters and I interpreted this news flash as being merely an announcement. We did not realize the seriousness of the situation until mobilization occurred.

A few days later, all students at school were called into an assembly. The principal, Mr. Hoogwinkel, told us that he, Mr. Nierop and another teacher had to enter military service as a result of the war. Consequently, several classes had to be combined and it soon became evident that this consolidation caused the female teachers to become overworked. So it was decided that after Christmas vacation, our European school would remain closed.

As a youngster, I did not object to such an unanticipated "vacation." On the contrary, it was great not to have to go to school. I did

This chapter was submitted in Dutch and translated by Jan Krancher.

not realize that this unsolicited time off would last five long years. Getting that much behind in school can be a difficult obstacle to overcome, as became evident later on. My dad, being the administrator of the Kudus telephone company, was also mobilized and assigned to the Destruction Corps as an ensign. He was proud of this rank. But there was another change in the offing.

It must have been toward the end of February 1942 when Dad came home with the news that we had to evacuate. Mom had to pack a few suitcases with the most essential items and some provisions for use on the way. Of course we asked Mom what "evacuate" meant. She answered, "We have to go to a place where it is safer than staying here. Where that will be, I do not know yet." The worst news for us girls was that our toys did not fit in the suitcases, and so we had to leave them behind.

The next day, after supper, we left in a convoy consisting, among other vehicles, of two buses loaded with personnel of the telephone company and their families. Our destination was Surakarta, Central Java, where we would stay overnight. Dad, using his own car, drove at the head of the convoy. Mom sat next to him and we five children were in the back seat. Unexpectedly, the plan to stay overnight in Surakarta was changed and we drove throughout the night to an evacuation center in Purwokerto, Central Java, a village on the slope of Mount Slamet. We arrived in the late afternoon and were temporarily housed with a Chinese family. Two weeks later, we moved in with the Diaz family, Mr. Diaz being Dad's colleague. We enjoyed the fresh, clean mountain air and found it much more agreeable than the heat in Kudus on the coastal plains.

On March 8, 1942, the Dutch capitulated. This again was a strange word I never heard before. So we lost the battle, I gathered, but the war would last much longer. A few days later, the Japanese drove into town. We had to stay indoors. Dad was recalled to Kudus with his telephone company personnel to normalize telephone connections in that region. Two weeks later, he picked us up and we returned to our home where our dolls and other toys were awaiting us.

As soon as the Japs felt confident that they could manage the telephone traffic, Dad was interned again and locked up in the Jurnatan jail in Semarang, Central Java. That was the first blow for our family, since without him we lost our income. I can still remember Mom's sad countenance as she was forced to sell off our possessions in order to meet our daily needs. At first she disposed of excess dishes and silverware, but soon she had to get rid of Dad's nice desk as well.

We were astonished, when, after more than three months' imprisonment, Dad suddenly showed up. The Japanese needed him to restore the chaotic local telephone traffic to its former state of operation once again. He had to continue to work for 100 Japanese occupation *rupiahs*, a mere pittance. On this income, our family was barely able to live for a week. The Japanese allowed us to make extra money if at all possible, but Mom had to continue to sell her things in order to for us to stay alive. Commodities were getting more expensive as the war progressed, and goods were getting more and more difficult to come by. Medicines in particular were very hard to find.

Mom came up with a brilliant idea to open a small food stand on the front lawn, facing the street. We sold rice with side dishes. She did the cooking and I assisted. She, in turn, would help us girls with sales. We got up very early in the morning and made sure that the stand was already open for business between 5 and 5:30. We could count as our best clients the stream of Indonesian passers-by coming from the villages on their way to the market. Around 9 we were already sold out. Our "profit" consisted of the entire family getting a free meal.

We were indeed lucky that Dad, thanks to his knowledge and skill, could keep on working for the Japanese even though it was at very low wages. In this manner, we were more or less under the protection of the local Japanese authorities so we were not threatened with violence. Nevertheless, our health continued to deteriorate; we lost weight and were frequently ill. Most of our household goods were sold by now, and all we had left was our beds, three cupboards and a table.

The Japs were starting to intern 16-year-olds in November 1944. My brother Norbert was sent to Ngawi, East Java, but my older brother Ewald managed to stay out of camp, primarily because he locked himself up in his room and never ventured into the street.

Eventually, our beds and two cupboards had to be sold too, so we ended up sleeping on mattresses on the floor. Our clothes were now stored in only one closet. But when the need was the greatest, assistance was nigh. Around August 1945, Dad came home and soon there was not a single Jap in sight in Kudus. Norbert returned from internment, resembling a walking skeleton. Out of joy, I personally baked him a multi-layered cake. However, we rejoiced too soon, for another dawn was about to break, and a very unpleasant one at that.

After the Japs disappeared, the *pemudas* (politicized Indonesian youth) showed up, yelling "*Merdeka*" (freedom). By radio, they were whipped into a frenzy against the Dutch by their leader, Sukarno. At the beginning of September 1945, first the men and later the older boys disappeared into prisons. A few weeks later, the women and children were picked up and placed in a camp, an old, dilapidated cigarette factory in Gebog, a village at the foot of Mount Muria, north of Kudus.

We were already weakened by the Japanese occupation as a result of malnutrition and lack of medicines. To make matters worse, the housing was deplorable. Sanitary facilities in particular were insufficient. Within a very short time, the entire camp smelled like human excrement, attracting countless flies. Later on, latrines were constructed over a flowing stream so at least the waste was immediately swept away by the water. We were fed prepared meals, so fortunately we did not have to cook for ourselves.

My 12-year-old niece came down with jaundice and there was neither medicine nor a doctor in the camp. My mother, who cared for Maud, was advised by a fellow prisoner to feed her three head lice in the morning with *pisang mas*, a certain variety of banana. She tried the remedy, and the result was unbelievable: Maud was cured within one week.

After being in Gebog for a month, we were transferred to a camp at Langsee, a dilapidated sugar cane factory near Pati, the residential capital, in Central Java. The facilities here were just as bad as Gebog, but we were given more freedom and were reunited with the men and boys. Here food had to be prepared by the internees themselves. The availability of food was limited, resulting in most internees becoming even weaker. There was a camp store where we could buy fruit and vegetables, but because of the high prices, we could not afford these commodities.

Fortunately there was a nurse in camp. She managed to obtain medicine and bandages by way of the Red Cross. The younger boys and girls were saddled with the chore of cutting wood and hauling water for use in the kitchen. This was heavy labor because our bodies were already very weak. The older folks kept the camp area clean.

Christmas and New Year's were not celebrated because we were not in the mood. Besides we were totally deprived of news from the outside world. One evening early in 1946, an Indonesian appeared and gave a speech to the gathered internees. His message was that we could choose between becoming Indonesian citizens or remaining foreigners in our land of birth. If we were to become citizens, we would be released immediately. But if we maintained our Dutch nationality, we would be transferred to another camp. Most elected to retain their Dutch citizenship, so a few days later, this group was ordered to get ready for departure at midnight. At around 1:30 in the morning this group which included my family, left on foot for the railway station in Pati, arriving around 6:30. Late that same afternoon we boarded a train and left for Ambarawa, Central Java. After an all-night ride, we reached this town at 8:00 in the morning.

After waiting several hours, we were transported by truck to Camp Baju Biru and billeted in the so-called children's prison. Food and housing were very poor in comparison with conditions at Langsee.

We were here barely one week when our group was trucked away again, this time in the direction of Surakarta. We found temporary housing overnight in a Red Cross shelter. After a while, we heard that we were to be flown to an area protected by Dutch troops. This was obviously great news, but somewhere deep down we did not believe it right away. So we had to await what would happen. Very early the next morning we were transported to the airport. Was it for real this time?

It was only after we recognized that the airplane on the tarmac was a Dakota, manned by a Dutch crew, that we felt assured that our freedom was close at hand. We were soon airborne and at long last landed at the Kalibanteng airport in Semarang, a few hours later. We saw the tricolor. We were now convinced that we were finally delivered from the darkness and destitution of war and had re-emerged in the light and life of peace and prosperity.

ABOUT THE CONTRIBUTOR

Mathilde van Kempen was born in 1930 in Madiun, East Java. After completing European elementary school, she attended middle school in the Indies until about 1946. She did not graduate because she got married to Frans John Nicolaas Ponder in 1948 in Semarang, Central Java. They have three sons and one daughter. Mathilde is a house wife and loves to cook. She is now studying English while living in Amsterdam.

BAREND A. VAN NOOTEN

The Mouse-Deer and the Tiger

When an army of 60,000 Japanese troops landed on the island of Java on March 1, 1942, and gradually made its way into the interior, our family was staying in the West Java countryside, about 60 kilometers south of Jakarta. We had fled there a month earlier from town, where heavy bombardments and frequent air combat between Japanese and Dutch East Indian planes made life dangerous. Here, far away from the coast, we owned a small bungalow in an idyllic mountain setting where clear, fresh brooks ran through grassy hills and beautiful, rosy-cheeked Indonesian children were playing in and around the small village. About a dozen modern bungalows made of stone and wood dotted the hillside.

These dwellings were mostly owned by affluent Dutch and Chinese civilians from Jakarta. Before the war, they used to come here on weekends to find relief from the sweltering heat of the coastal plains. A few old pensioners had settled permanently, waiting out their last days.

The name of this idyllic place was Sirnagalih, although the general vacation area was known as Megamendung. From the town of Bogor, it was some 16 kilometers along the highway leading south to Bandung, a stretch of road that we were to come to know very well.

This is the story of how the members of my small colonial community experienced the Japanese invasion, and how they tried to guard themselves against becoming victimized. Thousands of people all over the Dutch East Indies in those same months of February and March 1942 were facing similar crises. Too often these ended in humiliation, tragedy, and even bloodshed, while our family managed to cope and emerge relatively unscathed from the first encounter. If the incidents by themselves do not add up to a determining episode in the war against Japan, the story nevertheless deserves to be told, because it follows a very ancient motif.

It is a modern enactment of the old fables in which a weaker creature outwits a stronger one, in this case a mouse-deer triumphing over a tiger. It pivots around one woman's heroism in the face of overwhelming odds. It deals with her ingenuity and strength of character which resulted in the ultimate rescue of some 20 Dutch-Indonesians from assaults by roving Indonesian looters.

When a major war, like a gigantic horrible cloud, casts its shadow over the land, people change. In this conflict, many people who were widely known prior to the war as paragons of virtue and responsibility, leaders and wives of leaders, often failed to live up to that image when faced with a crisis that frightened them. Conversely, many simple folk who had hardly ever attracted the serious attention of the community at large displayed such strength and integrity of character that their fellow victims looked to them for leadership and moral support.

But that is only part of the story. The change that affected the people around us also had to do with attitudes that slowly were transformed under the pressure of the new circumstances. Attitudes towards the Japanese and Indonesians were suddenly called into question. Little did we know about the Japanese that had not been pounded into our subconscious by years of government propaganda. "Japanese" conjured up an image that was both hateful and ridiculous. The caricature of the Japanese soldier presented him as a short, subhuman barbarian with pronounced Mongolian features. At the same time Japanese technology was supposed to be far inferior to ours. We knew how quickly Japanese toys fell apart and hence—or so our leaders told us—the same must be true of their machinery.

Morally, the Japanese did not rate high, either. They were supposed to be cunning, treacherous, and exceedingly cruel. So the idea that a Japanese could be an individual with a character of his own, perhaps even a likable character, was absurd and even unpatriotic.

On the other hand, the Indonesians were our friends. They were living happily, or so the story went, in a society rightfully dominated for centuries by the Dutch. The Indonesians played the role of children of the wise, white parents from overseas and were ever grateful for the many superb technological innovations that the colonials had brought about: railways, cities, plantations, mines, public health and education. Hence it was inconceivable that these true friends of long standing would ever turn against their benevolent masters. In my family, at least, the question was never raised what price the subjected people had to pay for the largesse bestowed upon them.

But now the fact that the Japanese had swept down from across the ocean and were conquering our land within less time than it took for corn to mature struck an uncomfortable note. It clashed with the "truth" that we had learned to accept: the supremacy of the cultures of the West versus the supposedly inherent inferiority of Oriental thinking. So this story also has to do with prejudice.

Japan was the enemy, and now the enemy was just over the horizon. The local radio station was slowly changing its war coverage from purple descriptions of Dutch victories such as, "In Serang on the island of Java, the invading enemy was chopped into pieces" to announcements of tactical withdrawals and regrouping in strategic locations.

At night we listened to the military wavelengths where real-life events, often highly dramatic, were played out. Code names "kite" and "tiger" represented two military outposts, one of which suddenly went off the air with a loud crash one night after an appeal for assistance.

Reliable news was hard to come by and was replaced by rumors. To add to the confusion, now and then a Japanese plane would fly over—a bomber on its way back to its base, or a navy Zero, a fighter plane, spewing its ammunition over dirt roads. One of these fighters even made a dive and took a potshot at my brother as he was swimming in our little backyard pool. At the same time, from the vantage point of our bungalow halfway up a hill, we could see troop movements in the distance on the highway. These were units of the KNIL, the Royal Netherlands Indies Army, in retreat, listlessly winding their way along the asphalt road from Bogor to Bandung. On March 5, the Japanese occupied Bogor, and three days later Java capitulated.

The rumor mill was now grinding out one horror story after another: Patrols of Japanese commandos were systematically moving about the countryside to round up stray enemy. On their way they invaded the houses of Dutch civilians, pillaged what they could, raped women, and responded to any resistance with swift brutality. Not content with their own depredations, they also encouraged the Indonesian populations to storm into the houses after they had left and loot and plunder at will. The mob eagerly availed itself of the opportunity to get rich quick, so the Japanese patrols acquired a crowd of hangers-on which followed them from house to house.

It is still unclear to me how widespread those practices were, but we were soon to find out that the rumors contained a lot of truth. For us, huddled together in a little house with no protection against these unknown dangers, rumors were all the news we had. We children, three brothers, were between seven and eleven years old. There were also four adults: my mother, her sister, our nanny, and Ambri, a tall young man from Jakarta who had been a servant in our household for many years. Our nanny, Tiene van Gestel, was an Indo (i.e., of mixed Indonesian and white parentage). She had been with us since our childhood and was more a member of the family than a servant.

At night, by the light of an oil lamp in the dining room, we tried to devise ways to escape from the impending danger. One plan after another was considered and rejected as being unrealistic. Some of the plans we dreamt up were ingenious.

My aunt, for instance, suggested that even though we could not hope to oppose the Japanese, we might at least try to keep the Indonesian robbers away. But how? We could transform our house into a place to be avoided, a place known as a haunt where dangerous ghosts lurked. At her insistence we implemented her plan that same night. By the light of the waning moon, Ambri stole outside onto the terrace of our bungalow. On his head he had placed a footstool to add to his height, and over him my aunt had draped two white sheets that entirely covered him and the stool. A flashlight in his hand completed the ominous specter.

The effect was dramatic: a seven-foot ghost, slowly gliding across the terrace, making ghost-like gestures with his hands and head. Dressed in black, my mother followed closely behind him clutching a revolver in her hand, just in case a nonsuperstitious villager might appoint himself ghostbuster for the night. As is the case with almost all rituals, we never found out whether the charade was effective.

That was the last time we laughed for a long time to come. Although we talked and plotted until well into the night, nothing positive emerged. In fact, we all became very anxious, and when the meeting broke up everyone was close to tears. There seemed to be no escape from a fate that would humiliate and degrade us and which would remain an ugly memory for the rest of our lives.

My mother was never one to give up, however, even if she had to admit that she was at her wit's end. She was concerned that the next day she and her household would fall victim to a pitiless enemy that was a thousand times stronger than all the people in the community combined. Early the next morning, she called us all together and explained the situation as she saw it.

"There is no hope for us," she said, fixing her intense blue eyes on us. "The Japanese are going to do terrible things to us and we would be better off dead." Already panic stricken, we children stood speechless, more horrified than words could express. "Therefore," she continued inexorably, continuing her fixed gaze, "I have decided to kill all of us when the Japanese start in on us. You know that I have a gun. I will shoot all three of you in the back of the head and then kill myself."

Frankness was one of my mother's sterling qualities! I know that I broke out in tears and ran away to the children's room. We children never questioned what she proposed to do. This was perhaps because in some way, we, using our infantile minds, felt that she who had given us life was entitled to take it away again.

Next my mother asked Ambri and our nanny to find their own way to Jakarta. There was no reason for them to stay since they could easily pass for Indonesians. She entrusted Ambri with the valuables, including a kilogram of gold, to keep for her until she returned to Jakarta, if we escaped. Ambri slipped away along little known paths leading to the north. They told us later that they had kept away from the main roads, reaching Jakarta safely in a few days.

As the day wore on, we saw from the terrace the first Japanese commandos turn off from the highway unto the gravel road, linking the vacation cottages. A handful of them walked slowly to the first house, stopped outside and then went in.

A crowd of some 50 Indonesians had gathered outside the house waiting for them to reappear. After half an hour they came out and made a hand signal, at which time the mob ran inside and began their part of the day's "chore." Soon beds, furniture and other household goods were thrown out on the lawn. The Japanese military, meanwhile, ambled over to the second house to repeat this performance. My aunt observed,

"If they continue at that rate, they won't be here until noon."

When this observation trickled into my mother's consciousness, it stirred a sudden idea, a brilliant stroke of insight that might give us a chance to avert the imminent horror. She quickly called a family council and announced, "We are going to make them eat!"

I should add here that my mother had been raised in the Dutch

East Indies, spoke Indonesian fluently and had amassed an astounding amount of incidental knowledge. She had very little formal education and had always disliked school intensely. Through deft manipulation of her teachers and parents, she managed to be expelled from the third grade of the elementary school in Semarang, Central Java. She spent the rest of her childhood reading and educating herself. She grew up to be a petite, beautiful and individualistic young woman with a great force of personality and an uncompromising belief in her own dignity. After she had married my father, who had studied Japanese, she had learned a few phrases of that language from him. All these facts are of relevance to what follows.

"One of the things your father taught me," she continued as she addressed her puzzled, dispirited audience, "was that in Japanese culture, the guest-host relationship is sacred. If a man eats at your home, he will not do you any harm because he has accepted your hospitality. It is a code of conduct that nobody violates. We are going to make the Japanese eat at our table and hopefully they will spare us. It is our only chance!"

Within minutes the new plan was put into effect. My mother and aunt disappeared into the kitchen, we children tidied up the house, and my mother laid out our best eating bowls and silverware to honor our expected "guests." She placed her revolver on top of the sideboard for all to see.

Soon heavy steps sounded outside the door. Shouting and laughing noises came from the mob of looters who were standing on the gravel road, brandishing their newly acquired possessions. We could plainly see them through the windows. We children locked ourselves in our rooms adjoining the dining room and took turns peering through the keyhole. My mother stationed herself at the front door with her sister behind her. She opened the door and saw three people, two Japanese and one Indonesian interpreter.

My mother bowed down very low. From the vast storehouse of her memory she extracted a Japanese phrase which in translation would come through as, "Please, honored gentlemen, come in, sit down, and partake of our humble meal!" As my aunt described this incident later, the expression on the faces of the commandos was one of total astonishment. They had temporarily lost the initiative; and presumably, the prospect of a warm meal sounded very enticing to them. They nodded to the interpreter who then announced that they would accept the invitation. Both were young and rather short of stature. One of them may have been a subaltern officer; the other was a soldier. They were armed with sidearms and long swords in leather scabbards.

It was now my turn at the keyhole. I saw my mother and aunt come into the dining room holding a large bowl of steaming white rice and a delicious-smelling fish preparation. They politely looked away while the soldiers and the interpreter loaded the food into their bowls. With fascination I watched as they took their first mouthful. They seemed to approve! It was either that, I remember thinking, or a bullet in the back of my head.

Seldom since that time have I enjoyed watching people eating more than during the next half hour. The meal went off splendidly, and no chef, in my opinion, could have boasted of a greater culinary accomplishment than the couple in the kitchen. These cooks watched with rapt attention as their "guests" wolfed down the meal and started on their dessert and tea. The meal ended up with two well-deserved belches and the soldiers got up to continue their journey. As predicted by Mother, they did not search the house, nor did they touch the revolver which was within a few inches of their grasp.

Never one to give up the initiative, my mother asked through the interpreter whether she could request a favor from the honored "guests." She asked for a pass that would allow her to leave the mountain community to set out for Bogor the next day. They listened, discussed it among themselves, consented, and handed her a piece of paper with Japanese writing on it. Next, she asked them to keep the mob away from the house.

By that time we boys had opened the door to the dining room. I still vividly remember looking through the open front door. There I saw the commandos walk up to the menacing mob, pull out their long swords and brandish them over their heads. The interpreter announced in a loud voice that this house was under the protection of the Japanese army. Anybody who dared to loot would be decapitated.

This story shows not only how the mouse-deer outsmarted the tigers, but also how our preconception of the Japanese as murderous automatons needed revision. True, all throughout the subsequent years of suffering we met any number of enemies who lived up to the pitiless, even murderous stereotype. But these two commandos showed a different side of their character. Even though they were soldiers of a warring country, they possessed the civility to set aside their hostility for a few minutes. Thus they were able to meet the enemy on a personal level, in the role of guest and host. The image they conveyed was that of two citizens of a civilized nation who, in spite of temporary difficulties, were at ease interacting with like-minded people in another civilization. I like to think that was the case here.

On another occasion, my mother had managed somehow to save us from being attacked by looters, but many of our neighbors had not been so lucky. Their homes had been ransacked; a few had been beaten. The question facing us now was what to do next.

The events of the next few days are not easy to recall. I have pieced them together from personal memories and from conversations long ago with my mother when she was still alive and, more recently, with my two brothers. The day following the visit from the Japanese commandos was a day of great confusion.

Relief for having been spared a dreadful humiliation at the hands of the invaders alternated with uncertainty and anxiety about the future. Temporarily at least, we enjoyed a reprieve from attacks by marauding mobs, but how long that would last, no one knew.

Confused thoughts coursed through my head. The order of the world as we had known it appeared to be completely upset. The ransacked houses and the fearful expressions on other people's faces, the break in daily routines, the sudden enemy planes thundering overhead, all were reminders that some cataclysmic change had taken place, threatening to paralyze us. Our serene mountain setting, once a place where people had lived in harmony with nature and each other, had been transformed. It now had become an arena where a few among us were singled out as targets for the greed and malevolence of often unseen predators.

I felt as if we were walking along the edge of an ocean. A huge wave had just struck the beach and had retreated. Now we found ourselves in the short, peaceful interval before the next wave would crash down on us. The wave was invisible, but it was surely out there. It was a menacing presence lurking in the seemingly placid ocean ready to pounce on us again and again. The only thing that should concern us now was finding a way to cope with its inevitable, furious impact.

An old Indonesian saying states that a man who does what is expected of him is a good man, but one who does more than that is worthy of high praise. This story will show that the saying holds true for women as well.

Most of the people in our community responded to the invasion of their privacy and the violence they had witnessed and endured with predictable bitterness, resignation, hurt, and grief. But not so my mother! She had already determined that staying in the mountains was equivalent to courting further violence and even murder. So she went to the neighbors and told them what she had decided. "We are going to Bogor as soon as possible. We will take along anybody who can walk."

We did have a car in the garage, but it would have been very dangerous to drive it down to Bogor. Clearly, the Japanese were in complete control of the road and would have impounded the car immediately. No, the only way to get to Bogor was by foot. Even so, we were exposing ourselves to unknown dangers. It was by now abundantly clear that many among the Indonesian people would be unsympathetic to us. Their reaction to meeting up with a group of helpless, disheveled white people walking down the highway was entirely unpredictable. But it was the only chance we had.

The air was brisk and cool when we started out the next morning at daybreak. Four or five other people from the Sirnagalih community had joined us, mostly young women with their children. Some 20 Dutch remained behind because they had been injured or were too weak, too sick, or too terrified to walk that distance.

As my mother said good-bye to the Flemings, an elderly couple who were still dazed from the shock of the previous day, I heard her promise that she would be back soon. She further said that she would move them to safety eventually. I did not understand how she could make such a promise. She was not in the habit of making idle promises like that, the way people do to put anxious souls at ease, but I could think of no way that she might persuade the Japanese to provide for their evacuation. But a child accepts mysteries and paradoxes, especially if they have the authority of a mother's word.

The trek to Bogor took eight hours. To avoid attracting attention, we blackened our faces, arms and legs with soot. Additionally, we had stained our hair with black dye, and we spoke as little as possible as we walked slowly along the side of the road. We children wore pajamas to conceal our white skin, while the women had simple cotton dresses with long sleeves on. There was little traffic—an occasional horse and buggy or ox cart—so there was mostly vast emptiness. The sky was clear, and as the day progressed the air got warmer and warmer. An early-morning walk in this part of the country is usually a great treat. But not this time! We children were scared and did not look around very much. As the day grew hotter, we walked in the shade of the local large-leaved trees lining the road.

At times, convoys of trucks full of Japanese troops rolled by without paying much attention to us. Only once were we stopped by a Japanese foot patrol. My mother showed the permit she had obtained from the commandos the previous day. She explained that we were on a mission of mercy. They motioned us to continue. Occasionally, an Indonesian man or woman would exchange greetings with us or engage in a brief conversation. But nothing stands out so much in my memory as the frightful sense of desolation that pervaded the atmosphere around us.

The countryside appeared nightmarish as we were walking in slow motion like determined, alien puppets in a landscape of invisible terror. The most noticeable smell was that of acrid smoke. The Indonesian villages appeared peaceful enough, but many of the large Dutch or Chinese dwellings that lined the road did not. Doors had been pulled off their hinges; windows had been shattered; personal belongings were scattered about on the grass; dogs lay dead; statues were pushed over; and fountains lay still, full of litter and filth. Some houses were on fire; others were just smoldering, as if too tired to bring their own destruction to its inevitable end.

In her own yard a middle-aged women in a dressing gown was standing forlornly and silently staring at the wreckage surrounding her. Twice we children were told to look straight ahead and not sideways into the yards lining the street. That may be the reason, I suppose, that I do not remember seeing any human bodies, as was intimated by the adults. Time has advanced more than 50 years since I walked that road, and many details have become rather blurred. However, the memory of the apocalyptic landscape is still sharply etched in my mind.

Halfway during the trip we were attacked. A young Indonesian had been trailing our party for some time, ambling on in the rear of the column as if belonging to it. My aunt and brother were walking side by side. As they crossed a small bridge the strange man suddenly lunged forward, brandishing a knife. He caught up with my aunt, cut the string of the purse she was carrying, and snatched it away. He continued past the bridge, turned down a steep river bank, and disappeared from sight.

The robbery took only a few seconds. My aunt cried out and held up her hand, bleeding from a cut the young man had inflicted upon her. But she was not seriously injured, and the purse contained no valuables. Nevertheless, this episode had a debilitating effect on all of us. We became increasingly anxious about the prospect of making it to Bogor. Would we get attacked again?

Unaccustomed to walking more than just a few kilometers in the heat, we children soon got tired. As time wore on, we became utterly exhausted and asked to stop for rest every few minutes. My mother had to tell us over and over again how desperate our situation was so that we would keep on going. By the end of the walk the three of us were just stumbling on by sheer power of will.

Late in the afternoon we arrived in Bogor in a reasonably unscathed condition. The exception to this was that the soles of our shoes had worn out, and most of us were by now walking on bare feet. We eventually found lodging with relatives of one of the people in our party.

The morning after our arrival, my mother set out immediately to find a way to get back to Sirnagalih. She wanted to make good on her promise to evacuate the remaining Dutch people. She was determined to obtain an official pass that would allow her to move the invalids to safety in her own car. It proved to be much more difficult than she had imagined.

Before long it became clear that the social and professional networks that our family had built up over the years were no longer in effect. Friends in places of power and authority, relatives, police inspectors, military personnel and their spouses—these had all but disappeared.

The Japanese had not yet established a civil authority, and her attempts to approach the officials who were nominally in charge unfortunately met with no success. That is all I know about her activities that morning, but when she came home at noon, her mind was made up. She was going to approach the military commander in the Palace himself and petition him for permission to evacuate the Dutch civilians from Sirnagalih.

Those who are familiar with Indonesia or have lived there know that Bogor was more than a cool hill town far removed from the malaria-ridden plains of Jakarta. Ever since the governor general of the Dutch East Indies selected it as a site for his new official residence some two centuries earlier, this town had stood as a symbol for the established civilian power.

The residence, then known as "The Palace," still stands to this day as a large, sumptuous building with high ceilings, wide terraces, and floors made of polished marble imported from Italy. It was a place visited by foreign dignitaries from all over the world. They attended the many formal evening parties on the terrace or in the glittering ballroom. It was also the place were statesmen made important decisions that would influence the lives of millions of people scattered over the 3,000-plus inhabited islands, some as distant as 2,000 miles away from the capital.

Scientists the world over visited the magnificent botanical gardens surrounding the palace. Tourists by the thousands came to look at the water lilies so large that one leaf could support the weight of a baby. The Japanese immediately had moved in and made it into the regional army branch headquarters. Its commander was the target of my mother's urgent mission.

That afternoon we watched her leave in a horse-drawn carriage. There are no witnesses to what happened that afternoon, but this is how she described her visit to the Palace afterwards. The carriage dropped her off in front of the building and she walked up to the gate. Her appearance was unconventional, to put it mildly. Wearing the same clothes she had on the day before, and barefoot, she definitely did not look like the type of person who might request admission to the palace.

However, I should add that she had a very forceful personality, a quick wit, and a way of inspiring others to have confidence in her. She therefore persuaded the guard that she had urgent business with the commander, and he let her in. Heavy at heart and intensely frightened, she walked on her bare feet over the long driveway. This approach led from the gate to the marble front steps, passing through the columns of tall white pillars that lined the vast front lobby.

Here she was stopped by another guard. She requested to see the commander and was kept waiting for a long time. To her great surprise, when the guard returned he ushered her into the commander's office.

In a steady voice, she presented her petition in Indonesian to the commander who was seated behind his desk. It was translated by an interpreter. Again to her amazement, the commander reacted positively. He ordered a servant to bring him something out of a sideboard. It turned out to be a Japanese flag, about 12 by 10 inches in size, which he laid down on the desk.

He then proceeded to scribble a number of Japanese characters with ink on it. He motioned to the interpreter to hand it to my mother. The interpreter explained that this flag was the pass she needed and entitled her to use her car for transporting sick people over the highway. It should be displayed on the windshield. As she backed out of the room, she thanked the commander with a deep bow and made her way back to the steps. With a great sense of triumph and relief she took the horse-drawn carriage back home.

So much for my mother's account! Arriving at home, we saw her emerge from the vehicle, smiling and holding up the flag. Without losing time she began preparations to return to Sirnagalih. I cannot recall how she got there. However, I vaguely remember her getting a ride with a man, perhaps a member of the clergy, or else she may have taken a horse cart. What I do remember clearly is that she came back the next day in her own grey 1939 Chevrolet coupe, along with four women and children, refugees from Sirnagalih.

The very same day she made three or four more trips. By evening the Dutch people who had been stranded there had been evacuated and brought back to Bogor. For a few of them it had been too late. My older brother remembers her telling him that during the night one or two of the Dutch had been buried alive by the Indonesians. But the pass had worked its magic, for although she had been stopped many times, the signature of the military commander granted her immediate passage.

In this way my mother had first led us to safety. Then, like the mouse-deer, she ventured into the lair of the tiger. And finally, she rescued the weak and sick people from Sirnagalih. She had thus proved that she was capable of accomplishing much, much more than would otherwise have been expected of a women of her stature. The efficacy of the Indonesian saying, as described earlier, was born out. She certainly deserved high praise.

In fact, the only reward she ever received was the eternal gratitude of all of those people whom she rescued. And that is perhaps all she wanted.

For us, her descendants, looking back five decades into the past as the twentieth century comes to a close, the motivations for her actions are not always completely clear. However, by and large, during that time of transition and also during the remainder of the war years, she staunchly adhered to her own principles of correct living, regardless of the price she had to pay for that position.

One of these principles was loyalty to her fellow victims of oppression. As she saw an opportunity to rescue the weak and vulnerable, she exposed herself unselfishly to potentially great personal risk and danger. But in the process, she nevertheless gloriously carried off her missions.

ABOUT THE CONTRIBUTOR

Barend A. van Nooten was born in Larantuka on the island of Flores in 1932 from Indo-Surinam parents, both of whom could pass as white. Before the war he lived in Magelang, Central Java, and Bandung and Jakarta, West Java. He spent time in civilian prison camps in Cihapit and the 15th Battalion barracks, both in Bandung. After the war he found shelter in Wilhelmina Camp, Singapore; the Miramar Camp, Wellington, New Zealand; and a private beach cottage south of Brisbane, Australia. He went to the Netherlands in 1946 and to Canada in 1953. He has lived in California since 1960.

He enjoyed elementary and higher education in the Netherlands, graduating in 1951. He attended the University of Toronto in 1958 and the University of California at Berkeley where he earned a Ph.D. in Sanskrit in 1963.

He has written two books and numerous articles, mainly dealing with Sanskrit language and literature. He is presently a professor emeritus and lives with his wife in a quiet rural setting five miles west of Petaluma, where he continues to write.

WILLY RIEMERSMA-PHILIPPI

Imprisoned in Our Own Home

It was during elementary school exam time in Semarang, Central Java, in 1942 that the seriousness of the Japanese threat to our way of life became clear to me. The Japanese forces came closer and closer to the Indies. Everybody was closely following the news on the radio. The Japanese army and navy kept on winning more and more battles. Then they invaded Malaysia. Our army, air force and navy fought desperately to keep the Japanese at bay.

If the situation became very critical, my parents decided, upon advice from other people in town, to evacuate to the mountains. They thought it would be safer there, away from all the tumult and the fast approaching enemy. We stuffed our homemade backpacks with only the bare necessities and left town. My parents had rented a big house in the village of Tampingan, Central Java, from a village chief. Our entourage consisted of father, mother, three daughters, two elderly single sisters and one servant.

The first day in the village we felt as if we were on a prolonged vacation, far away from town and school. But we were also removed from extensive radio and newspaper coverage. The only news we received was by way of hearsay and rumor. It was awfully quiet everywhere.

The first month we were there, my father decided to collect his pension in town. But he came back within an hour, very upset, confused and agitated. He told everybody who wanted to listen that the Japanese had invaded the islands and that Semarang, Central Java, was occupied. A bridge over a canal leading to town was blown up by our own troops. The Dutch East Indies had lost the war! What were we going to do now?

Villagers from the mountains started to riot. There was no police force to maintain peace and order. Town people who had evacuated to their bungalows in the mountains now came fleeing through the village on their way back to town. They advised us to do the same. It was no longer safe in the villages. Many of the mountain people now suddenly became our adversaries. Unfortunately, there was a lack of transportation, so we just stayed inside.

One night, Mother overheard a conversation between our villagers and those from the mountain. They were asking questions about us. Our village chief explained that we were refugees from town and that we had neither any money nor valuables. They replied that they suspected there were young girls inside and that they might prove valuable assets to them. My mother almost went out of her mind with worry so she tried to get us out. Since she was Indonesian, she did all the wheeling and dealing.

The people suggested that if my father would become a Moslem, nothing would happen to us. My father was willing to do that to protect us, but Mother objected because she knew what it meant to become a Moslem. According to their customs, a man or a maturing boy would need to be circumcised.

At long last, she found a taxi driver, but we could not all make the trip together. So it was decided that Father and the three girls should go first. The driver would then double back to pick up Mom and the rest of the party. The taxi driver wore a disguise to resemble a bandit in order to ward off any potential terrorists. Unfortunately, upon approaching town, we could not go any farther than the destroyed bridge.

We had to cross the canal on an improvised ferry. We kept very quiet, not knowing whether we could trust the taxi driver. My mother, however, had promised him a big reward if he took us safely to town. It was getting late in the afternoon and he still had to drive back to the village. When we arrived at the other side of the canal, we hired a horse-drawn carriage. It was strangely quiet in town. There was hardly anybody in the streets. Japanese flags were flying on all of the tall buildings.

We felt much relieved when we reached home. The house was intact, and we waited there for Mother. As the evening hours went by, we became very worried. They did not yet show up. We did not know what might have happened or what to do. Going to the police would have been useless. Who made up the police force anyway? We could not sleep all night. We cried and prayed for Mother's safety.

Early the next morning the party finally showed up. We were so happy to be together again. Mother explained that the taxi driver had not dared to make another trip at night. He preferred to wait until the next morning. Unfortunately, there was no way to notify us in town about this decision.

Now we had to plan for the immediate future. The Japanese did not believe in releasing well-deserved pensions, so my father had no longer an income. We had to find another way to make a living. Two of our brothers were in the army and became prisoners of war, as we found out later. European men and boys 17 years and older were also thrown into prison.

My father was left alone because he was too old and needed special medical care. My oldest brother, who was employed by the Dutch State Railroad, was kept in service to build and repair damaged bridges. That was fortunate for us. He could send my parents money to pay rent and utilities. We only had to take care of our food.

Mother was a good cook and started a small catering business. Most of the housewives in the Indies did not know how to cook and for that matter, were not very adept at doing anything around the house. For these chores, just about every household had at least one servant to do the housework, including cooking. At a reasonable charge, mother prepared meals for housewives in this predicament. She did not make much profit but at least we got a share of those meals. She also took orders to prepare special delicacies such as boneless stuffed fish fried in coconut oil, and other typical Indies snacks.

My older sister and I were the healthy and strong ones. Together we had to make all the deliveries on a bicycle. Sometimes this was difficult, especially when we had to ride uphill. But we never complained. We kept promising ourselves that when the war was over, we would catch up and get all those nice things we missed out on. We dressed in rather unattractive clothes and did not use makeup in order not to attract undue attention. Besides, I was not yet allowed to use makeup anyway.

A general warning was given to all Dutchmen. Once a Japanese had his eye on a certain woman, he would pursue her and eventually take her as his mistress against her will. We did not want to take any risk, as we wanted nothing to do with the enemy.

There was a shortage of rice during those war years. We received dried tapioca roots or other rice substitutes. When rice was available, it could only be bought with distribution coupons. All supplies were confiscated by the Japanese military for use by their own people. Other foods, such as bread and butter were also unavailable.

People started to invent many new recipes from whatever edible commodity they could find. There was also a dire need for other items, so we started to sell off clothing, furniture or whatever was of value to the buyer. From the proceeds we could purchase other necessities. All of a sudden certain items which were useless before the war became quiet valuable, such as empty bottles and any type of container.

Nobody was allowed to listen to radio broadcasts. All radios had to be registered, and foreign stations were sealed off. We could only listen to Japanese broadcasts. A cousin had given us some valuable items to keep before he was imprisoned, and one of these was a radio. But we did not have the documents for it, so we could not prove who owned it. We were afraid that neighbors or others might betray us if they knew that we owned one. In those days, you never knew whom to trust. Some even betrayed their close friends or relatives for money or special favors.

In 1944 Father became very ill and had to be hospitalized. Never in the past did he openly demonstrate love for his children. Now that he was in the hospital, he was worried about his family being at home alone. We visited him daily, riding our bicycles a long distance from town. One day he told Mother to take money which he had hidden and pay for transportation to get to and from the hospital. We then realized how much he actually loved us, especially since he expressed his great concern about our health and safety over and over again. Two weeks later he passed away in his sleep. He never had a chance to see his two sons again. They, in turn, did not know that their father had died until we told them after the war.

Dutch education was prohibited by the invasion forces, and all schools were closed during the occupation. We could attend Japanese school and learn their language, but we refused to consider this option. We did not want anything to do with the enemy.

Mother was illiterate and realized that she had to learn how to read and write. When Father died, she became the head of household. Since she had to be able to read in order to sign documents, she secretly took lessons from my first grade teacher. Nobody was supposed to know what she was doing. If this had been discovered, she could have been jailed for disobedience of the rules. I really admired her for her strength and courage.

We experienced a couple of air raids but really did not know exactly what was going on. Most of the time we kept ourselves locked up. Mother did the majority of errands herself. The situation in town became critical again, and we did not know for sure what to do about it. We did not get any news other than what the Japanese fed us. Sometimes we heard from people who secretly listened to foreign radio stations how the war was progressing. One rumor had it that the Allies were advancing and had defeated the enemy. The Japanese had already lost the majority of the conquered territory, but we never knew who or what to believe.

One day in 1945 we heard gunshots throughout town. The tumult and shooting kept coming our way. Then we heard a lot of commotion next door. Our neighbors were Indonesians but we were not acquainted with them. Suddenly we heard a women crying and begging someone not to shoot. Nevertheless a shot was fired and the woman cried and wailed loudly. We also heard harsh Japanese soldiers' voices.

We thought that we would be next. We were so afraid and did not know where to turn for help or how to escape our impending fate. When the soldiers came to our door, Mother opened it and bravely faced them. All they wanted to know was whether there were any Indonesian soldiers or men in the house. Mother convinced them that she was Dutch and that there were none inside except herself and the small children. They believed her and left for next door. They were Dutch also and did not harbor any Indonesians either, but they had a boy of 14 who was my best friend. The primary purpose for the search turned out to be an attempt to find soldiers or potential soldiers.

Then at last the news came that the war was over. Japan had surrendered after atom bombs were dropped on Hiroshima and Nagasaki. There was chaos all around, and armed Indonesians took Japanese soldiers as well as civilians captive. How they came into possession of weapons, we did not know. The Japanese apparently did not keep their earlier promises to grant the Indonesians their independence. At the time, they only did this to ensure Indonesia's cooperation during the war. But when Indonesians started to kill Japanese prisoners by shooting through prison windows, some survivors overpowered the Indonesian guards, took their weapons and broke out.

The Japanese also freed Dutchmen from imprisonment, provoking fierce fighting between the Indonesians and the Japanese with the Dutch civilians caught in between. Of course we knew nothing at that time and had great fear of what would happen next. When the Japanese soldiers searched our house for Indonesians, they advised us to stay inside for our own safety.

Then one day we heard knocking on the door and when Mother opened it, a British-Indian Punjabi soldier, assigned to the British Army, stood there. He asked a question in English. Mother did not understand what he said and called me to assist in interpreting. I could not speak or understand English either, but I had always had an interest in my brothers' English lessons when they were still in high school. With the aid of an English-Dutch dictionary and after a lot of struggle, I finally could figure out what he wanted. He wanted to know who lived there. He also advised us to stay indoors and explained that British troops had landed and taken over control from the Japanese military. They arrived before our own men were released from prisoner of war camps elsewhere.

The Punjabi also told us not to worry. His patrol would come by every day to check on the Dutch living on our street. What was so incredible was the fact that the patrol was supposed to consist of defeated Japanese soldiers. Despite the Japanese surrender, the soldiers were very disciplined and accepted the temporary British command. I was not aware, however, whether this practice was also prevalent throughout the entire country. I only knew it was the case in Semarang.

The Indian officer kept his word. He came by every day to see that all was well with the Dutch families. One hot afternoon he asked for a glass of water. We handed it to him through a slit in the door. His men also wanted a drink, so he asked for a pitcher of water but did not allow his patrolmen to approach. I then saw for myself that the patrol consisted of Japanese soldiers. Now we knew for sure that he was really concerned about us and wanted to protect us.

In September or October 1945, many of the Dutch troops finally returned from imprisonment. My second brother, an officer in the army who was previously detained in a camp in Sumatra, also came home. Nevertheless, we still did not dare to go outside since the situation in town was not yet safe.

In December, my other brother, who was in charge of evacuating women from the interior to the coastal towns, advised our family to go to a so-called protection camp. It was located on the other side of town near military bases, and it was safe there. Again we loaded up our backpacks and suggested to our close relatives that they come along. In this manner we spent New Year's Eve 1945-1946 in a camp, in safety. There were numerous people in this camp, and we were guarded by British troops and Dutch military.

After New Year's Day, the camp director announced that we had to evacuate to either Burma or Singapore. They expected more fighting in town, this time between the Indonesian Army in the interior and returning Dutch troops. These troops had just landed from Holland and elsewhere after a delay of about three months. Some of these men were anxiously waiting in Malaysia, after being released from POW camps, for permission to re-enter the Indies.

We were transported by trucks to the harbor of Semarang where we camped in huge storage sheds. Everybody slept on mattresses, spread out on dirty floors in buildings without any partitions. The complete lack of privacy sometimes created difficulties, especially at night and in the morning when we had to get dressed and undressed. And we had to take turns using the improvised bathrooms as well. Once a small fire broke out in our barracks, caused by someone carelessly smoking a cigarette on his mattress.

Then came the news that Burma was overcrowded and could not accommodate us. Our new destination would be Singapore. We all had to put the name of the new destination on our packs. The only bright moment during this involuntary camp-out was the 11 A.M. break. The British would serve chocolate to everybody. We had not tasted this beverage for such a long time, and it was delicious. There was plenty for everyone who wanted a second helping.

A couple of days later news came that Singapore could not have us either. We had to try to get to Surabaya in East Java instead. We could not understand why they decided on this particular city and again we changed the destination label. But not long thereafter, the authorities announced that we would stay in Semarang after all.

We could now return to the protection camp, originally a Catholic school, once again. There were half decent living quarters, formerly used by the clergy, and we were assigned a small room. I liked these arrangements much better.

All this time I had secretly kept my pet rabbit. I hid him and kept him alive by sharing whatever edibles I could get hold of. The few people who knew my secret were kind enough not to tell the camp staff.

I was more than happy with that small room. I struck up a friendship with one of the kitchen helpers to make sure that he could provide me with fresh vegetables for my pet. I loved him very much. He was not just an ordinary rabbit. On the contrary, he liked to eat sweets and to drink coffee with cream and sugar which my father used to give him at breakfast. He was spoiled rotten and always wanted my undivided attention. He would not even let me lie down peacefully on the floor to read a book. He would jump up at me and sit there until I paid attention to him and played with him.

In April 1946, people were allowed to return to their homes once again. The town was now safe and secure. But our house had been burglarized and we did not dare to move in. Instead, Mother looked for one near the protection camps and found a large place in a narrow street. Nobody seemed to know who owned it or where the owner could be found, so the camp director gave Mother permission to move in.

Slowly things were getting back to normal again. Schools started up after a four-year hiatus. We were required to take several tests to determine how much we still remembered and what class we would be assigned to. I started higher education that year, and I had a lot of catching up to do. The classes were only in session for six months. They gave us crash courses, and some of those deemed less important were deleted from the curriculum.

It was not easy, but I made it through hard work and determination. The first school year, I studied at the light of an Aladdin oil lamp since our house was not yet connected to electricity. There were also not enough textbooks, so we had to share them with other students. I copied most of the lessons by hand. This made it a little easier to study when we discussed that particular chapter.

These war years were undoubtedly the hardest years of my life. I have had experiences that a person under normal circumstances would never have had, and I have learned from these experiences. I believe I am a better person because of what I endured.

ABOUT THE CONTRIBUTOR

Wilhelmina Christina Philippi was born in 1929 in Pekalongan, Central Java. Her mother was an Indonesian woman from a large wealthy Islamic family and she married a Protestant Dutch-Indonesian, against her father's strong objection.

She attended European elementary school in Semarang until 1942 when everything was disrupted by the war. After the war she continued her studies, graduating in 1949, and became a ground stewardess for the Royal Dutch Airlines which later became Garuda Indonesian Airways.

In 1953, she began working at the Consulate General of the Netherlands in Bandung and Semarang and stayed until 1957 when it had to close and all Dutch citizens in Indonesia had to leave.

She went to the Netherlands for two years and then emigrated to California in 1960. She and her husband have been living in San Jose every since and both are retired. They enjoy traveling and are active in Dutch community activities in the San Francisco Bay area. Willy loves to write and contributes regularly to *FOCUS*, a publication of the Netherlands Society of Northern California, Inc., of which she is the secretary and editor.

MARIA McFADDEN-BEEK

Ode to My Mother

This story is a tribute to my dear mother, Justine Simon-Beek. It was her strength, love and sense of humor that got me through three and one-half years of Japanese imprisonment which was filled with fear and illness. It was my mother who helped me put this period of time in its proper perspective. After all, it was wartime.

In November 1942, we were told to report to camp Cihapit in Bandung, West Java, with one suitcase each. My mother chose to take two large paintings by Han van Meegeren which were oil portraits of her and my brother, Pim. She simply cut them out of the frames, rolled them up and put them in her suitcase. The remaining space was primarily taken up with powdered baby formula. My youngest half-brother Andriaan was six months old. The older brother Kees was four and I was sixteen. During those confusing first months of 1942 we all thought that this fearful, disruptive period would only last a couple of months. How very wrong we were!

We started our three and one-half years of confinement in a small shop. After only one week, we were made to move again. This time we shared a very small house with a family friend and her bedridden mother. They occupied the only bedroom. My mother and the two boys stayed in the living room while I slept on the front porch.

I celebrated my seventeenth birthday in April. Bamboo fencing in Cihapit kept us inside, and there was only one gate. In the beginning, I would duck under the perimeter fence with friends to explore the outside world. We would return the same way or use a sewage culvert inside camp. We were usually loaded down with food, bacon being especially high on the wish list. But soon such escapades became very

126

risky. Once, as we returned from a scavenging trip, the Japanese guards were waiting for us at the inlet of the culvert. I was hit on my face with a flashlight and taken to the camp jail with two of my friends.

We were afraid that we would not be released. I shared a filthy cell with another woman. In order to sleep, we took turns, since there was not enough space for all of us to stretch our legs out at the same time. Lice were eating us alive. The latrine was visible to the guards. Using it was very humiliating and foreshadowed other indignities we would have to endure in the future. Miraculously, I was released after about ten days and returned to my mother and brothers.

From mid–1942 on, the situation quickly deteriorated. Hunger soon occupied all of our thoughts. Our food rations became smaller and smaller. We cooked on our small coal hibachi-type grill and it became more difficult each day to get charcoal, cooking oil and rice. I remember collecting large snails which we found in the vicinity of the sewage and waste-water ditches. Fried in oil, they did not taste bad and provided us with much needed protein!

Chickenpox also afflicted many in camp, and I contracted a solid case of it. I was 17, and as a consequence, I became very sick.

At the end of the year, groups of prisoners were moved around once again. We packed our belongings and were transported to Muntilan to a former nunnery. We were packed in open trucks and driven to the train station. There we were loaded like cattle onto railroad cars with shuttered windows. With the overcrowding on the train, the lavatories soon became too filthy to use. And there was no drinking water anywhere.

I vividly remember this particular transport. I saw my mother's legs and shoes turn red with blood. She had started to menstruate, and the blood was collecting in her shoes! She advised me not to talk about it, as it would upset the boys.

At Muntilan, classrooms had to provide space for 15 to 20 women and children. If you were lucky, you had sufficient space for a mattress or a bed. I preferred the floor instead. The ever-present lice did not bother me there.

By 1943, all of us suffered from many diseases as a result of over-crowding, malnutrition and inadequate sanitary facilities. Jaundice, beriberi, malaria, dysentery, and endless skin problems were rampant. Our scant food rations barely kept us going. In spite of these conditions, we were expected to perform many chores on a daily basis. Red Cross packages were not distributed to the prisoners, but instead were stolen by the Japanese guards.

Sometimes a nurse or one of the nuns was able to get medicine from base camp to treat the worst cases of dysentery or malaria. Weakened by fever and diarrhea, many inmates died. I was a member of one of the many crews assigned to carry the loaded bamboo coffins out of the camp to a burial site nearby. I still remember how surprised I was at finding out how heavy a dead human body actually was, even in an emaciated state. The sight and smell of body fluids seeping through the thin coffin bottoms was upsetting, to say the least.

My mother became very ill, and repeated bouts of malaria left her terribly weak. Still, she insisted on sharing her food with the boys. I never heard one word of complaint. Every day she tried to convince us that the war would soon be over.

A narrow creek running through the middle of the camp served as our wash site. Every other day, I would roll up a bundle of dirty clothes belonging to the four of us and take them there. I hated the dirty water and that tiny piece of soap.

Another chore I shared with others was working in the camp vegetable garden. It was a short distance from the gate and was a popular work detail. I cannot recall finding any semblance of carrots, onions, or anything that we grew in our food rations, however. We did occasionally steal a carrot or green onion, though we knew that if we were caught, we would receive a severe beating.

The boys in our camp who were big and tall physically were separated from their mothers and taken to the men's camps at Ambarawa. Some were only 11 or 12 years old.

The camp commander took sinister pleasure in constantly moving us around. We were never told anything about our destination, and most of the time it was just to a different room in the same camp. Although our possessions were few, the continual moving caused much fear and stress for our already weak and discouraged group. Often it meant ending up with even less room. It also created deep resentment from those who had to give up a section of their room.

One of the many silly duties we had to perform was the night patrol. It consisted of eight hours of inspecting a designated area of the camp. When reporting to the Japanese guards, we had to bow and report that all was well. I never understood the purpose of this assignment. Surely we could not escape. And if we could get out somehow, where could we go? With our white skin, blond hair and blue eyes we would not remain undetected in the native villages for very long.

Constant hunger, sickness, and weakness often overwhelmed us.

The thoughts of never getting out became persistent. But my mother never let on how worried she was. She never stopped telling us it was really only a matter of a little more time. She reminded us of all those wonderful things which would be awaiting us when the war was over.

All of us adapted in many ways to imprisonment and deprivation. We brushed our teeth with our fingers, using ashes from the kitchen fire as toothpaste. Our toothbrushes had long ago worn out. One bucket of water per person per day was hardly adequate for our drinking and bathing needs. The latrine was simply a board placed over a deep hole. When the pit was overflowing, it would be covered and a new one dug a few yards away.

There was a water well surrounded by a low concrete wall. Women had to stand in line to take a bath in full view of Japanese and Indonesian soldiers. On one special visit, a Japanese officer came by to observe. He found great pleasure in touching some of the women on their breasts and buttocks with his sword.

Around this time, strange new skin diseases started to show up, mostly on our legs and ankles. These appeared as tender red blotches which were very sensitive to sunlight. Those of us who worked in the sun began to wrap these areas of the body with bandages made from our clothes. What a sight to see—skinny, dirty, sickly smelly human beings. We were deeply humiliated.

We talked constantly of liberation as being "just around the corner," arriving "very soon." We heard little news about the war's progress, but rumors were rampant about the Americans fighting in the Pacific. There were stories about battles fought in the Philippines and Irian Jaya. As conditions in Muntilan worsened, the behavior of the camp commander became even more erratic than before.

We had to line up time after time. Women were pulled out of the lineup and beaten for no apparent reason. The guards ran around shouting and harassing. More rumors were whispered of possible moves to other camps. I was constantly worried about being separated from my mother and brothers. We had all heard, of course, about the special camps where young female internees were forced into prostitution for the Japanese troops.

In March 1945, hundreds of us were transported to Banjubiru, Central Java. The trip was a nightmare. The sight of a third camp, a former prison, was especially frightening. Camp #10 was terribly overcrowded, holding about 4,500 women and children. We found a small space in a former stable. Over the next few weeks, many male prisoners were added to this already overcrowded camp. They came from several camps in Ambarawa.

From these men, we learned that there was to be an imminent end of the war. For the first time, we heard about the unrest caused by young, militant Indonesians who were threatening to kill all of us in the camps. My mother now was terribly thin and weak, but her spirit was still high. She just knew that all this movement of prisoners was the beginning of the end.

And sure enough, on August 15, 1945, Japan surrendered. The war was finally over. For us, however, freedom had not yet arrived. Indonesia declared independence on August 17. A segment of the population reacted hatefully and with malice toward the weak and sick Dutch people who were totally defenseless.

We were convinced that the Americans would eventually liberate us. But at the very last minute, the task of liberating and protecting Allied prisoners and internees was delegated to British forces. This was apparently a political move, because the British wanted to reestablish themselves in Malaysia. As it turned out, they were quite unprepared to execute their mandate. They had to simultaneously disarm the Japanese, protect the Dutch prisoners, and fight the Indonesians. And there was no adequate transportation, no medical help, and insufficient personnel to manage such an enormous task. It was chaos.

How wrong we were to think we could just walk out of camp, find our loved ones, resume our lives, and continue our careers as before. Because of a lack of adequate troops of their own, the British forced the Japanese to "protect" us in camps from the violent young Indonesians. Our former guards and tormentors were now our protectors! How ironic that was.

We had no choice but to remain in camp for our own safety. It was far too dangerous to travel. Besides, we had no money and no means of transportation, and many were too sick to be moved.

In early October 1945, I was lucky enough to find a job with the RAPWI (Recovery of Allied Prisoners of War and Internees) as a translator during interrogations of Indonesian militants. In addition, I did the food purchasing for the British officers' mess. Two Ghurka soldiers were assigned to accompany me for protection. I was thrilled to be able to do something constructive for a change. I was also quite elated to be sleeping in a real bed with mosquito netting after all those years of sleeping on the ground.

At long last, my mother and brothers were assigned to transport by ship from Semarang in Central Java to the capital, Jakarta, in West Java. She was eventually repatriated to Holland for a reunion with my stepfather.

I was assigned a room in a hotel in Semarang which was taken over by the RAPWI command. But the situation in that city remained very tense. There were skirmishes with the *pemudas* around the clock. It was as though there was another war going on. I remember a trip in a Jeep with other RAPWI personnel to attend a soccer game. Gurkha soldiers were riding shotgun. Upon arrival, they completely surrounded the soccer field to assure a safe game.

A great deal of fighting took place between Ambarawa and Semarang. Even the sick were at risk from attack on their way from the mountains to the hospital in Semarang.

In December 1945, I finally made my way to Jakarta. With help from the RAPWI I was placed on a waiting list for evacuation to Australia. The Dutch government had arranged for some recuperation camps to be set up in the vicinity of Brisbane. But I did not stay at Wacol camp very long. Although the food was good, it still was another "camp."

I had immediately applied for immigration to the United States. My permanent visa was granted in late June 1946. With the SS *Mariposa*, I arrived in San Francisco, California, on July 26, 1946. This is a date that I cannot ever forget.

My mother died in 1976. Her painting now hangs on the wall in my living room after being repaired, cleaned, revarnished and framed. Often, when I look at it, all the memories of my beautiful, dedicated and courageous mother flood back. She taught me about priorities and love. She also told me to keep my feet squarely on the ground and to move forward always.

ABOUT THE CONTRIBUTOR

Maria Magdalena McFadden-Beek was born in Bandung, West Java, on April 22, 1925, of Dutch parents who came to Java in 1919. Her father was employed by the state railroad as a civil engineer. Her parents divorced in the early thirties and her mother remarried. Maria's stepfather, also an engineer, owned a consulting firm in Bandung until his internment in 1942.

Maria, her mother and brothers survived the war years and the Indonesian revolution. Before emigrating to America, she had a short stay in Australia. She found employment as a model for I. Magnin in San Francisco, later becoming an assistant in the Custom Made Salon. She eventually moved to southern California and worked in San Bernardino.

She married an air force officer, and after 22 moves in 20 years of married life, the couple retired in Oxford, Mississippi, in 1973. For 15 years they raised beef cattle and Appaloosa horses. McFadden-Beek gave riding lessons and still has a few students and show horses.

KAREL SENIOR

New Terror on the Way Home

After returning to Baros Camp #5 near Cimahi from the railroad camp Cicalengka around August 17, 1945, we found that the rumors were true. The war was really over. Japan had capitulated, but we still had no conception what the atom bomb was all about.

It barely sank in that my brother Hans and I had survived the railroad camp and now probably the war as well. Dad, whom we left behind in Baros Camp #5, also confirmed that the war was over. After some twisting and turning, a space was prepared for the newcomers. A number of people also had died in the meantime, so there was more space available. The food situation was much improved. We were given rice, and the soup was much more substantial.

In a central barracks near the gate, the Japanese guards, assisted by the *heihos* (Indonesian auxiliary forces), had built a storage shed. Guards were still on their posts. However, a rumor circulated that they themselves would not mind being interned in this camp or at least staying here until they could return to Japan. As a precaution, they had already stashed away extra food and textiles.

The prisoners were handed military towels every so often. Somebody must have had access to these linens. We stole other commodities and hid them in a cavity which was craftily cut in the bamboo pole of one of the sheds. Cans obtained this way contained whale meat. Without much comment, the content was incorporated in the soups. In this manner, we slowly regained our strength.

The average internee did not understand why we had to stay in camp. News traveled very slowly then. About one month after capit-

This chapter was submitted in Dutch and translated by Jan Krancher.

ulation, we saw our first Brit, who had parachuted in earlier. But what the Brits discussed with the leadership of the camp we did not know. In the meantime, there was a lively trade with the locals for extra food, a practice which was subtly condoned by the guards.

With a pair of shorts as our starting capital, my brother and I started to conduct trade ourselves. Hans knew of an Indonesian family who could deliver some kind of croquettes. On occasion, evening concerts were conducted by musicians of the former NIROM (Netherlands Indies Radio Broadcast Company). Somehow, they managed to keep their instruments in working order. During such an occasion, Hans and I warmed up the croquettes on a small wooden stove near the podium where they would perform. This treat went like hotcakes, and money came trickling in.

Baros Camp was sometimes called the "elite" or "VIP" camp because the occupants consisted of upper management personnel and those who could sustain themselves financially before the war. A few of the Internal Affairs people had already left camp to visit their former work sites. The natives had received them with open arms and this sounded promising. But they soon returned, mainly due to the poor food situation outside camp.

We found out that Mother occupied our old house again and that she was healthy. A family council was convened. With the croquette money, we could afford to buy a train ticket. I had once been employed as a coolie, using forged papers prior to 1943, so I was deemed the most logical person to check the situation out. After all, working as a coolie I had found myself rubbing elbows with the "common people," primarily Indonesians who performed menial tasks. Out of the three of us, I spoke the language the best. Dad was not completely up to par yet physically and neither was Hans after the treatment he received working on the railroad in Cicalengka.

Through his connections in the village, Hans managed to buy a ticket. Then both of us crawled out of the camp early in the morning on October 4, 1945. I was wearing my carefully safeguarded shorts which I carried with me throughout all the camps. I never traded them and had saved them for just such an occasion—to return home again. My shirt, in contrast, was shabby and all patched up. I did not own any shoes but had grown accustomed to going barefoot. We did not have any money for underwear either. Everything was invested in the train ticket and the croquettes.

As a valuable, tradable commodity, we brought with us all the towels we possessed, packed in a clean gunny sack. That was our only luggage, and I promised myself to use as few towels as possible. I did not know what I would encounter once I reached home. They could prove to be money makers!

Huffing and puffing, the overloaded train arrived at the station of Cimahi. People were hanging out the windows and clinging to the open train balcony. They were even sitting on the roof clutching their belongings, some holding on tightly to chickens, cooped up in baskets. I somehow ended up on the iron railing of the balcony with the bag of towels at my feet at the very edge of the last wagon. To stand among fellow passengers was impossible.

It was about 9:30 when the train laboriously got moving. The trip was breathtaking. I looked down into the deep gorges of the Priangan as we crossed the high bridges. Soon the train was approaching the lowlands of the northern part of West Java. It was October 4, 1945, the war was over, and I was on my way home—at least, so I thought.

I was in high spirits. The Indonesians on the balcony were friendly. However, they looked rather suspiciously at my crumpled shirt, my bare feet and my pants, made of a gunny sack material. My pale yet sunburned skin was the most noticeable oddity. Otherwise I could have passed as just another coolie, even though at approximately six feet I was on the tall side.

The slow train stopped at almost every small village. At each station, there were natives who stood guard with all kind of strange looking weapons. Upon a signal by one of the fellow passengers, they approached me and another victim on the train, whom I did not notice before. We were interrogated as to our destination and then frisked. In Cikampek, the major railroad interchange, where the train would swing towards Jakarta, the *peloppors*, Indonesian rebellious youth, appeared to be more fierce and were gesticulating wildly.

Several cars were disconnected and reconnected and there was a lot of talking and shouting. It seemed that the car I was in was getting emptier. I found a seat next to my fellow traveler who was in distress earlier. He was a dark, small Dutch-Indonesian about my age. At long last, the train was moving again, and I calculated that in another hour or two, I would be home. The train entered Tambun, one stop prior to Bekasi, about 30 kilometers before Jakarta.

During the usual searches, the situation suddenly turned very ugly. A furious crowd armed with sticks and swords stood on the platform, yelling that all Dutchmen had to get off the train. Pushed from the back and pulled forward, I found myself standing on the platform. With five other Dutchmen, I was taken, guarded by two well-armed men, to a large house.

We were again interrogated and searched in the presence of the crowd which had followed us. The towels, removed from the bag, caused a roar of laughter and soon disappeared. There went my capital, my pocket money, my trading commodity!

The six of us were taken upstairs and locked up in a large, bare room. As he took us aside, the leader told us that we were lucky that we were removed in Tambun and not in Bekasi. In Bekasi, every Dutchmen taken off the train who fell in the hands of the *peloppors* was murdered. When the crowd had calmed down, he assured us, we would be allowed to complete our travel to Jakarta. The door closed.

With these hopeful thoughts we sat down on the bare floor of an unfurnished room. There was one barred window. It overlooked a balcony which ran along the entire width of the building. Now and then a dark face would appear, staring curiously at us. In short, soft-spoken sentences, we introduced ourselves: four of us were Dutchmen from camps in Cimahi, one was a Dutch-Indonesian who was never interned, and one was a rather tall Ambonese who also was never in a camp. All of us were on our way to Jakarta.

We soon found out that nobody knew what to do with us. There was no toilet in the room. We had to rattle the door and ask politely, yet urgently, for permission to go to the bathroom. This was done under guard, obviously. We were even given food that day. It came from the kitchen for the "troops," an un-uniformed, undisciplined, wild and furious-looking gang. It was difficult to estimate their number, and they possessed an assortment of weapons. One of them brought up a pot of rice. We ate with our fingers off a banana leaf plate, a common practice in Indonesia. There were no accommodations for the night, so we just lay down on the bare tile floor in our pitiful clothes. The floor was hard but as longtime internees we were used to it.

We barely slept because of the constant yelling of the guards and because of the hard tile floor. In the early morning, several sinister characters stood in front of the window, looking at us as if we were monkeys. We moved to the other corner of the four-by-three-meter room, out of sight of those thugs. They were now asking for clothes. The day before, during frisking, they noticed that we were carrying a few garments. We ignored them but soon they started to threaten.

Eventually we relented and passed some items through the window to get rid of the beggars. But because of this gesture, the interest in us only increased. That afternoon, we were visited by some kind of gang leader who had somehow gained access to the room. He took away the last remnant of clothing, under threat of a sword. I realized full well that it was getting serious. Only the clothes I had on could I call my own.

In the early morning of October 6, 1945, it suddenly turned much quieter. Around noon, several excited young Indonesian guards appeared. With a lot of threats, they tied our hands behind our backs and took us out. We were taken to the railroad station again and boarded a train to Bekasi, where we found crowds yelling "*Merdeka!*" (freedom). It was a tall leap from the freight car onto the platform with our hands tied behind our backs. Mr. W. fell but stumbled bravely along. Would the execution take place in the center of the village, in the town square? We stopped just outside the station. The lead guard pointed his sword to a formless, bloody mass in a dry ditch. It turned out to be a corpse of someone who ostensibly was killed with a sword.

"That is your destiny," he commented.

Soon we walked through town, still surrounded by excited, talk-ative men, armed to the teeth with sharpened spears and swords. We had to doubletime to an official-looking building. It turned out to be the police barracks, where we were pushed into a two-by-two-meter cell. To our surprise, two Dutch boys also from Cimahi, Ruud and Koen, were already in there. The roof was tall and looked reasonably sound. Above the bare, once whitewashed walls, chicken wire was strung all the way to the unpartitioned brick roof. After a few days, we concurred that we would take turns sitting on the tile floor in front of the key hole. This was our only lookout.

None of the cells had a toilet nor washing facilities. By beating on the door and kindly yet loudly calling out, we made it known that we had to go. The toilets were located in the courtyard, covered with a roof. Toilet paper was unknown here. Fortunately we learned in the Japanese camp how to take care of ourselves by using tin cans and water. Such a can could always be found somewhere.

During the hottest part of the day, two or three prisoners were allowed to take a typical Indonesian "public bath." This was done within the partially walled enclosure behind the barracks. Under a stream of clean, cold water from a faucet, we cleansed ourselves. How many were allowed to bathe at the same time depended on the mood of the Indonesian guards. On one occasion, Ruud and I, together with the young guards, were allowed to swim in the brown, muddy water of the Bekasi River. The public bath water also ended up here.

Three men were in the other cells; a few Dutch ladies and children were in yet another one. When it was the women's turn to take a bath, the guards would position themselves on their haunches on the two-meter-high wall, taking in the scene.

One evening I was dragged out of the cell. The camp commandant read me the riot act and threatened me. Boys like me were fighting in Jakarta, I was told, and if I did not behave myself, it would not take much to snuff me out. The commandant thought that I was ridiculing his people because they heard laughter coming from my cell. After I offered my humble apologies, I was allowed to return to the safe cell. The others were sincerely happy that I had come back in one piece.

We realized that any day could be our last. Mr. W. fortunately lifted our spirits by constantly recounting stories about his navy career. For example, he told us how he started out as an ensign and about the assistance he later rendered with the construction of the long wave radio station high in the mountains near Bandung. There were also lighter moments when we had to suppress our laughter. We lost all track of time.

After each speech by "Bung [Brother] Karno" (official nickname for President Sukarno), which resounded throughout the camp, the guards were fired up again and became violent.

It must have been around October 13, according to our primitive calendar, that Mr. W. was called on the carpet. He returned with the news that we would be moved to the front lines the next day where the NICA (Netherlands Indies Civil Administration) troops were fighting. Mr. W. was expected to approach the troops with a white flag to persuade them to surrender to the Indonesians. If that were to succeed, all of us would be turned over to the upper echelon of the newly formed Indonesian Republic. If the NICA troops did not surrender, the Indonesians would get our hides. Fearful, we tried to get some sleep that night. The floor was unbearably hard and the brick which I smuggled in to serve as a pillow seemed even harder than the glazed tiles.

Would the Dutch troops surrender? And if not, what would be our fate? Mr. W. was trying to memorize all our names. At least he would be able to relay a message as to who we were and how many of us there were. How many of us were there, anyway? How many women and children were locked up in the other cells? We did not know!

Finally, dawn broke. Fortunately, one by one we were allowed, with some jostling, to visit the toilet first. Afterwards, the eight of us, with our hands tied behind our backs, were loaded in an open truck. We sat on the floorboard. One of the guards sat on the tailgate and another on top of the cab. And off we were to an unknown destination.

In the center of the town of Klendar, we had to stop in front of a closed railroad gate, next to an open market. It looked as if there were hundreds of people, many armed with bamboo spears. All of a sudden, several of them looked into the rear of the truck, where we were trying to hide.

"Dutchmen, Dutchmen!" they shouted. The throngs became immediately restless. More and more faces with fiery eyes jumped up and down next to the vehicle to get a glimpse of us. "Cut up those Dutch!" The cries became more insistent. The armed mass now formed a half circle around the vehicle. We lowered our heads even more and kept them between our knees. Terribly shaken, we just sat there while the rope cut deeply into our flesh. Then the train roared by. Peering sideways through the corner of my eye, I noticed that the majority of the passengers on the train were Dutch troops, armed with Sten guns, standing on the balcony. Real Dutch soldiers, so near, yet so far. Suddenly our vehicle lunged forward and again we were on our way. At long last, the tailgate was lowered and we got out. We were released and that was a relief. The rope had given me a few weals on my wrists which I massaged away.

With troop reinforcements, we were ordered to walk along for about 100 meters. Mr. W. was given instructions in the presence of G., who spoke Malay fluently. Mr. W. had to walk ahead by himself, carrying a white flag secured to a makeshift stick. He approached a couple of the NICA soldiers who were clearly visible, carelessly standing in the middle of the road, their weapons on their hips. He was supposed to ask them if they were ready to surrender. Only a few hundred meters ahead was our freedom! Should I dare to escape by running quickly to the other side? I decided I had better not because this could result in the death of those present as well as those who had stayed behind in Bekasi.

Mr. W. bravely proceeded to move towards the Dutch soldiers, waving his flag. They turned out to be Ambonese, loyal to the Dutch regime. A few of the *peloppors* had disappeared into the bush some distance back. They were now crawling silently alongside Mr. W., under protection of the vegetation. Mr. W. appeared to stay away a long time as we stood transfixed, staring at the soldiers who were looking our way.

Finally, after a discussion, the two Ambonese soldiers made way for Mr. W. to return to us. He somberly shook his head as he approached. G. and G.E. then went into a huddle, speaking in muffled tones. As soon as Mr. W. came close, they immediately walked with him to the two Indonesians who clearly were in command of the *peloppors*. The plan worked—G.E. was allowed to try once again to approach the Dutchmen with a white flag in hand, just as before. Again the *peloppors* crawled alongside him, but soon, with his head bowed down, G.E. returned.

He was halfway back when the NICA soldiers suddenly opened fire. G.E. dove into an empty ditch and ran back quickly. All of us, including the guards, escaped the rain of bullets as we ran towards the truck. I was sure the Dutch soldiers were aiming high because nobody was hurt.

The truck quickly spun around and lumbered away. We were back in the truck's bed again, petrified, our hearts beating overtime. In the distance, we could hear the frightening sound of the "coconut wireless" whereby natives would beat a stick on a hollowed-out tree trunk, relaying messages.

"We will not consider surrendering at all. We are not surrounded," was the Dutch officer's reply, according to G.E.

I was happy that both Mr. W. and G.E. returned safely, but what was awaiting us now?

Our truck stopped in Pondok Gedeh. We were met by a throng of heavily armed Indonesians. The men uttered wild noises and barely moved aside. They forced us to our knees. Shaking, the eight of us lay there quietly among a sea of brown legs. With loud voices, they commanded us to mount the steps. As I stood up, I was almost struck by one of those wild-eyed people. He pointed his spear towards my pants, the pants which I safeguarded throughout the war years.

"Out! Out!" he commanded.

And there I stood, naked from the waist down, with only a patched-up, sleeveless T-shirt on. It really didn't matter, we would end up dead anyway!

The slaughter would probably start soon. I wished that I would die quickly. I felt naked, like cattle, thoroughly humiliated, facing growling dogs. I was very scared to die a horrible death. Please God, let it be quick, I prayed.

Past the pillars, we had to stop. A strikingly well-groomed Indonesian military man dressed in an old KNIL uniform approached us with a drawn sword. He pointed the thing in my direction. Would he behead me in public like the Japanese used to do? With the tip of the sword he quickly lifted up my shirt. There was mumbling among the mob outside.

"Give him a pair of pants," he commanded.

In less than a minute, I was handed a pair made of the most primitive material, namely a jute rice bag. Then we were quickly shoved along and ended up in a rather large room with an open window. The door was slammed shut behind us. We could still hear the shouts of the masses outside. Everybody was trying to cope with his own fears. We lined up against a bare white wall. Nobody spoke, except for Mr. W., the perpetual optimist, who said, "We are still alive, aren't we?"

He had barely finished the sentence as the door flung open. In stepped the same well-dressed officer with several followers. Without making a sound, they led us to the outside towards the rear of the big white house. There stood a small vehicle with engine running. "Quick, quick!" he motioned. Soon we drove away from the noise of the *peloppors*. So there was not to be any lynching after all. We escaped again.

We stumbled back to the same place, the cell at the police barracks, which almost appeared inviting now. We immediately were offered some food. As if we were heroes, our guards told those left behind how we managed to run to safety under the rain of "NICA dogs'" bullets. That we barely made it to the front line and were almost slaughtered by the *peloppors*, they conveniently left out.

A few days later all Dutch people, including Uncle Latu, our old Ambonese friend, were transported inland. The 11 men, hands tied on their backs, ended up in Tambun again. We were placed in the same room of the large house. Now we had to share the same space with 11 men. We succeeded, after a lot of begging, in getting a hollowed-out piece of bamboo. We placed it in the farthest corner and used it as a makeshift bedpan.

Mr. W. continued to tell us that he had conveyed as many names as possible to the Dutch NICA officer. He had also warned them that any troop movement at the front would be passed along via the coconut wireless. Fear for those left behind had made Mr. W. return. It was the same story G.E. told. Regardless, it was great for them to be able to speak Dutch again. The Ambonese soldiers had warned the lieutenant against the *peloppors* who they saw sneaking along the berm. Only when G.E. had reached a safe distance did they start to shoot.

The question often came up whether anybody on the outside knew where we were. According to Mr. G., his Aceh wife, dressed in native costume, escaped the infamous October 4 train incident. She just kept on traveling. He was sure she would still be looking for him, and that gave us some encouragement. It was a dim glimmer of hope, but we clung to it. Those Aceh wives, it was claimed, were the bravest of all Indonesian women, and very faithful.

According to our calendar it must have been November 4, 1945, when again we were transported farther inland. The destination turned out to be the local headquarters of the newly formed TNI (*Tentara National Indonesia*), the Indonesian military in Cikampek. What happened to the women and children, we never found out. The eleven of us were locked up in a rather small room with only one door. We were allowed to go to the servants' bathroom and wash ourselves at the well. The food was somewhat better and the guards did not deliberately forget us. We were given tea in the morning and rice once a day. I was the only one who had to do hard work. It was great to be able to leave that crowded room for a little while. I had to mop the floor, crawling on my knees through the entire house.

One day I saw a few Gurkhas (soldiers from Nepal in the British-Indian army). They had their feet propped up on the table, just like the Indonesian officers in the front room. As I came by, mopping the floor, they noticed me and frowned but continued their lively conversation with the Indonesians. As our allies, they certainly did not do much for us in our case. I heard later that some of them just turned their weapons over to the Indonesians.

After five days, around November 15, we were transported again. Where were we going this time? Was somebody still looking for us? Weren't we already given up for dead?

We were unloaded in a makeshift camp, the former police barracks in Purwakarta. Quarters were located in the front and sides, surrounded by a wall two meters high with pieces of glass cemented on top to protect us from intruders and to prevent us from escaping. In the center of the yard there were trees and a grass lawn. We were allowed, in the afternoon, to roam around freely within the outer walls.

Mr. W., suffering from pain in the shoulder as a result of sleeping on the hard tile floor, was now afflicted with dysentery. I detected that typical odor and thus could make the diagnosis. Having this condition could be terminal. We decided that I, who had earlier survived this rotten affliction in a Japanese camp, would take care of Mr. W. We would have to be assigned a separate room and the doors needed to remain open. The commandant allowed Mr. W. to have a small mat to lie on and an iron ammunition box with two Bren gun ammo clips to sit on if he needed to go. After some persuasion, the Indonesians also gave us some old police reports, to be used as toilet paper. From experience we knew that the nightly toilet visits, often as frequent as 20 times or more, were very detrimental for an already weakened patient. And we were permitted to turn on the light in the "sick bay."

We admonished Mr. W. that he should not eat for a few days but only drink tea and water. The disease would then have a chance to run its course. Once he survived that stage, he would most likely survive, provided he would eat very slowly. We had no medicine here, as was the case in Japanese internment camps.

I lay on the floor next to Mr. W., often reading the old police reports. We frequently had a good laugh about their contents. Mr. W. had lost his glasses so I had to read to him. When he signaled that he had to go, I jumped up. The box was opened, the ammo clips placed on it and after the business was done, a few pages were ripped in half. Because of the stench, the clips were immediately removed and the box closed.

In the morning I was one of the first to get out. I would go into the yard to dispose of the contents of the box. I would dig a hole by hand as close as possible to the outer wall and far away from us. Next I had to clean the box, but I could not disinfect it. So I removed some ashes from the kitchen furnace, rubbed the box with them and washed it off. The alkali was supposed to kill the bacteria. This was important because I knew how contagious bacillary dysentery was. Then I let the box dry in the sun for as long as Mr. W. could do without it. This way the others would have minimal exposure and a lesser chance of being infected. I was in essence Mr. W.'s private nurse.

According to B.'s calendar, we left on December 2, 1945, on another transport. This time, it was a short trip southward towards the mountains. Just outside the village of Bendul, we got out and, following the truck on foot over a steep path, we reached a large house by the name of Villa Diane, a makeshift camp.

Some TNI prisoners were already in this small camp. They were predominantly Ambonese small farmers with or without family. As former members of the Dutch military, they were considered enemies of the new Republic despite being married to Indonesians. There were only two guards at the entrance and there was no wall or fence around Villa Diane. The lush growth of this perch made escaping in the dense jungle, where the population was in favor of the new republic, an unattractive alternative. The toilets, and especially the washing facilities, were wholly inadequate so we reverted to doing our business in nature.

In the morning we were given tea and towards the afternoon we received food, which was procured from barracks in Purwakarta and brought in by food carriers. Once a day we were permitted to go down to a small stream to take a bath. We followed the narrow path across the road until we reached the stream. Water cascaded over rocks and it was clear and cold. We went farther downstream to defecate, if permitted by the guard.

Fortunately the roof of Villa Diane was watertight. We were not bothered by the nightly downpours during the wet season. From our bedroom we had a great view of the edge of the slopes of the Priangan. Behind them was the endless lowland of West Java. Regularly, we saw airplanes flying overhead, heading towards Bandung. Would they know that we were here? Was there anybody among the Dutch, in or out of the camp, who knew that we were slowly wasting away, starving to death?

The Ambonese and other small farmers were regularly visited by their relatives. In this manner they could supplement the inadequate diet. The group which fetched rice in the valley sometimes could get something extra from the kitchen. The elderly gentlemen such as Mr. W. and youngsters such as myself were not strong enough for the journey by foot to get rice and carry it up hill.

We were still suffering from the aftereffects of life in the Japanese internment camp. I was plagued with scabies and lice. I asked a man with the only nail clippers in camp to shave me bald. This procedure took the entire morning. The gentleman was a Dutch-Indonesian who used to be a member of the itinerant opera, and he often sang with us. He would volunteer to sing "Figaro, Figaro." He could also somehow predict the future by studying the lines in the palms of people's hands.

"You are a sight for sore eyes" and "You look terrible" were some of the milder comments made about my appearance. But it did not bother me; at least my head did not itch. In the Japanese camp we used to rub our heads with petroleum after shaving, but there was no petroleum here.

Lice infestation was a story by itself. We thoroughly inspected our clothes, which was not a big problem since we hardly had any apparel to begin with. I did the searching for Mr. W. because he had lost his glasses. I gained some kind of reputation in this specialty. When Mr. W. felt that he was being bitten, he yelled, sat down, took off his pants and with his mat covering himself, he threw his pants towards me. Standing in front of the window, I would find the culprit and squash it between my nails. Since the dysentery episode I had developed a certain attachment to Mr. W.

At Christmas and New Year's, one of the Ambonese gave a sermon alongside the house, the regular meeting place on Sundays. His sermons were so passionate that they induced the entire congregation, including the visiting women and children, to sniffle and cry. However, the Ambonese people were not always as honest as they pretended to be. For example, they divided the food, mostly brought in by their own group, in such a way that they always benefited the most. We felt cheated. If we said something about it, they took a threatening stance and we were too weak to challenge them.

By this time, I was getting more and more depressed. On New Year's Eve 1945, I realized that I should not be so dissatisfied. So many people had died of starvation in China or for that matter elsewhere in the world. Why would I be an exception?

Once, between Christmas and New Year's, we were surprised by a serving of fried rice. We could eat as much as we wanted, according to our fellow Ambonese prisoners. But it was bad luck for our hungry stomachs. The rice was fried in citronella oil and was therefore not edible. It was heart-rending to have to throw out so much food. As former internees with much experience, we did not dare to eat it. If you got an upset stomach or probably diarrhea, it could mean your death. It would be better to go hungry one more day and dream about a luscious meal in Hotel des Indes, as was promised by W., than to take a chance.

After the "holidays," in early 1946, Mr. G's wife came as part of a group of visiting Ambonese. She had found us! We were all elated, but especially Mr. G. The guards usually did not interfere during these visits. She only spoke Malay and husband and wife were engaged in a lively discussion. Upon departure, she promised us that she would spread the word in the Dutch community. She would tell them where we were located and disclose our identity.

Towards the end of January 1946, it appeared to me that there were more visits from TNI officers. We heard that someday we would be turned over to the Dutch authorities in Jakarta. Only Ruud, G.A. and

I would be exempted because of our age. If we were to be released, we might just take up arms against the TNI. That was when Mr. W. stood his ground—either we all went or none of us would come along! That was a big gamble.

Fortunately, we found a compromise. The three of us would sign a pledge that we would not fight against the TNI. Obviously, we did that right away. We could hardly believe it when that very afternoon— it must have been February 5, 1946—we were taken to the empty mission hospital in Cikampek. Here we ended up in a large, empty hall with neat rows of bamboo cots covered with clean mats. We were given some food and clean clothes. We were issued new TNI uniforms, consisting of a black cotton short sleeve shirt and a pair of black cotton pants. I still felt uncomfortable and insecure. The guards kept milling around the door.

We would be turned over to the authorities in Jakarta. We got up early the next morning and were taken to the station where we boarded a shuttered train. We stopped in Jatinegara, the station before Jakarta, now occupied by the Dutch. All of a sudden our Indonesian guards just disappeared. We continued to the main station, where we stopped and were met by Red Cross personnel and Dutch troops. In a delivery van marked with a red cross as an ambulance, we were taken to the sickbay of the 10th Battalion barracks. The driver happened to be a former classmate of my brother at the Christian High School.

"Have you possibly seen my father?" he asked sadly. His father, too, was declared missing on October 4, 1945. We did not know his whereabouts and that was all we could tell him.

"I will notify your relatives," I promised him.

We were given a quick medical examination and a thorough treatment with DDT to get rid of lice. We took a shower, were handed clean clothes, and were even fed the almost unimaginable delicacy of real pea soup with pork. Delicious! But that evening in the barracks hospital I had to visit the toilet often as a consequence of overindulgence.

The next day, Dad was there waiting for me. It was February 4, 1946, after four months' imprisonment and being considered missing, that I finally came home—slimmer, at 45 kilos, but alive and well. Dad and Mom were happy as could be. Mom cried a lot the day before, my Dad told me. Family in the Netherlands wanted them to come home earlier and face the fact that I was probably already dead. But Mom stuck it out. She did not leave because she just knew that I was still alive.

How happy I was—123 days after departure from the Japanese camp—to be finally home. Mother and Father also could barely stop expressing their joy. We thanked God for my miraculous homecoming. Mother would touch my skinny body and break out in tears. I got my own room back with a real bed with sheets, pillows and mosquito netting. Despite the fact that I was very tired, I could not sleep in the very soft bed. I slept better on the mat in front of the bed, but with a pillow this time. I had many visitors who heard that I had returned to the land of the living.

Our old cook also came by every so often. She did this during the Japanese occupation too, even after Mother had to let her go. The stooped old native woman had predicted that the boy was not dead because the orchid which I took home once was still blooming. There was a lot of shooting in Jakarta. It affected me. At night I cried out with fright, and I still felt rather riled up and afraid every time I saw a large group of Indonesians.

I saw a doctor who gave me a lot of vitamins. And with the extreme good care provided by my mother, I was soon doing well. I was often served soft rice, cooked in bouillon, sometimes including spinach. My mother also spoiled me with all kinds of delicious, nutritious snacks. I quickly gained weight and became stronger. That was fortunate, because I wanted to go back to Holland as fast as possible.

ABOUT THE CONTRIBUTOR

Karel Hoekendijk, a.k.a. Karel Senior, was born in Jombang, East Java, on July 27, 1926. He married and has one son and two daughters.

He moved to Jatinegara during elementary school when his father, as principal of the Dutch-Chinese school, was transferred there. Another transfer brought the Hoekendijk family to Jakarta, where Karel received secondary level education. In the third school year, the Japanese invasion took place, and he was interned in July 1942 as a 16-year-old.

In 1946, he repatriated to the Netherlands and returned to school; in 1948 he graduated from college in Haarlem. Subsequently, he followed several courses in the medical field, leading to an M.D. degree.

He became a practicing physician in 1956 and became self-employed in 1988. He retired in 1993 and now lives in Enschede, the Netherlands. He contributes regularly to Dutch and Dutch-Indonesian magazines.

HENDRIK B. BABTIST

The Protectors Abandoned Us

On November 14, 1928, I was born in Bogor on the island of Java in the former Dutch East Indies. My father was a Dutchman from Emmercompascum, a village in the province of Drente, the Netherlands. He went to the Indies for military service. My mother was a descendant of another Dutchman who was married to an Indonesian woman.

We moved often because of my father's military assignments. I remember vaguely such places as Cimahi, Singkawang, Semarang, Candi, Yogyakarta, and Magelang.

In Magelang, Central Java, I went to a school operated by Catholic nuns. As kids, we often got into fights with those of other schools because of our perceived sense of superiority. We also tangled with those of the nearby orphanage, operated by Pa van der Steur. "Steurtjes," as his charges were often called, were like one big family. If you had a fight with one, you got yourself into big trouble. We quickly learned to quit messing with them and to try to stay on friendly terms.

When the Japanese attacked Pearl Harbor, the Dutch government in exile was the first to react by declaring war on them. The Dutch were completely unprepared, and the Japanese wiped out the Royal Dutch Navy, Air Force and Army in rapid succession.

Magelang was a military garrison town. It was vacated by the troops which moved to the coastal area to face the oncoming enemy. Most of the soldiers never returned; the majority died in Japanese internment camps. One of them was my father. He performed slave labor while building the Pakanbaru railroad in southern Sumatra.

Meanwhile, back in Magelang, my mother was expecting her

eleventh child and my oldest sister was also eight months pregnant. Both babies were born within a month of each other and both mothers had been totally dependent on their husbands. Now they had to try to survive with all these children without any income.

Not long thereafter, the Japanese started to round up all women and children of Dutch descent, locking them up in various camps. We wound up in Rawahseneng, a place in the mountains above Temangung, a nearby city in Central Java. Many other families from Ambarawa, Salatiga and Purworedjo also joined us there.

Rawahseneng used to be a coffee plantation and agricultural school operated by the Jesuits. Its Indonesian name means something like "Pleasant Meadow," but it was far from pleasant for us. The barracks and dormitories were packed full with close to 300 women and children. They became slave laborers, working the fields, planting corn, sweet potatoes and vegetables. Coffee plantations in the vicinity also needed constant care such as weeding, pruning and harvesting. In addition, we raised pigs which were kept in sties scattered throughout the camp.

Being one of the bigger boys, I was assigned the more strenuous tasks such as fertilizing the fields and preparing the soil for planting. Fertilizing required two of us to fill a large bucket with the contents of septic tanks. This bucket was then suspended from a bamboo pole and carried uphill and into the fields a couple of miles away. At the site, other prisoners would use the liquid waste to water each plant individually. Tilling the ground was done the old fashioned way with a *pajol*, a wide-bladed pick. Doing such chores all day was back-breaking work, and later on in life I developed many back-related problems.

Nevertheless, those of us in Rawahseneng could consider ourselves lucky in comparison with many in other camps. At least we could often sneak out into the surrounding jungle to supplement our food with edible weeds, mushrooms and breadfruit. After a rain, we could catch flying termites, which were a delicacy when roasted. On occasion, we would even catch a snake or a wild chicken.

Once, a black panther broke into a pig pen and fought it out with a large boar, tearing up the entire shelter. Several pigs took advantage of the breach in the fence and escaped. We caught one of the piglets, took it into the jungle and butchered and roasted it.

In general, one tends to remember mainly the happier aspects under such circumstances. Nevertheless, life at Rawahseneng was no picnic. Food was insufficient, there was no medication, we slept on wooden boards infested with bedbugs, and we had to constantly battle lice which had infested our clothes and hair. Because of malnutrition, I developed several large tropical sores on my legs. They were very painful and festered; I had to literally spoon the pus out of them. I also survived several bouts of malaria and dysentery. We were very isolated and had almost no contact with the outside world except with Indonesians from a nearby village.

One day we heard the sound of several large planes flying high overhead, and the Jap guards became very nervous. About two weeks later, we heard the planes again. All kinds of rumors started circulating that Japan was losing the war. Not long thereafter, the Japs just disappeared from the scene. Where did they go? We were cautiously optimistic and happy but were afraid that they were pulling some kind of cruel hoax on us. Most of us actually had given up hope, but some ventured out to Temanggung and returned with the good news. The war was indeed over. It was a strange sensation.

For the past three and one-half years, all we had thought about was when it would all be over. And suddenly the day had arrived. It seemed too good to be true; it was anti-climactic. The main question now was what to do next.

We came to the conclusion that the best thing to do was to return to Magelang. Several families pooled their resources and hired an ox-drawn cart to carry our meager possessions. We walked alongside the cart for about 45 miles. Arriving in town we came to the cruel realization that we had become homeless. We had no money even to rent a room, and there were no organizations to assist us. We found utter chaos. In desperation, we went to a church and the pastor put us up in a school building, one family to a room.

This happened in September 1945. All we could do now was to wait. We were awaiting news from my father and my sister's husband, and everybody was becoming more anxious as the days passed. The only military men who would show up were a small British contingent, consisting of British-Indian Sikhs and Gurkhas commanded by British officers. Before these troops appeared, our only protection against Indonesian insurgents was a few Japanese soldiers who were commanded by the Allied forces to guard the Dutch citizens. We found out later that the Dutch were not allowed by the Allies to restore order in their former colony, a very critical issue in the early phases of liberation. It was the British who took over the operation, such as at the local army hospital and at nearby camps.

In the meantime, two of my sisters found temporary employment as nurses' aides. I became a courier between the camp and the hospital. Thus we were at least able to provide food and other necessities for the rest of the family.

After about one month of minor skirmishes with Indonesians, more and more *peloppors*, youthful Indonesian freedom fighters who let their hair grow long as a sign of rebellion, started to show up in Magelang. Most of them came from the nearby town of Yogyakarta. Taking advantage of the uncertain political situation, they forcefully pressed their demands for independence and were often very brazen since there was no authority to keep them in check.

One day they captured me and took me to the local jail were others were already imprisoned. They put about 50 of us in a cell intended for no more than 10. We were the lucky ones. Several others who resisted were instantly killed, bayoneted with sharpened bamboo spears. Among those murdered were the local priests and their staff. After killing them, the marauders chopped their heads off.

Women and children living behind the parsonage were subsequently terrorized. Among the unlucky ones were my mother and family. Fortunately, they were able to escape eventually, fleeing to the protection camp guarded by Gurkha soldiers, a distance of two miles through alleys and back roads. Several days later, these Gurkhas also freed those of us in jail and took us to the same camp. All others from Magelang who were fearful of the *peloppors*, whether Dutch, Dutch-Indonesian or Ambonese, sought refuge in there as well.

More and more of these insurgents started coming into town, and before long they even started to attack our camp. We were completely surrounded and cut off from the outside world. Food and supplies eventually had to be parachuted in. Many of the Indonesian youth were killed in these attacks, but they kept on coming, giving the Sikhs and the Gurkhas no reprieve. These activities went on for about three weeks.

One night these British-Indian "protectors" just left and abandoned us to the mercy of the Indonesians. They killed those Dutchmen in camp who were suspected of being involved in fighting them. The women and children were taken to what used to be Pa van der Steur's orphanage. Eventually they were freed in exchange for Indonesian prisoners of war. Men and older boys were herded off to another camp where my brother Piet and I ended up.

The first three months we were put on a real starvation diet of one cup of starch, made from tapioca flour, per day. This concoction makes excellent glue but becomes watery when salt is added. Many died during that time. The first ones to pass on were the big guys, those who were used to large meals. They were buried in shallow graves because we, the grave diggers, did not have the strength to dig deeper graves.

I again contracted tropical sores which were excruciatingly painful. I was almost incapacitated. They festered so badly that they would expose the bone and the stench was horrendous. Because of this disease, I was placed in a makeshift sickbay with several others with the same afflictions.

Every morning as I would wake up, I would find out that two or three of my barracks mates had died during the night. Eventually, the guards increased our food portions somewhat and gave us rice and corn. I recuperated and the wounds healed slowly. Any dogs, cats, snakes, rats or other edible creatures which dared to venture into camp did not live long. We learned to eat all kinds of animals, including lizards, grasshoppers and snails.

One night, my friend Joop Antoni and I captured a dog in a makeshift trap. But while butchering the animal, we got caught ourselves. In the excitement, we made too much noise and attracted the Indonesian guard's attention. He took us to the guard house. Seemingly everyone started beating us and continued doing so until we eventually passed out. After we came to, they made us stand at attention in front of the guard house for hours on end. At the change of the guard, the new shift would beat us first before asking what our offense was. The next day, after beating us senseless again, they finally had mercy on us and let us go. So we survived this episode too, but we lost a couple of teeth in the process.

One day some Indonesians brought a Dutch-Indonesian gentleman and what was probably his daughter to the guard house. After a while we could hear her cry out several times in Indonesian, "Forgiveness, please sir, forgive me." We never saw or heard from these two people again.

Sometime in early 1947, the Indonesians loaded us like cattle into trucks and took us to a former sugar factory called Barongan in Yogyakarta. Nearby there was a women's camp and at times we could catch glimpses of the inmates, but we were too far removed to be able to communicate. It did not take long before they were relocated to another camp anyway.

While walking through the city, I saw hundreds of *peloppors* marching with brand new Lee Enfield rifles. Not only had the British abandoned us in Magelang, they apparently had supplied the Indonesians with weapons too. At Barongan, the treatment was considerably better. We received more food; there were chunks of meat in our soup and occasionally we were given salted fish.

In April 1947, they put us on the train to Yogyakarta and we traveled via Cirebon to Jakarta. It must have been in Krawang that we finally entered Dutch controlled territory. I remember crying when I saw the Dutch flag flying again. But I observed a regrettable incident right after that which made me sad. A Dutch soldier was kicking an Indonesian with his heavy boots. That was uncalled for.

Arriving in Jakarta, the capital city in West Java, we were first taken into a large building where we had to take off our clothes. We were then thoroughly sprayed with DDT powder in order to delouse us. I heard later that the women and children received the same treatment prior to their return to civilization. After this, we were allowed to shower and we were given new clothes and shoes. The first members of the family to meet us in Jakarta were my oldest sister Rie and her husband Cor. They were already reunited earlier after her release in 1946.

Cor had survived slave labor in the coal mines of Japan. My father, on the other hand, died in July 1945 in Sumatra, just two months before the bomb was dropped on Hiroshima. My mother and my eight brothers and sisters had survived and were waiting for us in Bandung.

Although he looked like a 14-year-old kid, my brother Piet was drafted into the Dutch army shortly after our arrival in Bandung. My turn to serve my country came the following year, after our family had decided to repatriate to the Netherlands in 1947.

These are some of my recollections of what happened in the former Dutch East Indies during and immediately after the war. I did not personally recall much of the Bersiap period. But several of my countrymen also suffered greatly during this very tumultuous time.

ABOUT THE CONTRIBUTOR

Hendrik B. Babtist was born November 14, 1928, in Bogor, West Java. His carefree days came to an abrupt end in 1942 and he endured five years in Japanese and Indonesian concentration camps. After he was freed in 1947, his family was repatriated to the Netherlands.

In the Netherlands he joined the Royal Dutch Navy and served seven years as a machinist. He saw service in Indonesia and Korea as part of a U.N. force. After stopovers at San Francisco and San Diego, Hank decided to emigrate to the United States. He got married before he left.

He worked as a ranch hand in Montana and eventually came to California where he and his wife lived for 30 years in Santa Ana. Hank worked as a welder while his wife did drafting for several engineering firms. He received an A.A. degree in industrial supervision. His professional career was cut short when he developed serious back problems which resulted in his being declared totally disabled. The Babtists decided to sell their California home and purchase lakefront property in Hot Springs, Arkansas. They now manage several rental units and have a home on Lake Hamilton.

PIETER H. GROENEVELT

The Bombs That Saved My Life

My mother whispered in my ear, "Don't give up now, Peter. The Americans are coming!"

Two and one-half years of starvation had finally taken its toll on my tiny body. Only bones remained, covered with skin on which the tropical ulcers did not want to heal as a result of prolonged malnutrition and absence of medication. My number had come up at last—or so we thought. Some of my friends had already been carried out of the concentration camp to be buried somewhere in unmarked graves. Many such graves dot the jungles of the island of Java in the Dutch East Indies.

It was early August 1945. The camp doctor, herself a specimen of skin and bones, told my mother that there was no hope for me. She was asked to withhold whatever little extra bits of food there were in order to save another child which would still have a chance for survival. But my mother did not give up that easily. She kept praying and whispering in Dutch, "*Niet opgeven, Pieter. De Amerikanen komen eraan!*" ("Don't give up, Peter. The Americans are coming!").

The camp was Banjubiru #12, located in Central Java. It was my fourth concentration camp after having survived three others, all on the island of Java—Sumowono, Ambarawa and Muntilan.

During the year 1942, after the Japanese invaded the Dutch East Indies, almost all Europeans on Java were eventually interned. The women and younger children were placed in camps, segregated from the men and older boys. For the next three years, life in these concentration camps would become increasingly harsh and inhumane. The

155

women were forced to do hard physical labor, such as carrying or rolling boulders from one end of the camp to the other and back again. Food and clothing became progressively scarce.

By 1945 food consisted of little more than tapioca, while outside the camp it was plentiful. Women and children walked around in rags towards the end of the war, although at least one nice dress was often stashed away to be worn on the day of liberation. These rare pieces of apparel proved later to be very valuable as barter.

At night, lying on their primitive bamboo cots, riddled with bed bugs and lice, the women, their empty stomachs gnawing with hunger, used to torture themselves by calling out the name of various foods. Someone would say "beefsteaks!" and the inhabitants of the barrack would respond by moaning and groaning. After the noises had died down, another would exclaim "ham!" and the moaning and groaning would start all over again. For the younger children, who did not know what those foods represented, this was a rather odd kind of conversation. Nevertheless, they dutifully moaned and groaned in unison with their mothers.

The daily roll calls on the sweltering hot pavement were exhausting, being either boring or frightening, depending on the camp commander's mood. It started with his yelling "*Kiotske!*" (Attention!), followed by "*Kere!*" (Bow!). And there we were, standing at attention and bowing down like pocketknives being opened and closed, dressed in rags, and on bare feet. It was a pitiful sight of human wrecks. Some days we were made to stand while bowing for a long, long time until the commander finally would yell "*Norre!*" (At ease!). That would be followed by counting in Japanese, "*Ichi, ni, san, shi, go, roku,*" and on and on it went. This cadence still drones through my head even now.

In the tropical heat women would often collapse, but were then kicked to encourage them to stand upright once again. When the commander was in a cheerful mood, he was nice to the children, but when he was in a bad mood, he kicked and beat up women. On one particular day, he was always in a very good mood. He was extra kind to the children then and sometimes even brought each a small present. That particular day was Emperor Hirohito's birthday, April 29.

In order to continuously destabilize our lives, we were frequently forced to moved from concentration camp to concentration camp and often even within the camps. At bayonet point, the internees were packed like sardines into shuttered train cars, often previously used for transportation of cattle. These train rides were indeed torture: for hours on end we rode without any food, water or bathroom facilities, our sweating bodies sticking together. Surrounded by filth and swarms of flies, most of us clutched some precious belongings, be they a photo album, a bible, some toiletries, or whatever. By this process of reinternment, only whatever the weakened bodies could carry would constitute the sum total of possessions the survivors would have at the end of the war.

At some often unknown point of destination, the train would stop and the internees were finally let out. An agonizing march to the next camp would inevitably follow. When this relocation took place during daytime, the oppressive heat, thirst and hunger would further torment the already weakened internees. We would merely drag ourselves along, moving between two rows of bayonets poised to inflict pain at any provocation. On the poor souls' arms and legs, flies would set up camp, preferring open ulcers upon which to feed.

When such a march would take place at night, it usually happened when it was pitch dark. There were blackouts everywhere because the Japanese feared bombardments by the Allies. Through heat and cold, through rain and mud, we would march, children often getting lost. I still hear my mother's warning voice,

"Hold hands, children, hold hands!"

Upon arrival, we would inevitably be locked up again in our new "home." Immediately divvying up the available space, the internees were desperately trying to cope with an ever-increasing crowdedness. More and more thousands of women and children would be crammed into fewer and fewer camps, resulting in unbearable living conditions.

With the ever-dwindling food supply, new survival skills and tricks were soon developed. The women on night patrol would set up traps in order to catch frogs. An old pillowcase was propped open by means of an upright stick. A small burning candle inside would attract a curious frog. Upon hopping inside the contraption, it would knock down the stick, causing the pillow to collapse. The critter would extinguish the candle and entangle itself in the darkness, thus signaling the women that dinner was assured for that day. Frog meat was a real delicacy. My mother told me that it resembled calf's meat in taste—whatever a calf was.

I became a master with the slingshot. All camps were surrounded by plaited bamboo, nailed down to bamboo poles and reenforced with barbed wire. Outside the camp there were high trees which sometimes bore edible nuts. With my slingshots and an appropriate-sized stone, I occasionally managed to hit a couple of these nuts, causing them to bounce into the camp. Thus, we had a snack for the day. We kids had plenty of time on our hands with hardly anything to do, so we had to be inventive.

Life in the camps also had its rituals. One of these was the daily visit to the "hospital." It seemed as though my oldest sister was always in the hospital. I often accompanied my mother on her daily round. In one of the camps, the route led us through a narrow passageway. On one side there was a dark, damp prison cell in which a woman who had gone mad was locked up. While hanging with her head and arms between the stiles of a small window, she would yell obscenities at every passerby. This picture became a returning scene in a kaleidoscope of nightmarish concentration camp memories that haunted me for several decades.

On one of these trips to the hospital, I saw an open keyhole in a locked door in the bamboo wall. I approached it and peeked through it. On the outside I saw half-naked white men swinging native hoes, guarded by Japanese soldiers with bayonets at the ready. I called to my mother, "Mom, look!"

She came running, bent over and looked, hoping to get a glimpse of her husband. Who knows? Maybe my father was among them. But we had no such luck. Within seconds an extremely angry guard appeared and pulled her away. He kicked her shins with his heavy army boots and punched her in the face with his well-exercised fists. It was a beautiful display of the martial arts, practiced on a defenseless woman. My mother crumpled into a heap under the blows. I ran screaming for help. Ever since, any time I see people being trained in the martial arts, it causes shivers to run up and down my spine. The thought of losing my mother was one of my greatest fears. She was the only reliable adult I knew. My father was already gone, taken away a long time ago.

Once a year, the guards rounded up all the boys who had become old enough to be separated from the women. This could happen as early as twelve years of age, or sometimes even as early as age nine or ten. These boys were then lined up. Before being ushered out of the camp, as an exercise in human cruelty, they were allowed to march through the camp to wave good-bye to their relatives, often with little hope of ever seeing them again. Amidst a lot of crying everywhere, the thought of an impending separation scared the hell out of me. Fortunately, I was only seven and my mother somehow survived the beating.

At one time I landed in the hospital myself as described previously. Some women had organized something resembling a school. One day, I climbed out of the upper section of a bunk bed to attend this school, holding my "notebook" in one hand while grabbing the rungs with the other. Sudden weakness caused me to miss one of the rungs, and I fell backwards, landing with my head hitting the stone floor. The concussion was severe.

I was told that I had to lie horizontal in bed without a pillow for six weeks. If I were to move my head even an inch, I would never be able to learn a thing in later years. So there I lay, completely immobile for all this time, while the flies and bedbugs had a field day attacking me without any fear of repercussion.

By mid–1945 hunger and filthy conditions were overwhelming. One day I was squatting over a gutter to relieve myself as a result of never-ending diarrheal episodes. A small stream of water passed by, carrying the excrement of those squatting upstream. Watching the brown, watery liquid float by, I all of a sudden realized how ironic the situation was. I was squatting there in a camp called Banjubiru, which in Indonesian means "blue water." I was sick, hungry and lonely. I then said to myself, "Life cannot get more difficult than it is now. If I ever encounter any challenges in the future, I will recall this particular moment." And I still do. I was only seven then.

There were unsubstantiated rumors that in the event the Americans landed on Java, the occupying forces would first kill all the internees. They then would fight to the death to avoid the humiliation of having to surrender. This was known as the *Bushido* code of conduct, originally a code of conduct for the Samurai or warrior class in Japan which evolved as early as 1192, though the term itself was not used until the sixteenth century. It became the official philosophy of education for Japanese of all classes until the post–World War II period.

By early August 1945, some 3,000 women and children were desperately clinging to life. However, the atmosphere in camp was slowly changing. The women no longer had to perform heavy work, and the food supply was virtually cut off. So the majority of them lay listlessly on their cots, many of them near death.

Conditions in the camps changed suddenly on August 6. We were not informed at that time what had transpired in Hiroshima, but we guessed that something cataclysmic must have taken place. Then came the eighth day of the eighth month of that cataclysmic year of 1945. It was my eighth birthday, but there was no party planned at all. And neither were there any presents or surprises. Besides, most of the women had forgotten what a celebration was, and almost none of the children knew what a real birthday party was all about. My youngest sister, for example, was only three weeks old when we were locked up in 1942. On the 9th of August, the second bomb fell on Nagasaki.

The camp guards did not inform us about these events, nor did they show any overt emotions. Out of the sight of the prisoners, however, I imagine they must have shed tears just as I did a while earlier. "Nagasaki, oh my beloved Nagasaki, it has been turned into rubble," they must have moaned. I had tears in my eyes only a little while earlier. "Mother, oh my beloved mother, she has been reduced to rubble."

It took six agonizing days longer before the Japanese capitulation took place on August 15. Thereafter, there were six additional hungry and worrisome days before we were "liberated."

On August 21, 1945, I returned from an eerie, quiet place far away to an unfamiliar surrounding where people were laughing, chickens were flapping their wings, and there was a fresh scent of tropical fruit in the air.

But soon the island of Java was in turmoil again. Apparently there was nobody in charge after our "liberation." The women and children were trying to determine what had happened to their male loved ones. Day after day the Red Cross posted lists with names, divided into two categories, "alive" and "dead." We waited and waited in great anticipation.

Finally, sometime during the fall of 1945, my father's name appeared on the "dead" list. He had been captured, and as a POW he was shipped to an island far away as a white slave in a Japanese coal mine. The name of the island was Kyushu. He died there on January 21, 1944. For him the bombs were dropped too late. We children were told, "Daddy is not coming back." My mother sat down and cried, and we sat beside her and joined in her crying.

A few years ago, my middle sister in the Netherlands sent me a birthday present while I resided in Canada. It was a small book which had just come off the press at that time. It was the printed diary of a Dutch concentration camp doctor who was a POW himself. I immediately turned to January 21, 1944, and saw this entry: "21 Jan at 9:35 A.M. Private P.H. Groenevelt, camp #81, died of pneumonia."

After reading this for the first time I truly believed that my father would not return. This happened on August 8, 1985. The book describes the horrors the prisoners had to endure during the boat trip from Java to Kyushu. On this island, the weakened prisoners had to work in the heat of a coal mine. After the shift, they would cool off in the freezing Japanese winter air without the benefit of proper clothing. Pneumonia was the inevitable and often deadly outcome.

The title of the book is *Fukuoka 9*, the name of the concentration camp. It contains a map of the island, showing the location of the camp as almost exactly midway between Hiroshima and Nagasaki.

Every year on August 6 and 9, many thousands of people somberly stand around the cenotaphs of Hiroshima and Nagasaki, praying for the souls of those for whom the bombs fell too close. May they also say a prayer for the souls of those for whom the bombs fell too late. For us as survivors, it was the bombs that saved our lives.

May all of the inhabitants of this planet say a prayer on those memorable days, too: "Military imperialism, never again, and never again an atomic bomb!"

ABOUT THE CONTRIBUTOR

Pieter H. Groenevelt was born on August 8, 1937, in Klaten, Central Java, and during the war he was interned in Japanese concentration camps together with his mother and his three sisters. After the war he was transported to a protection camp in Semarang and later to Jakarta.

In March 1946, he was shipped off to the Netherlands and lived with his grandparents in Harderwijk. His family lived in poverty for four years. He completed elementary school and after his mother's remarriage, they moved to Arnhem, the town made famous for the movie *A Bridge Too Far*.

He completed high school, graduated from college, and was offered a job to work for the U.N. Food and Agriculture Organization in Africa. For political reasons the job was canceled and he continued his college education earning a Ph.D. degree. In 1969 he went to Canberra, Australia, and in 1973 he moved to Canada to work for the University of Guelph, Ontario, where he is currently professor of soil physics.

JAN VOS

Memories of an Indo Boy

The occupation of the Netherlands by Germany started with drops of German paratroops on May 10, 1940. We received the news in Jakarta one afternoon after the sounding of the siren at the News Agency building. That same afternoon, all German and Austrian citizens were picked up and interned. The German language as subject of instruction was forbidden in all schools. Youth organizations catering to Germans were disbanded. Besides the use of the newly invented slogan "The Netherlands shall rise again," fundraising activities to benefit the Spitfire Fund, and the formation of City/County Guard and Voluntary Training Corps, life in the Dutch East Indies went on as normally as can be expected under the circumstances.

Slowly but surely, however, the Air Raid Protection Service became more active and construction of numerous air raid shelters was started. We all received wafer-shaped pieces of rubber which were to be placed between the teeth in the event of a bombardment to prevent concussion. Japan gained more and more prominence in the Pacific. Being totally dependent on petroleum imports, Japan sent delegations to Jakarta in 1940 and again in 1941 to try to negotiate increasing the import and having their commercial interests permitted to explore and develop new oil fields. With the exception of some minor concessions, these delegations were sent home empty-handed by the Dutch government under the leadership of Dr. Van Mook of the Department of Economic Affairs.

December 8, 1941, was a very significant date not only for the United States, but also for those who lived in the former Dutch East Indies. As a member of the ABCD (American, British, Canadian and

162

Dutch) front in the Pacific, it was not surprising that the Netherlands declared war immediately after the attack on Pearl Harbor. The next day, barricades were erected at all strategic locations in Batavia, later to be called Jakarta. My friends and I witnessed this from a bridge in front of Admiral Helfrich's residence. Waterloo Square, for camouflage purposes, was being transformed into a complete separate section of the city. Although enormous quantities of bamboo and a roof covering made of dried palm leaves and bamboo matting were used, the construction itself did not take long. Radio Tokyo mockingly claimed that it had prior knowledge of these camouflage attempts.

Compulsory and voluntary applications for the armed forces and the Air Raid Protection Service were solicited on a large scale. The ladies had created several auxiliary organizations and later they were also in charge of running the people's kitchen. Strips of paper in the form of a cross were glued on windows of the Vincentius building in an attempt to hold the glass together in case it shattered during bomb explosions.

At 15, I was too young to join the armed forces, so I volunteered for the Air Raid Protection Service but wound up serving at the fire department instead. With Vincentius friends and "outsiders" I was taking up my post near the provincial public works building. The main command post was located at Kebon Sirih Street and our chief was Mr. van Wetering. It was gratifying to learn later that radio messages emanating from this command and designated as "Radio Tiger" and "Cornelius Zutphen Marie" actually meant "navy commander" for the Navy.

Our sector post was the Vincentius recreation room where our recruitment meant, among other duties, regular training with Sigmund fire pumps, towed by a municipal disposal truck. In the evening we assisted the members of the Air Raid Protection Service auxiliary police. We would stop any vehicle which had insufficiently dimmed lights. We would also yell, "Lights out!" at those residents who forgot to turn off their house lights.

Sipping coffee with cream while smoking cigarettes through a "Zeuspijpje," we often sang with the accompaniment of a guitar such favorites as "My Bonnie Lies Over the Ocean," "Give Me Five Minutes More," "Oh Johnny, Oh Johnny, How You Can Love," and numerous other English tunes.

More army trucks, marked with the familiar Department of War red, white and blue license plates, were now on the road. We could see the evacuees' overloaded cars and trucks transporting their household effects toward the villages in the interior of the island. In general life went on as usual, but the word "temporary" was always in the back of our minds. Circumstances were constantly changing.

Then came the evening in mid–December 1941 at about a quarter to ten. The siren on the roof of the Rex movie theater sounded for the first time. However, they were our own planes so an "All Clear" was soon called. This first experience must have made a lasting impression on everybody, and there were many more real air raids to follow.

Most who were there will undoubtedly remember the Japanese bombers which flew in formation over Jakarta, resembling silver birds, unaffected by our anti-aircraft guns. The subsequent attacks by fast flying navy Zero fighter planes did not do our morale any good either. It was difficult not to wonder whether our Glenn Martin bombers and Brewster fighter planes, sent to Singapore for the defense of Malaysia, might have played a significant role defending the Indies in those days. In reality it is unlikely that they would have made a difference.

It was at this time that we saw many posters with the slogan, "It is better to die while standing upright than to live in a kneeling position." Nonetheless capitulation of our armed forces seemed inevitable after the landing of the Japanese invading forces, followed by the declaration by General Ter Poorten that Bandung was an open city. Meanwhile, Singapore had fallen on February 15, 1942, and the battle of the Java Sea on February 27 and 28 had been fought and lost with the historical command, "I attack. Follow me!" uttered by fleet squadron commander Karel Doorman. Total surrender of the Dutch East Indies was a *fait accompli* on March 8, 1942.

Riding our bicycles with friends of Vincentius, we saw our first Japanese soldiers. They stood guard in front of the telephone company and at the palace of the governor-general. They were wearing those peculiar "sun rags," strips of cloth attached to the back of their caps. Their helmets were covered with webbing and had leaves stuck to them. Small Japanese flags displaying the words of well-wishers painted in black were attached to their long bayonets which were fixed to their rifles.

The next Sunday we walked the streets and were stopped by a Japanese navy officer in front of the Department of the Navy. Together with Indonesian passers-by we were put to work. For several hours we had to burn all of the documents stored in the archives. In spite of their nice promises to get us rice and other foodstuffs, they did not see us return for a repeat performance!

The Vincentius boys who still had families were sent home in the middle of 1942 for lack of funds to run the facility. I ended up staying with my mother, sisters and their children in Bogor (formerly known as Buitenzorg). Being the spouse of a military man, my sister could only receive her "delegation money" once. She had to pick it up at the post office in the Botanical Garden. But the Japs stopped these payments at once. From then on there was no longer any income for her, so she started to sell clothing and furniture. By now most European men were already interned.

For me this meant no more school and becoming an "assistant of domestic affairs." My mother and sisters took care of the cooking, while I did all the dishes, sweeping and mopping, buying food at Pasar Anjar market and babysitting. I also picked up rice once a month from the rectory for ourselves and two other military families. My sisters were approached by KNIL officers' wives who asked us if we would like to sell them and their friends snacks once a week. This way the Japs would not object, but it was actually financial assistance in disguise.

On Fridays, I had to go to the market to buy groceries. My mother made a popular snack, tuna fish and small portions of sweet rice, topped off with brown sugar and coconut. On Saturday morning, my sister Bertha would visit the homes of the officers' wives to sell them these snacks. Mother taught me how to iron using banana leaves and how to check how hot the iron was using my finger without getting burned. At that time all kinds of rumors were already circulating.

Prisoners of war in Bandung were allowed to have a visit from their spouses, so Bertha with her two sons and my mother traveled there. Because of a demolished bridge at Sukabumi, they had to wade through a river to get to the train connection on the other side. In the meantime, Japanese and Indonesian government officials visited us frequently encouraging us to register, resulting in our officially reporting to the Residency Office in mid–December 1942. This was the beginning of our internment process.

Men and boys were billeted for a few days at a police station and for one month at a school. The next day we were being transported in trucks to Kedungbadak, a camp situated on the city's outskirts, on the bank of a river. The guards were our former Bogor policemen. The camp consisted of a large estate house, a pavilion and four large barracks. There also was an open hall, a small hot water kitchen, a hospital and a barracks with shower and toilet facilities.

In the early morning we were allowed to play basketball on the field along the river or even wash our clothes in the river. However, when one of the internees escaped, this activity was prohibited. He was an ex–police officer from Banten and we did not hear from him again.

At the entrance, there was a separate pavilion in which 30 British subjects were housed. Between this building and the main gate, I once was allowed a brief visit with my mother and my four-year-old niece. They brought me a parcel and only a handshake was permitted. I often wondered who arranged this exceptional visit. Could it have been my mother's courage and coolness that prompted this meeting?

There were many rubber trees in camp and also several wrecked cars. Our Japanese camp commander's name was Matsuoka, a short old man with a deep tan and Hitler-type mustache. Judging from his Samurai sword, he must have been of nobility. Everybody considered him a "good" Jap. His young assistant was Matsumura, nicknamed "the slapper." He used to be a taxi driver in Tokyo. The very first time I came to hate the Jap was the morning after arrival in camp. They confiscated our precious personal documents and family pictures and just burned them.

The assistant residents, district officers and other high officials were housed in the large hall, called the "House of Lords." The three longest barracks behind the estate house were interconnected by covered dining halls containing permanent tables and benches. In the front section of the center barracks, young men were billeted along both sides of the building. My room supervisor was a former plantation administrator.

Rice and other meals for the Japanese were brought in by a Chinese. Our food orders also came with the same cart. For breakfast the selections were duck eggs and pineapple jam. The cast iron oven doors of the hot water kitchen served as our bread toasters and other meals were also prepared here. From time to time one could even buy special dishes such as pork pickled in vinegar. Food always seemed plentiful at first. Later on, however, rice was supplemented with pieces of sweet potato. In the corner of one of the long barracks one could select from a wide variety of dishes prepared by a *kongsi*, a select group.

There was essentially no work to perform. Once in a while we were sent to the kitchen to wash kitchen utensils. Boys took turns to be servers for the Japanese. A few rubber trees were cut down and the wood was delivered to the regular kitchen and hot water kitchen.

We could attend many different classes, though white tiles now replaced slate and paper. Material from wrecked cars was used to build a lathe. With this tool, many useful products were fabricated such as pieces for a chess set. Aluminum from cars had many uses, the most important one being that of making camp numbers, those assigned to each inmate. The most beautiful ones were those fastened with rivets onto aluminum plates, covered with wrinkled silver foil and colored cellophane, all placed within an aluminum frame.

An unforgettable exhibit of artistic pieces by talented internees was held at one time. One could admire the rosaries, statues and wood carvings. We also often played chess and card games. Sukabumi ex–police officers were constantly busy making peanut butter. The production process was quite ingenious and interesting. My sleeping companion formed a *kongsi* with two young ex–police officers. They operated a coffee shop at our window. The ingredients for a tasty cup of java were coffee extract mixed with canned milk powder and hot water.

I myself sold "Aroma" cigarettes which were made from a blend of Virginia tobacco and black tobacco, soaked in leftover coffee to which a pinch of honey was added. The mixture was then dried, rolled in a special kind of paper and cut to size. The proportions were of my own invention and hence were considered proprietary. Later, during forced transport, I exchanged some of these cigarettes with a guard for one of his cigarettes. He found the taste to be great.

Dr. Mansveld of Economic Affairs was able to construct a miniature golf course out of a transmission and other parts of wrecked cars. It was placed in the corner of the camp and was unbelievably nice. A bike rack consisting of pieces of wood and aluminum was transformed into golf clubs. He also built a deck tennis court. Strips of fabric were twisted around cables and these served as rings. Young and old enjoyed this game. Finally, we built a "bowling alley," though the number of bowlers was kept to a minimum because of the poor condition of the structure.

Besides the regular parties in the barracks, accompanied by guitar music by two brothers, we were allowed to form a band and perform once a week among the rubber trees. With his hands cupped in front of his mouth, someone would imitate the sounds of a steel guitar. Someone played an actual guitar, another the ukulele, and yet another a cello which had to double as a big bass. I provided the beat by hitting an outstretched bundle of dried coconut palm leaves. In our repertory we had "Sweet Sue," "J'Attendrai," "Harbor Lights" and "Hawaiian War Song." An ex-employee of Goodyear sang cowboy songs in an authentic country and western voice. One of them was

"I'm an Old Cowhand (from the Rio Grande)." A piano player and a violinist performed a concert in the open hall once a week.

I was glad to have Harry as a friend. He amused us with his opera singing. His favorite song was "Oh, Sweet Mystery of Love." He also told stories and joked with his Technological High School friends. As a native of Jakarta, I could appreciate his practical jokes.

One night, after the "lights out" signal, he pulled one of his tricks. He connected aluminum plates, spoons, cups and other objects to a string and strung it along the barracks wall. Then he tossed the end of the string as far away as possible after giving it a strong tug. The noise of the falling objects was invariably followed by angry remarks like "*Potverdorie*" (Dutch for "Darn it"), "*Potverdomme*" ("Damn it") and worse.

He could also grab your attention by his lip, hand and arm movements as he mimicked old folks talking to each other at some distance. He would dream up stories with the funniest settings to enact in this manner.

One evening we were enjoying a group performing a radio cabaret program featuring some unforgettable characters. The youths' favorite was Gijs L. from Bogor. He sometimes impersonated a gorilla by changing his facial expressions and the way he walked. Mr. D. from Depok helped a lot of people with his engraving machine, creating an "Only a few more days" sign. And then there was the man known as the dog killer of Bogor, who patched the holes in his pants with strips of fabric soaked in fresh latex, tapped directly from rubber trees. A small old gray man called Charlie sang a song of lamentation, "I Am Sick of the Mess Here." Mr. C. from Depok demonstrated his tough cold remedy by "inhaling" water from a glass. There were two gentlemen with long hair and beards, dressed in brown uniforms like those worn by our air force. They sometimes dressed in white tabard and would then resemble Rasputin. We often wondered whether they were real air force servicemen or just impersonators. It is worth mentioning that the son of General Van Heutsz also lived in our barracks.

Matsumura was the camp's dispenser of punishment, which he administered with a bamboo stick. Dick and Jack v.d.A.'s father once had to take a blow to his neck with the Samurai sword which was still in the scabbard. The sword penetrated the sheath and caused a long gash.

On another occasion, Alex, the middle son of Mr. V. from Suka-bumi, punched Matsumura on the jaw. He could not bear witnessing his father being slapped by him merely for dismissing his roommate too soon during roll call. After the punch, Alex realized what the consequences would be, so he ran to Matsuoka's living room to explain. He had not yet finished apologizing when Matsumura burst into the room with pistol drawn, aiming and pulling the trigger. Alex was very lucky; the pistol misfired. Matsuoka ordered Matsumura to calm down. Fortunately this incident never became a *Kempeitai* matter.

We often received *Kempeitai* visits, especially from a man called Matsuda. He dressed in a gray suit and an Indonesian hat. He always greeted us with exaggerated politeness but he could probably be considered the worst executioner around. Matsuda had no qualms at all torturing a Jewish dentist, for example. The torture took place in the commander's living room. He drove needles underneath the man's fingernails and toenails in order to extract a confession.

Through the holes in the bamboo fence, we always watched the detained inmates, led away by the *Kempeitai*, walk to the Grote Postweg. If they turned to the right, we could expect them to return. If they turned left, we would never see them again.

Our arrival in camp was followed by the appearance of many individuals as well as several groups. Sometimes these groups would consist of persons recently released by the *Kempeitai*. After having been administered strong electric shocks, they would walk around with outstretched fingers for some time thereafter.

One kitchen worker kept staring at his family picture for long periods while sitting on his mattress. Being much older now and knowing what it is to have a wife and grandchildren, I can sympathize. I can better understand, too, why tears would well up in old folks' eyes as they listened to such hymns as "Ave Maria" and why they could not contain themselves as they secretly attended night mass at Christmastime.

Then there were two days in 1942 when we were supposed to leave camp for an unknown destination. We had to march with our belongings to a waiting train at the station. We left through the side gate, between rubber trees and two rows of *Kempeitai* soldiers and policemen. With shuttered windows and doors—one of the guards cracked the door a bit—we were transported to Cimahi.

Internees from various other camps were arriving at the same time. Camp 4, consisting of the 4th and 9th battalion barracks, was completely packed in no time. There were separate sections for the Chinese and the so-called "Ball Boys." These were the men who were wearing the Japanese red ball arm bands. I believe that they were either pro–Japanese or anti–Dutch.

The first few nights I slept in Block VI barracks across from the rice kitchen. Then I was moved with a group of Bogor people to the horse stable adjacent to the clinic, near the graves of executed soldiers in Block III. Next I was sent to the washing shed of Block VII, and finally, through intervention of an old friend, I ended up in Block IV with most internees from East Java.

In Camp 4 there were approximately 10,000 men. Right from the start, food was scarce and of poor quality. With so many strenuous outside duties, we had to work harder too. The Japanese handed us former KNIL uniforms. We were assigned chores at the Bergartillerie, Cimindi Hospital, and at Gunungbohong in addition to several other sites.

Beatings were primarily administered during these types of duties. An exception was when a dagger was stolen out of a room at the main gate. The offender was suspended for many hours from a hook on a bell-rack in the camp, his toes barely touching the ground.

For the old and infirm, the dying process was now accelerating, and younger and younger inmates were dying. Burials at Leuwigajah cemetery were performed utilizing bamboo coffins and were attended by family members and a *heiho* (Indonesian auxiliary force) soldier. How different it was from our first death at Bogor, where Commander O'Hara paid his last respects dressed in a coat, with Samurai sword on his hip and a black armlet on.

Healthy, younger men were able to smuggle Mido watches, Arrow shirts and Pyramid handkerchiefs, and this earned them some money to buy extra food from the camp store. From the camp distribution center, we received small quantities of sugar, tea, and coffee, mixed with roasted corn, brown sugar and fruits. One time we got so many small cayenne peppers, we had to wash them quickly, cook them with salt and preserve them in glass jars for future use in salsa.

There were not many recreational activities but we walked a lot, especially after supper while smoking a cigarette. Cigarette supplies soon dried up, so from real cigarettes and lighters we regressed to smoking dried leaves, lit by an orange colored fuse lighter. After that supply was gone, we used a wad of sago palm wool lit by a spark from hitting a steel plate against the edge of a piece of flint. Later we became very proficient and merely pressed a burning cigarette against that of someone asking for a light.

I only remember one concert conducted by the famous violinist George Setet. He walked around twisting a miniature leather whip in his hand to keep his wrist exercised. During his concert, we young-sters were ordered to leave the hall as we were too rowdy. But we still wanted to have a good time, so we diverted the attention of the camp police by staging a mock fight. The combatants imitated the sound of real blows while mixing it up in the vicinity of the woodshed fence. By doing so, we could secretly steal wood for our cooking fire.

On the wall near the small cemetery hung a colorful picture drawn by a POW artist. It depicted a complete rice table with roasted suck-ling pig, fruit, and all the trimmings. Because of the pervasive need for food, we had to limit the time we spent looking at such a drawing.

Harry L. surprised me one night as I lay in the barracks. He brought me several packages of a special rice dish covered with fried onions. He had smuggled it into the rear of the horse stable via a wrought iron–covered window. How he managed to contact the Indonesians at the kitchen of the prewar officers' residence remains a mystery to me. But I had to eat the rice right away so as not to get caught.

In early 1945, lack of nutrition took its toll. Friends my age came down with beriberi. Whether they survived until the liberation I never found out.

Camp 4 was very large, and my friends and acquaintances were scattered throughout the camp. At one time we were asked to rou-tinely urinate in oil drums that were cut in half and placed at several strategic locations throughout the camp. The collected urine was taken to Technical Services in the corner of the 9th Battalion camp. After undergoing certain chemical processes, the liquid was turned into a rich "vitamin drink" intended exclusively for use by the aged. I personally had a chance to sample this drink, and I must say that it tasted like palm wine.

I recall one incident that is funny now but was a bit painful at the time. In the horse stable we had collected all the necessary ingredients for preparing a pot of vegetable stew. As soon as the guys found out that I would be going to the Sunny Farm in Cimahi for duty, they came up with a plan. A sock with a zipper was fastened on the inside of my working pants so that I could smuggle in cayenne peppers.

Initially, I was assigned as a grass cutter and had to work a few hours in the large field behind the camp. The grass clippings were loaded into what used to be a military ammunition cart and hauled off. Even now, when I smell the scent of fresh grass while mowing my lawn, my thoughts race back to this Cimahi incident.

As fate would have it, after arrival on the Sunny Farm dairy, I was assigned to work in the cayenne pepper and sweet potato fields. I had no qualms about making a considerable quantity of peppers disappear into my sock—and while I was at it, to eat a goodly number of fresh sweet potatoes. However, on the way home, the Japanese guard suddenly made the four of us run. He also had us push hard on the back of the cart which caused the "driver" to be lifted into the air.

Is it necessary to recount what happened to the peppers stashed away in the bag, and the effect it had on me? Suffice it to state that it was especially painful when certain parts of my anatomy came in contact afterwards with the cold Cimahi water.

Once the Japs reported in the *Nippon News* that Allied planes did fly over Surabaya, and this news gave us renewed hope. Towards the end of 1944 or the beginning of 1945, a group of young boys arrived in the camp. They were children of navy personnel and were considered to be too old to remain in the women's camp.

In May or June 1945, a new work detail for railroad duty was assembled and scheduled to go to Cicalengka. Although I was considered a permanent worker for our block distribution center, I was nevertheless assigned as a crew member. In this town, a country road led to the camp which was a former roof tile factory, consisting of sheds with newly constructed walls and floors of bamboo matting. The food was worse than that at Cimahi. We were fed rice mixed with local weeds and a few drops of coconut oil. We considered this a royal meal.

A wide ditch was dug along the entire perimeter of the camp, surrounded with bamboo poles lashed together. We were supposed to stand or squat on this contraption and use it as our toilet. A visit to these facilities was to be avoided as much as possible, especially at night. Strong howling winds would be blowing across the open plains, causing all kinds of problems.

Bathing accommodations were nonexistent. Very early in the morning we would walk in groups of 100 towards our work station, carrying hoes on our shoulder, to work on railroad berms. Our Japanese guard, nicknamed Brown Bear because of his peculiar walk, was actually no bully at all. After eating his lunch, consisting of rice and a piece of fish which he kept in a netted bamboo box, he would usually take a nap underneath a bamboo bush. One day the little guy kept on sleeping long beyond the usual time. Some of us could not resist the temptation to explore the undisturbed buffalo watering holes and to take a dip in clean water for a change.

The guard was awake when we returned, and a long sermon preceded the inevitable beating with a hoe handle. Now our nice, docile guard became just another Jap! But it was all worth it, and fortunately our stay in Cicalengka was short lived.

Our one day of rest per week was suddenly extended to two. There was now time to dry the mattresses and to search out and destroy our small eternal companions, the infamous bedbugs which took up residence in the cracks of the walls and the creases of the mattresses. What a luxury!

From returning auto mechanics who had visited Bandung, we learned that a drunk Japanese soldier had told the story that the Japanese emperor in Tokyo was considering calling a cease-fire. In reality, it must have been the acceptance of the unconditional surrender in mid–August 1945.

After a few days of rest, we were ordered to return the camp to its former state within two days. Then we were transported by train to our base camps. En route to the station, the natives smiled broadly and some even gave the thumbs-up sign. Despite the shuttered windows, we noticed that the lights were on in Bandung as before the war.

Back in Cimahi we had to await confirmation of the declaration of peace. We received more food, and the Chinese on the outside were allowed to come into camp and open a restaurant in one of the front halls. They would serve very simple meals. Out of boredom, I applied for a job in the vegetable kitchen. After being accepted as an apprentice, I had to perform the dirtiest job, that of separating the sweet potato leaves from the long stems. After gaining more experience with such tasks as cutting and chopping vegetables, I had the honor of replacing the boss for a day. This involved, among other chores, the distribution of tropical fruits, such as papayas and bananas.

We never heard the official word about the Japanese capitulation. Everywhere the Japanese bullies were already forcefully transferred. We had a short visit from a British major, accompanied by a Dutch army officer. After a quick tour through the camp, he climbed onto a chair in front of the camp office and explained the reason for the delay of the arrival of Allied troops. He further recommended that we stay in camp under the protection of the Japs.

One day Dutch Liberator bombers, marked with the red, white and blue colors and orange triangle, flew low over the camp, tipping their wings as a salute. Pamphlets were dropped, requesting us to form a cross made from white sheets and to place it on the field behind the camp. This would indicate the location where medicines could be dropped. Seeing these planes definitely gave me a lump in the throat.

I was also proud to read a short report on the bulletin board about a successful mission by a Dutch submarine operating along the west coast of Sumatra. The crew received an expression of thanks from SEAC. (South East Asia Command) in Ceylon, now called Sri Lanka, with the bottom line reading, "A job well done!" Not long thereafter we saw several Dutch troops in khaki uniforms walking around Cimahi.

Eventually we were given train tickets by the Red Cross to go home. Many of us remained in camp, however, because we did not know exactly where our family was. One morning I left for Bandung through a hole in the fence, wearing new sandals made of sheet rubber. I was not familiar with Bandung so I got lost for a while. I first went to the Borromeus Hospital on Dago Road instead of Kosambi, my ultimate destination.

What transpired during the transition period to Indonesia's independence movement, the so-called Bersiap period, most Dutch and Dutch-Indonesians are quite familiar with. It was the defining moment for the majority of us and the start of a new chapter in our lives.

ABOUT THE CONTRIBUTOR

Jan Vos was born in Surabaya, East Java, in 1926 of Dutch-Indonesian parents. He attended elementary and secondary school in the former Dutch colony. He fulfilled his military duties as a conscript soldier in the Royal Netherlands Indies Army and was attached to the Topographical Department. After the service, he was employed in Jakarta for six years.

He has been married for more than 41 years. After spending 29 years in Indonesia, including the Japanese occupation and the Indonesian independence movement, the family emigrated to the Netherlands in 1955. He found suitable employment but decided to emigrate to the United States in 1961 with his wife and four-year-old daughter.

From 1961 until retirement in 1987, he was employed by Ford Motor Company in Des Moines and Los Angeles. Two other daughters were born in the United States.

FEITE POSTHUMUS

An Unlikely Friendship

Salatiga is a small town in Central Java where the climate is ideal—cool, sometimes cold mornings and warm days. The pleasant, dancing breezes would cause the branches of the tamarind trees in front of our house and the banana trees in our back yard to wave. There was practically no humidity, making the days so comfortable that it really felt like paradise. Even during the monsoon season, we could play in the rain in our swimsuits. The nights, however, could be chilly and we often covered ourselves with a blanket, if only a very thin one.

In Salatiga, most people, whether European, Dutch-Indonesian (Indos), Chinese or Indonesian, were acquainted with each other. It was a town where I could buy something for a dime, or at the most a quarter, and tell the store owner that my dad would pay for it later. He did, but not until he had lectured me about my spending habits.

Once, I remember distinctly, a circus came to town, but one without elephants, tigers, or other animals. There were only a few jugglers, magicians and clowns. It was just wonderful, and all this for only 25 cents. For a *pasar malam* (Indonesian night market or fair) we had to travel to Semarang on the north coast of Central Java.

Then our rustic little town in paradise was rudely awakened by the sounds of war in December 1941. My parents knew what was about to happen long before I did.

My brother was 18 years old when the Dutch government declared war on Japan. He was called up for military service and left in late December 1941. Early in 1942 we heard that he was assigned to the navy. My mother wrote him to say that no matter what, he should not sign up for submarine service; that prospect scared her very much. He

175

responded that he would decline and would become a telegraphy student instead.

My father listened to the shortwave radio broadcast emanating from England and Australia. Because he could speak and understand English, he could tell us that the Japanese had sunk two of the most powerful British battleships and were advancing rapidly down the Malaysian peninsula towards Singapore. He was very concerned since Singapore was our Allies' last bastion against the Japanese onslaught. The Dutch in the colonies sent all their air power, which was not much to begin with, to Singapore to assist in its defense.

To a kid of 13, my father's news bulletins about the war sounded like a Flash Gordon story in my ignorance of what the consequences would be. Then came the news that Singapore indeed had capitulated and the Japanese were advancing towards Sumatra, Java and other parts of the archipelago.

We were in school at the Tuntangse Weg in Salatiga, but we were not aware what tragedy had already taken place on the ocean. The Battle of the Java Sea was valiantly fought but was ultimately lost by the Dutch. Except for the bomb shelters we had built, the blackout curtains we fabricated and extra food supplies we gathered, life went on almost as usual until March 1942. That month, the Japs invaded Java.

The result was total chaos. First we had Allied troops passing from Semarang through Salatiga—British, Australians, Dutch and others—attempting to form a second front around Surakarta, or at least that was what they told us. Eventually the Semarang "*stadwacht*" (city guard) also showed up. Because we lived close to the church square and next to the office of the assistant resident, all convoys happened to stop at this location.

My parents invited the exhausted Scottish, British, and Dutch KNIL soldiers into our home. My mother fed them, served tea and soup, and let them bathe during this two-day period. I was roaming around, admiring their weapons. Of course I also noticed that Ambonese soldiers had set up posts behind the above-ground tamarind tree roots along the roadside. What a retreat that was—no enemy in sight and two days of rest!

Then came a wave of civilian refugees from Semarang, a town abandoned by the army and the city guard. As a consequence, the citizens became vulnerable to attacks by Indonesian vandals and looters. These refugees alleged that there had been a bloodbath in town. Bojong, the main street, was supposed to have been flowing with blood.

They claimed that there were looters everywhere and the citizens were fleeing by car, bus, or bicycle. Some even walked the 30 miles to Salatiga.

We must have housed 20 or more people during that particular week. They were sleeping on floors, sofas, divans, and beds. I, as a youngster, was jumping all over the place, enjoying the excitement without realizing how serious the situation was.

After a couple of days, a Mr. W. announced that he was returning to Semarang to see for himself what was actually happening. With a busload of brave volunteers from Salatiga, they departed. Upon their return, he reported that no bloodbaths or other terrible things had taken place. Some homes had indeed been looted, but in general there were no major problems. So the evacuees from Semarang decided to go back, and our household returned to normal again, but only for a short time.

Every morning, the Dutch flag was raised on the pole in the assistant resident's front yard. We could observe this daily ceremony from our living room. My father remarked after the affairs of March 8, "Well, the Dutch flag is still there!"

However, one morning it was the Japanese "red ball" flag which was hoisted. My father's comment was then, "Good God, we are in trouble now!" And he was right.

Shortly thereafter, the phrase *"Japs Uit Nederlands Indie"* (Japanese Out of the Dutch East Indies) or JUNI was coined. There was still hope for deliverance, though. Most people were of the opinion that it would be all over in a short time—American, British, Australian and Dutch soldiers would be fighting against Japan, so how could we lose?

In April 1942, after the first Japanese troops arrived in Salatiga, we were subjected to *hormat* (bowing) regulations at the Jap guardposts, at the marketplace and on the main roads into and out of town. Of course we, as kids, could easily get around these Jap positions, but we were confronted by the locals who would immediately recognize me as a being a *totok*, or pure Dutchman.

During that month, too, the Japs demanded that all Dutch adult male residents in Salatiga report to the assistant resident's office. They were told to bring a suitcase and to expect to go to Semarang for a two-day meeting. The purpose for this gathering was to determine the future of the administrators, self-employed, and other nonmilitary personnel. My mother had packed a suitcase with canned food, clothing, and other necessities, so my father was prepared for a long stay. She realized that this was not going to be a two-day affair but rather an internment for my father.

When my father left with his suitcase, my mother and I followed him in order to say good-bye properly, but a Jap soldier stopped us with his bayonet. All we could do was to wave at the truck as it went by. A family that had recently arrived from the island of Borneo, now called Kalimantan, lived three houses away from us. Not only was the woman's husband interned, but the Japs also evicted them from their home. My mother invited Mrs. B. to stay with us. What else could one say or do under such circumstances but lend a helping hand? Thus, we ended up sharing our house with three complete strangers, a mother and her two children. Charity was needed more than ever.

In late May, we heard that the Japs allowed visitors to come to the civilian men's camp in Semarang. My mother and Mrs. B. went by bus while the lady's son, our Indonesian servant and I went on bikes. There was no space on the bus for us.

When we met my father, he was a mental wreck; we barely recognized him. He kept asking to see my hands because he heard that the Japs had cut off my fingers. He kept touching my hands throughout the visit. This incident took place only two to three months after he was interned. What had they done to him? That was the last time I saw my father alive.

Dad was a man dedicated to education. He was involved in the lives of Indonesians and felt very badly that his students did not want to go to the MULO (more extended lower instruction) or to follow other higher education opportunities. Instead, his students only wanted to run the Indonesian shops owned by their fathers. This attitude obviously was a great disappointment to my dad. He was such a great man!

During the following months more restrictions were imposed on the Dutch people. They could no longer leave town. My mother, however, managed to obtain a permit from the Japs to go to Surabaya, where my father was subsequently interned. We had friends there, so we were allowed to go. As a 13-year-old kid, I found the train ride exciting. I had a different perspective from the adults of what was happening. It was an adventure for me, but it must have been desperation for my mother.

Once in Surabaya, my mother found out that she could not visit the camp in which my father was interned after all. We could walk by and see the internees but we were not allowed to visit. This was sheer torture.

So we returned to Salatiga. In August or September we were ordered to go to the old KNIL camp in order to receive "protection" from attacks by Indonesians. At least, that was what the Japs claimed. It is interesting to note that we were never threatened by any Indonesians in the past and our maid and house boy were still with us all this time. We had to leave everything behind in our house—chairs, table, suitcases, bed, linens, divan, etc.—except for some basic furniture. Friends of ours helped to move my father's library and other items to a friend outside, who was at that time not threatened with internment.

The "camp" was the officers' camp of Salatiga, where we were assigned to live in unoccupied houses and share them with others, often two or three families to a house. But our designated family never showed up, so we considered ourselves fortunate. We were allowed to go in and out of this camp, passing the Jap sentry at the gate, but all our activities were monitored by them. As we passed by the gate, we often heard the cries of Indonesians or citizens of other nationalities who were tortured or punished by the Japs. What they did or how they were treated, I did not know. Rumor had it that the Japs cut off the hands of thieves or hit people with bamboo poles to punish them for their alleged crimes.

In late 1942, all the women and children in our camp were rounded up and put on transport to another "protection" camp. Again, we could only take a few suitcases and personal belongings such as a bed, table, and chair, and only one item per person, in addition to mosquito netting and some bedding. We arrived in the town of Ambarawa in Central Java. The orange zinnias my mother picked and waved were in defiance of the Japanese, orange being the color of the Royal Dutch family (House of Orange). Who cared about such niceties at that time anyway!

We arrived in Camp 7 in Ambarawa, an old converted Dutch police camp, and were assigned to a former horse stable. What a riot it was to attempt to find a place, assemble beds, contact acquaintances and so forth in barracks meant to board horses. The sleeping spaces were separated only by blankets and bedsheets. We found a spot next to people we still have contact with to this day.

In this camp we could cook our own meals. and we especially enjoyed the *nasi goreng* (fried rice) prepared by the H. family, our neighbors. The neighbors on the other side were just as kind. We were all from the Salatiga camp but were not well acquainted with one another.

Matters soon went from bad to worse. The view to the outside world through the barbed wire fence was eventually blocked by a woven bamboo screen. Guardposts were erected on every corner. No contact whatsoever with the outside world was allowed, but of course there were still clandestine encounters with some friendly Indonesians.

Often there were Japanese inspections of the barracks during which everybody was ordered to line up outside. All suitcases were opened and laid on top of the bunk beds while the Japs went through everything we had. They often confiscated items such as watches, jewelry, money and other valuables. They stole anything they wanted under the poor excuse that they were looking for radios and weapons. On such occasions I usually managed to escape to the "bathrooms" (nothing but planks over a ditch) carrying a pouch that contained my mother's jewelry. I reported to the *honcho* (head) of our barracks that I was sick.

I believe it was mid–1943 when things started to get really bad. Suddenly our camp was placed under military supervision, which meant that stricter rules and regulations were imposed. Up to that time we still had some sort of school, worship, entertainment, and other social activities, even though they were technically not allowed. Now we were forced to listen to a Jap proclaiming the might of Hirohito and similar propaganda, and the message was translated into Malay and then into Dutch. The bottom line was that from now on, we were subject to Japanese military rule.

Boys who were 18 years old or older were immediately removed from camp, and I lost one of my friends this way. Those 11 years and older were placed in a separate boys' barracks. Big, tall boys, regardless of age, had to line up outside camp and were given work assignments. Then came the quest to find a boy who could shout the loudest. Since I qualified and was the skinniest of the group, I was picked to conduct the daily calisthenics. Every morning it was *"kokomin taiso— ichi, ni, san, shi,"* etc. I had to lead the drills for about half an hour, and then everybody had to perform other daily chores.

One of my jobs was to take the garbage out through two gates, one leading to the camp and the other to the outside so that there was a space between them. As usual, I wore on the belt strap of my shorts a pin with the phrase *"Nederland zal herrijzen"* (The Netherlands shall rise again) engraved on it alongside a very small Dutch/British flag.

Early one afternoon, an Indonesian freedom fighter in service to the Japanese, spotted the pin and reported me to the Japanese commander. Oh boy, was I ever in trouble! The Jap wanted to see everything I had in my pockets. Among other items, they found small notes from my girlfriend.

As a consequence, her mother was called in and so was the Dutch camp leader. All this time I was sitting on my haunches and the Japs were deliberately stepping on my feet. I was apprehended at about two or three in the afternoon. This charade went on until about two o'clock the next morning. The camp leader, my girlfriend's mother and the Jap commander were also in attendance. Not knowing what to decide, the Japs let us go finally, apparently not wanting to lose face. I was the last to leave.

However, as soon as I came through the gate leading to the camp, my friend B de F. handed me another, similar pin which I still have in my possession to this day. I did get a long lecture from our Dutch camp leader. She was a lovely lady who had to go through these motions, regardless of how silly they were. I still had the friendship of my girlfriend, and we all played bridge with her and her mother many nights thereafter. From then on, Kano, one of the Jap camp guards, a really nice guy, kiddingly called me "*Sinjo* [boy] Molly." Molly was my girlfriend's name.

Once my mother became ill and had to be admitted to the hospital. But since we did not have medicine or other equipment, the Japs allowed her to go to the hospital outside the camp. Kano took me there to visit her once or twice. Unfortunately, there was nothing they could do for her, so she was sent back to our camp hospital where she slowly withered away. She was a strong-willed Jewish woman who had often defied the Japs by not bowing on cue. She was my sweet mother, the one I loved dearly.

Then one day, as I was working outside the camp, digging shelters for the Japs on the side of the road, Kano showed up and shouted, "*Sinjo* Molly, *sinjo* Molly, come quick." He escorted me to the camp. My mother was dying. During the conversation, she expressed her fear that my brother might have already died and that I probably would not see my father again. She was so concerned about my well-being. She told me, just before she died, that a Mrs. S., a good friend in camp, would take care of me even though I was barely acquainted with her.

My mother passed away on July 14, 1944. As it turned out, my brother was indeed reported missing in action by the Dutch navy on June 8, 1944, during a bombing raid over France. My father died in Batavia, later called Jakarta, in a men's camp on July 5, 1945. Her fears certainly materialized.

Mrs. S. took good care of me after my mother's passing. When word came that all boys 11 years and older had to leave the women's camp, she provided me with a rolled-up mattress and packed my suit-case. It contained pictures of my family torn out of albums because of space limitations, plus the pouch with some of my mother's jewelry. So sometime towards the end of 1944, these boys of 11 (and some as young as 10), trotted off to a new camp.

The new camp, Camp 8 in Ambarawa, was a former Dutch Catholic school campus which comprised a church, classrooms and dormitories. The exception here was that we kids were not confined to barracks, but were housed everywhere, including on the inside of the church. As we were assigned a building, we settled down as best we could. We settled on the bare floor, rolled out our mattress and unpacked our suitcases. Kano showed up again in this camp, passing along little notes to and from parents in other camps. He kept these notes inside his very ugly Jap baseball cap, an ideal hiding place.

The water supply in camp at one time was abruptly cut off, and the toilets became a nightmare. Even to this day I still have dreams about overflowing toilets. How messy that was!

At another time, the Japs asked for volunteers to go to Bandugan, a camp where vegetables and other food crops were grown for distri-bution to camps surrounding Ambarawa. I signed up—the Japs prom-ised us twice our food ration—and off we went. We were crammed into an Indonesian resort cottage with thirty others in a space originally meant to house only four. One of our daily tasks was to cut terraces out of the hillsides with spades. We were to construct straight paths leading to these cottages, similar to those in existence in Japan.

We also had to empty septic tanks from the surrounding cottages and fertilize the fields with the liquid contents. All of this work was accompanied by many "*bageros*," a Japanese curse, and with the inevitable beating by the guards. There were no *heihos* or Indonesian guards here. They were all Japs.

Unfortunately, the Japs could or would not give us the promised double food rations. They claimed it was due to transportation irreg-ularities. However, their own Jap contingent in other cottages did not face the same problem. They obviously ate well.

We continued to spade, to plant and to cultivate. The first har-vest of sweet potatoes and white radishes always went to the Jap camps. We learned about this arrangement later from those in Ambarawa camps, who never saw any of those crops.

A couple of months after this agricultural experience I developed a sore under a callous on my heel. So when the Jap asked for any volunteers to return to Ambarawa to unload transport train cars coming from other camps, I stepped forward, hoping to find a cure for my ailment.

One train arrived sometime during the night from a Bandung men's camp. The Japs had shipped out all old and invalid men, those who could no longer work. We had to unload them and take them to this decimated Camp 8, the same camp with plenty of space. There were dead bodies on the train, but as 15- and 16-year-olds, we could not do much with these corpses. We took them off the train and left them on the platform, hoping that some Jap outfit would eventually take them away for burial. At times, I still dream about that dreadful experience.

Meantime I arrived in Camp 8 with that festering sore on my heel. The doctor lanced it without the benefit of any anaesthetic; I had only a handkerchief to clench between my teeth. Subsequently, I was assigned as a hospital attendant by a Catholic sister who was acquainted with my mother and me. This position gave me the privilege of being able to place a bucket of water in front of those waiting in line to use the toilet. And it took many hours to collect the water.

I had to spend much time performing cleanup chores, particularly that of trying to keep the hospital bathrooms clean. These facilities were used extensively by diarrhea patients. Additionally, I had to take care of patients with soiled diapers, clean bedpans and even remove corpses. There were so many bodies, and I was only 16!

At long last, the Japs recognized the fact that the water situation was the major cause of all these illness and deaths, and they moved the entire boys' and old men's Camp 8 population back to Camp 7. This new camp provided us a living space of six by two feet. We slept in bunks which were three tiers high. If someone in the top bunk became sick and had to throw up or had diarrhea, those in the lower levels suffered. Bedbugs were another major problem. No one could apparently eradicate these critters and stop them from attacking us at night.

The death rate was so high that there were not enough regular wooden coffins. The ones we had were made of bamboo and were stacked up outside the "mortuary room," with fluid often dripping from underneath. These primitive coffins were carried by boys to an ox-drawn carriage and taken outside the camp for burial at the local cemetery.

The last few months of the war—it must have been July and August 1945—were the most stressful. Rumors about liberation and about Indonesia becoming independent combined with the high death rate and the Japs' progressively clamping down on our camp activities to make the situation very tense.

But suddenly we were given more food, the outside work details ended, and towards the end of August, a Jap officer told us that we were free again. This message was translated into Indonesian and then into Dutch. Japan had indeed surrendered and the war was over. But now what? Here we were, still in Ambarawa Camp 7. Many male adults were leaving for an unknown destination and so were some of the boys who were contacted by their mothers in the meantime.

We decided to stay inside the camp, awaiting word of when and where to go. Mrs. S., my mother's friend from the Salatiga camp, got in touch with me. She told me to come to town and report to Mr. L. He was an Indo who lived through the war years without being interned. Nevertheless, he suffered dearly outside the camp because of his national origin.

We left on foot from Ambarawa to Salatiga carrying only a suitcase. On the way, I met a girl who was originally from a plantation in the Salatiga area, and we continued our journey together. A native carriage came alongside and the Indonesian driver offered us a ride. He told us how bad the Japs had been and how glad he was that the Dutch would soon return. What could we tell this man? Times had changed in the interim, and we did not know whether the Dutch would even come back at all. In fact, we had heard the cries of "*Merdeka*" (freedom) all over, even before we left camp.

Arriving in Salatiga, I went straight to the designated home while my companion joined her family. We were welcomed by Mrs. S., her daughter and the L. family. I was not acquainted with the latter family, but they were true Christians who wanted to save me. During the time I stayed with them, they took me along to attend services at an Indonesian Christian church, but I could not understand a word of what was being taught.

One night, after dinner, there was a knock on the door. Ten to twelve armed Indonesians asked how many males were living at the residence. The obvious answer was that there were only two. They responded, "Well, you have to come with us to register."

So Mr. L. and I went along and we were taken to a school. To our great surprise we met many other male Indos and Dutch friends, also recently returned from prison camps, in addition to others who were never imprisoned during the war. They were caught in the dragnet this time.

Ironically, all of a sudden, we were internees once again. This time we were supposed to be the enemies of the newly formed Republic of Indonesia. What did we do wrong? So in October 1945, when the world at large was liberated from war, we Dutch were sent to jail in Salatiga, our heavenly paradise a mere five years ago. Again we were interned, twenty persons to a cell constructed for only six. If you wanted to change your sleeping position, everyone had to turn simultaneously. If you had to go to the bathroom, you were supposed to sing a song, the rule of our cell. In this manner, we heard many, many songs.

Finally, after a week of this Bersiap torture, we were released and brought to a house belonging to a Chinese that was previously used as a Japanese internment camp. The accommodations were terrible. There were many, many people to one room, sleeping on the floor. But in general the contacts and interactions with the Indonesians outside the camp were good. The guards, former policemen, even let some of the internees leave at night to visit their wives and family.

In October 1945, towards the end of the month, the Swiss Red Cross organized repatriation of former internees now living at the Chinese house. There were numerous Dutch and Indos who qualified, but unfortunately many more Indos were left behind. They were not liberated until 1948 or even later.

Then we were transferred to Ambarawa with other women and children. On our way, we were stopped at a checkpoint between Indonesian and British occupied territory. Shells from 10-inch guns on British navy ships off the coast of Semarang were buzzing overhead. There was no doubt that there was still a war going on around us.

We arrived in a camp—not in Ambarawa, but in Banjubiru, which was protected by British officers and Gurkha troops, a British-Indian tribe in the service of Britain. We were shot at almost daily by Indonesian snipers who were positioned around the camp. Several persons going to the kitchen for food were hit by bullets. A woman cried because a bullet penetrated her bamboo barracks and went through the only dress she owned, hanging on the wall. We saw Indonesian freedom fighters try to scale the bamboo fences in an attempt to harm us, but several were shot dead by the Gurkhas and left hanging there.

After a couple of weeks, the British decided to move us to Fort Willem II camp in Banjubiru, a so-called safe haven. The transport of women and children was again bombarded and shot at, but this time few were injured. As it turned out, Fort Willem II was also under constant attack by Indonesian insurgents. I still have in my possession as a souvenir a grenade head fashioned into a lampshade and many smashed bullets extracted from the barracks' walls. The Gurkhas protected us well, and it was to their credit that there were few casualties in this camp.

Finally, in December 1945, the British allowed us to go to Semarang, which was under their control. In open trucks, women, children and some men were transported from Banjubiru, a distance of about 30 miles. After all the hardship and turmoil we went through, being moved from camp to camp, having been shot at repeatedly and having endured other dreadful experiences, we finally arrived in Semarang. On the way, we passed a group of Japanese soldiers walking along the same road. Of all people, one among them was Kano, who had done so much for us kids in Camp 7. We waved at each other and he shouted to us in which camp he would be stationed. It was a school where I formerly attended the third and fifth grades, so I knew where it was located.

Once in our camp, I met friends of my parents with whom they had been acquainted since 1929. They took me into their little house in a native village and treated me as a lost, and now found, son. From there I went on a special mission to visit the school, now a British-controlled camp for Japanese soldiers, in search of Kano. The British were so kind to allow me to meet with him. He brought a carton of cigarettes as a present, but I had nothing to exchange with him.

Kano told me that he was previously assigned to an Irian Jaya post after his Camp 7 and 8 tour of duty. He was wounded and returned to Java where he became a prisoner of war. And now here we were, former enemies, sitting on a green patch of grass, talking in a mixture of Indonesian (Malay), Dutch and English, yet using very few words but a lot of gestures. We both knew full well that all was over.

With other friends in these camps, we reminisced about our hunger suffered in various camps, where we ate mice, rats, snakes and whatever we could catch. We remembered our torture, the curses and Jap abuses, the kicking and hitting, the withholding of food for days on end. Then we talked about the lack of medicines, sugar, salt and other vital substances needed at certain times during the internment; the stacks of leaking bamboo coffins in which our camp people were laid after their death; the suffering under a tropical sun; the sick we attended to in a so-called hospital without medicines, and our futile attempts to keep them clean. We remembered the overflowing toilets; the boys who were being abused by adult Japanese soldiers or by very frustrated soldiers who did not know that kids do not behave like soldiers.

The Bersiap period started right after the Japanese surrendered, with Indonesian youth attacking unprotected women's camps. Fanatical Indonesians killed innocent people who happened to look European, including an Indo friend of mine. Yes, it was all over in January 1946, except for the tumultuous period, which lasted through 1949 and much later for some Indo families.

In this short overview, I have recounted only a few details of the suffering and agony which those in and outside the camps experienced in that hellish four-year period. Books can and have been written providing more detailed information. This is just my account, one of the many which had to be told.

ABOUT THE CONTRIBUTOR

Feite Posthumus was born on May 5, 1929, in Rotterdam, the Netherlands, while the family was on leave. His father was employed as a teacher in the Indies. Both his father and mother were Dutch. They traveled often between the Netherlands and the Indies, and Feite was educated in both countries. A few months old, Feite came to the Indies in 1929, went to Holland in 1936 and again back to the Indies. He stayed there until 1946 when he returned as an orphan to Holland, a country which he actually did not know.

K.A. Peter van Berkum

Saved by a Stranger

By September 1944, I had already spent a total of twenty months in three Japanese internment camps on Java. In this one, in Bandung, our *kongsi* (self-support group) was busily fixing bread pudding, our tradition for birthdays and other special occasions. At sixteen, I was the youngest of our group of five. The others ranged in age from 18 to 22.

We had lived in these barracks, one long hall, with 120 other men for about eight months. Our *kongsi's* designated area of ten feet was located along the right outer wall of the building in the rear. Each man was allotted a two-foot space. We were fortunate to be assigned this area because it had a window without glass but with shutters. When there were no Jap guards around, we often used this window as a makeshift entrance or exit since it was a long walk to the official entrance.

People were assigned even to the space in the middle of the hall, leaving only two narrow pathways on either side. This caused occasional problems at night since stepping on a fellow prisoner was seldom, if ever, appreciated. To prevent such accidents from happening, a rope was strung above the center of the pathway, similar to the catenary of a streetcar. When you had to go out at night, you would walk straight to the end of your mattress, grab the rope, turn left and follow it to the door. This contraption was a godsend.

I remember what happened during one terrible night before the rope was installed. It was pitch black and I got hopelessly lost. I ended up crawling on hands and knees, bumping into all sorts of mysterious objects, both warm and cold, until a kind soul oriented me and led me to the door.

Our living space, small as it was, was nevertheless our castle. The two older men of our *kongsi* had been able to scrounge up folding camp cots somewhere which we used to partition our living space; the others slept on the floor, in between the cots. During the day, we rolled up the thin camp mattresses. On the floor underneath the mattresses, we had laid mats woven out of palm leaves. We stretched them to the edge of the pathway in order to delineate the outer limits of our territory.

With so many people crowded together in such a small space, marking your boundaries was no luxury. We always sat on the concrete floor. On the wall, on either side of the window, each of us had hung some sort of shelf. Materials were very scarce, so the shelves often looked like Rube Goldberg devices.

Our dress code was shorts, patched so many times that they would stand up by themselves and not because they were dirty! We also wore used wooden clogs to get around.

It was our *kongsi*'s custom to save one thin slice of our daily bread ration—one-third of a three by four by nine inch loaf—in order to be able to cook bread pudding for special occasions. Nobody cheated.

At first our bread had been as hard as a rock, but later, when one of the chemists in camp succeeded in culturing yeast out of human urine, it actually looked like bread, was more digestible and even tasted pretty good, at least to our starved palates. From money we earned on work details we had been able to buy a small packet of flour necessary to bind the pudding.

Our barracks was built in the shape of the letter H. Between the legs of the H, there was a covered laundry room, long since without water, but containing a gas pipe. Somehow we had been able to loosen a connection, and when the gas was lit, it burned with a strong flame. For a pan, we used a 10-gallon kerosene tin, ubiquitous in Southeast Asia, which had been fashioned into a bucket for laundry purposes. We also used it as a cooking pan since we had nothing else large enough for our present purpose.

Arie and Dick were the cooks. The others were lookouts, since what we were doing was a very serious offense: stealing gas from Emperor Hirohito. Discovery would unquestionably lead to a severe beating. One of us was posted at the entrance to the laundry area, the others on nearby corners. Matters were made somewhat easier since we were required by the Japs to shout "*Kiotske!*" (Attention) as soon as a Jap came into sight. Thanks to this practice we always knew well in advance that a guard was approaching from afar. Sometimes, however, the Japs would sneak around out of uniform, which posed a definite hazard. Fortunately, everything went fine. Nobody got burned and neither did the pudding.

Only when the bucket, carefully wrapped in a pair of mattresses to keep the pudding warm, was put away was the danger finally over and we could all breathe a bit easier. From that moment on, what followed would be fun. We flopped down on our mats and took our afternoon nap. The longer we slept, the faster the time would pass. We would make sure we were washed up before the evening meal call. This meal would usually consist of a cup of soup and our bread ration. The "soup" was nothing but warm water in which floated the same kind of greens that I used to feed my rabbits. If you were very lucky, you might get a goblet of fat. You had surely hit the jackpot if you found a minuscule piece of intestine, which, of course, had to be examined and admired by everybody.

Each person had his own routine for eating his ration. Some just gobbled it all up, others savored it slowly and chewed forever on what was chewable, and still others ate what was warm and saved the bread, or part of it, for later as I did.

The routine of serving food was another story again. There would always be some people who were very hungry or just impatient waiting at the serving station long before the designated time. As soon as they spotted the carrying team, consisting of two strong well-fed guys carrying a bamboo pole on their shoulders from which hung the heavy steel drum, they shouted, "Food's up!" Quickly a line would form in numerical order; everybody had a number and each serving session started at the next higher number after the last had left off.

The servers, mostly respected men in the barracks, were elected to this position by majority vote and were regularly rotated. They in turn were supervised by independent referees. This matter of serving the prisoners was a most serious business. After all, we were hungry all the time, if not starving.

On the big day we all saved our bread and then waited impatiently until seven o'clock to start the "big bash." When that moment arrived, Arie, one of the cooks, carefully unwrapped the mattresses from around the bucket, while Jan, the keeper of our treasures, unearthed the sugar, which we had not seen or tasted for about four months. But just two weeks earlier a two-ounce block of dark brown palm sugar had been distributed to each of us, at which time, after a quick, restrained lick, the lump had been surrendered to Jan.

Finally, the long awaited moment had arrived. It was my seventeenth birthday, and because of that I was allowed to serve myself first and load up my bowl. There was plenty for everybody to go around: each could have his fill. The pudding did not smell particularly delicious and the taste resembled that of bread and water, but it still was a treat. The sugar was usually eaten separately.

We had a good time in performing this ritual and it took several hours before even the most voracious among us finally would admit that even he was stuffed. But that was what it was all about—to have the privilege to serve yourself and to eat till you were ready to burst.

That night for once we went to sleep without feeling hungry. In general, we slept well, except for the many trips down the streetcar wire.

We now leap forward in time to October 15, 1945. The war with Japan was over. My older brother Bob, my fifteen-year-old sister Carla, my two little brothers, ten and eight years old, and I were living in a garage in Surabaya. Except for Bob, we had all been born in the former Dutch East Indies, now Indonesia. Until the beginning of World War II we had enjoyed a happy youth, living as a white minority among a huge native population.

The streets had been ominously quiet that day; there was barely any traffic and hardly anybody walked by. The armed Japanese soldiers on the streetcorners, strangely such a reassuring sight up till then, had disappeared overnight. Indonesian rebels had somehow disarmed them and thrown them into prison. The only disturbance of the deceptive calm was the movement of an occasional band of *pemudas*, or young revolutionaries, armed to the teeth, riding in a truck or walking by in small groups. The eerie and sometimes ominous sound of the clanging of sticks on hollow metal lampposts, slowly coming nearer and then again receding in the distance, had kept us awake most of the night. We were expecting the worst to happen!

Over the back fence we had heard rumors that these rebels were picking up all white men and doing terrible things to them. We had been back in our hometown for only two weeks. Prior to that, Carla, my mother and our two little brothers had been interned in a women's camp in Semarang in Central Java for two and a half years while Bob and I had spent that time in a men's camp in Bandung, West Java.

After Japan's capitulation in August 1945, on learning that my mother was very ill, I left my camp for Semarang, followed by Bob, only to see our mother die a few days after our arrival. Years of deprivation and starvation had taken their ultimate toll.

After having returned to our hometown in a convoy of 300 survivors, the Red Cross had put us up in a garage. The Japs had been ordered by the British admiral, Lord Louis Mountbatten, commander-in-chief for Southeast Asia, to protect us, the white population, from the rampaging revolutionaries. These extremists had taken advantage of the power vacuum created by the sudden surrender of Japan to unilaterally declare the independence of the Republic of Indonesia.

It was getting close to darkness. Maybe we would be lucky and would not be discovered after all. But just as we were beginning to feel a sense of relief, the *pemudas* showed up. They banged on the door and yelled at us to open up. There were five of them—excited, menacing, wild-looking teenagers, *runcings* (bamboo spears with very sharp, hardened tips) in hand. One held a pistol at the ready, aiming at my brother. He wore a Japanese officer's uniform and jack boots, and a Samurai sword was hanging from his belt. There was nothing to do but to go with them, leaving Carla and the two little boys by themselves in this lawless city. They would not even allow us to say proper good-byes.

Carrying our rucksacks, which we always kept ready, we were marched to an idling truck around the corner. More *pemudas* were awaiting us in the bed of the truck, surrounding a few more Dutch boys and men. Dicky P., a classmate I had not seen since the beginning of the war, was among them. He looked as scared as I felt. We did not dare to say anything and just stood there, waiting for things to develop.

The truck finally took off. A few blocks away, we stopped in front of the local police station near the Keputran *kampong*. This native village was entirely surrounded by the city and was known to be a hotbed of rebellion. We were prodded off the truck and herded into the station. In the back room, about 30 whites and Dutch-Indonesians were surrounded by a crush of *pemudas*.

It was totally dark by now and the air was filled with a great noise of excited and menacing natives. We still had no idea what was going to happen to us. We just stood there silently. Every time one of us said anything he was prodded with sharp and deadly *runcings*.

During the ensuing hour more prisoners were brought in, and finally, after some loud decision making, we were shoved outside where a large crowd had gathered. Fortunately, they moved aside and allowed us to board another truck. There were a lot more of us this time so we were pretty well squashed together on the truck bed. At least now we would not fall when the driver took a sharp turn too fast, as he did with great frequency while constantly keeping his hand on the horn. Our armed guards, hanging from the sides of the truck, triumphantly shouted "*Merdeka!*" to the masses lining the streets, waving the red-and-white flag of the newly self-proclaimed republic.

Although I had no idea where we were going, I noticed we were driving toward downtown and not toward the Simpang Club, where earlier that afternoon, many of my friends had been clubbed to death as they were standing, arms held high, in the broiling tropical sun. All of a sudden Bob whispered, "I bet they are taking us to the Werff-straat." This was a prison in which he had spent eight months several years ago.

The streets were dark, lined with mostly young natives armed with a variety of weapons, shouting, "*bunuh Belanda!*" (Death to the whites!), to which our guards responded with their exuberant shouts of "*Merdeka!*"

Bob was right; they were taking us to the Werffstraat prison. When we turned into the plaza in front of the prison, the dark, high walls and watchtowers ominously rising up on the left, a blood-curdling, menacing roar rose from the massed crowd, until then not immediately evident in the darkness.

As the truck slowed it was surrounded by this mass of screaming people. I saw only a blur of brown, sweaty faces with contorted, wide-open mouths. They were shaking clenched fists and brandishing all sorts of weapons. The guards had by now jumped off the truck, and a narrow path began to form from the back of the truck to the open gate of the prison. The entrance hall was dimly lit by a weak, bare light-bulb and burning torches. In this flickering light I could clearly see many men, armed with an amazing variety of weapons, lining the walls.

There we were, a bunch of scared men and boys, huddled together for protection from the seething mass of humanity below us. As the men surrounding the truck started to prod us off with spears, the roar swelled into a deafening crescendo, "*bunuh Belanda!*"

The men near the front started pushing us towards the gate and those near it had no choice but to jump off. Immediately the crowd started in on them, beating, hacking, stabbing with sticks and bayonets, and using axes, riffle butts and spears. The prisoners ran as fast as they could, zig-zagging and ducking to evade the onslaught. It was a miracle that most of them actually reached the entrance to the prison. As they disappeared into its eerily lit maw, more armed men were waiting for them.

Suddenly, while being inexorably pushed to the rear of the truck, I had the strange sensation that I had witnessed this scene before, in a movie about riots in British India. There had been that same eerie light in the darkness with flickering torches and faces while British soldiers were running the gauntlet. But there was no time for such reflection. I saw Dicky lying on the ground, not moving, and people jumping over him to get to the safety of the prison.

Suddenly, Bob turned around and yelled,

"Hold your rucksacks over your head, try to stay near me and don't stop to help—*run!*"

I jumped down, over Dicky and over others lying on the ground. I tried to run zig-zag and almost immediately lost sight of Bob. I received blows all over my body and felt a searing pain in my back, but I managed to stay on my feet until I reached the entrance hall where I was hit below my rucksack, on the back of my head, over and over again. Finally, I started to lose my footing, but with a desperate loping gait I was able to take a few more steps. When I finally crashed down, I found myself well beyond the entrance hall where the beating seemed to have subsided.

I must have lost consciousness because when I came to, I was on the ground, still clutching my rucksack. A soft, kind voice said, in Malay, "You are all right now, sir. You are safe now, sir, no more beating." The voice belonged to an old, dark skinned, native guard, probably a Moluccan. He helped me get up and directed me into a dark corridor from where I was eventually pushed by another guard into a cell already packed with people.

It was pitch black and amazingly quiet when I first entered. There was no room to sit or lie down, so I slowly wiggled myself down, paying no attention to the objections of those I pushed aside. I had no choice since I was passing out again. I finally ended up with my rear on the concrete sleeping bench and I just leaned against the men around me. At one point, I quickly withdrew my hand when I touched something warm, moist and slimy. I later learned that it was my neighbor's intestines hanging out of his abdomen.

There was a lot of moaning and groaning with an occasional cry of pain, but everybody seemed to be polite. The smell in the cell was a mixture of sweat, blood, urine, feces—in short, the smell of fear. The man with the exposed intestines died quietly during the night; he never said much and finally did not respond to my whispered questions.

When daylight finally broke, we found ourselves to be with about 50 men in a cell meant for only 10. Most of us were fairly seriously wounded, and three were already dead. I felt sore all over and had several gaping lacerations on my scalp; my shirt was stiff with dried blood. My back ached terribly when I moved.

By about ten o'clock there was a commotion outside in the corridor. The cell door was flung open by an Indonesian soldier who ordered the wounded to follow him. In the first-aid area, to my great relief, I found Bob, though he was barely recognizable due to the swelling of his face. He had no recollection whatsoever of what had happened to him the night before.

As it turned out, we were to spend 25 additional days in a cell. On November 10, 1945, we were liberated by a platoon of Gurkha soldiers under the command of a young Dutch officer. He had been alerted by a Moluccan prison guard that the revolutionaries were planning to torch the jail that particular night.

Could that have been the same man who so kindly helped me up after my frantic dash through the mob?

ABOUT THE CONTRIBUTOR

K.A. Peter van Berkum was born in Surabaya, East Java, on September 24, 1927, and attended grade and elementary school in that town. During the war, he spent almost three years in women's camp "De Wijk," Bubutan prison in Surabaya and the 15th Battalion Camp in Bandung. Subsequently, he was imprisoned for one month in the Werffstraat camp in Surabaya during the Bersiap period.

Upon return to the Netherlands in February 1946, he completed college in the Hague, followed by medical school at the University of Leiden, graduating in 1952.

He came to the United States that same year and has conducted a private practice in internal medicine and rheumatology in Baltimore, Maryland, ever since. He retired in July 1989 and lives in Maryland. He is married and has three children and six grandchildren.

RITA LA FONTAINE-
DE CLERCQ ZUBLI

Disguised as a Boy

Eight months prior to the Japanese invasion of the Dutch East Indies, my family moved from Cepu on Java to Jambi, Sumatra. My father had received a promotional transfer to become the new postmaster for the town.

My younger brother and I started school immediately and quickly made new friends. But gradually, our friends began leaving town. Since I was only 12, I had no concept of world events, but I was told that people were leaving for safety reasons. There was talk about a war and restlessness was in the air. Adults were whispering and acting frightened, as if in anticipation of a dreaded event.

Then one day, without warning, it happened. It seemed as though the entire town were on fire! Clouds of smoke hung overhead, tangible evidence of what was actually occurring.

My father and the postal workers began disconnecting and dismantling all radio and telegraph equipment, as instructed in the final orders received from headquarters. Confidential material was burned in several oil drums, contributing to the already heavy smoke in the air. Three radio towers on the premises were rendered useless.

Looting erupted everywhere, especially around the town's warehouses. It was the end of an illustrious era and the beginning of a tumultuous, never-to-be-forgotten chapter of our lives. A few days later, planes flew overhead so low that the ground trembled beneath our feet, and the house shook on its foundation. Pamphlets were dropped. The nation was informed that the enemy was nearby and

196

closing in. Radio broadcasts kept the public informed about the location of the approaching enemy troops and dispensed information and instructions.

As part of a government-organized evacuation effort, a bus arrived at our house one morning to pick up our family. The plan was for my aunt, who lived with us, to take my two brothers and me and flee to the west coast of Sumatra. From there, an attempt would be made to reach the relative safety of the isolated offshore islands. When I realized that my parents would not be coming with us, I refused to leave. My brothers went along with my decision.

Surprisingly, my parents did not object to our remaining with them. My mother seemed actually grateful that I had taken this stand. She had been so terrified by the thought of the family being separated that she had left everything to chance and had never mentioned the evacuation plan to us. She even admitted that she had not told us about it for selfish reasons. From here on, everything began happening rapidly.

The day after the bus incident, our parish priest came by the house carrying a package under his arm. He presented my parents with a plan to protect and shield me from enemy soldiers and suggested that I be disguised as a boy. The plan seemed incredible! My father even joked about it, claiming that it would be a welcome idea since I had always wanted to be a boy anyway. After a lengthy discussion, my parents approved the plan.

Once the proposed disguise was agreed upon, I realized that I would have to undergo a serious cosmetic change, beginning with a drastic haircut. My hair, my pride and joy, reaching to my waist, was my best feature. Now it became the first element to be altered in the progressive steps towards my transformation. Initially, I could hardly bear the thought of losing my long hair, but the idea of the chance to live as a boy sounded too inviting. And to know that I would never have to sit through another painful combing session after a shampoo made the offer even more attractive.

After the painful and emotional experience of a haircut of this nature, my life as a boy officially commenced. I had no idea what the future had in store for me, but I fully intended to enjoy the transformation!

In the meantime, the Japanese army had occupied the town of Jambi. Before long, a high ranking officer of the *Kempeitai* (the Japanese military police) and his entourage arrived at our home. The officer introduced himself as a former store owner in town.

Speaking fluent Dutch to my parents, he informed them that the family would be picked up within the hour and taken to the police station for registration. We were to take along clothing and other necessities, including all legal documents, for a stay of ten days to two weeks. There was no further discussion on the subject.

Before he left, the officer took it upon himself to tour the house. Upon entering our dining room, he was halted by the sight of a portrait of my mother at a younger age. The portrait was of special significance to my father, who always insisted of having it hung in a spot where he could admire it every time he sat down for a meal. Knowing the woman in the picture was my mother, the officer complimented her. His first impression must have had quite a compelling influence on him, because the portrait found its way onto the wall in his study, where I saw it hanging a few months later.

During the wait to be registered at the police station, we were confronted with the first unpleasant consequence associated with my transformation. I was approached by my teacher after my mother informed her about the situation. When she asked what to call me, I was dumbfounded. A name to go with my new identity had never come up or been discussed! My mother was unable to reach my father to discuss the problem, as he had just been called in for the interview. There was nothing any of us could do but try to remain calm as we waited for him to complete the interview process. In the meantime, inside the registration room, my father had the situation well in hand and had come up with the name of Richard for me.

Later that afternoon, we were taken to the three-room school building across the street where only a few weeks before, I had made new friends and played my accordion while singing popular songs out of the songbook *Kun je nog zingen, zing dan mee* (*If you can sing, sing along*). It quickly became evident as we entered the premises that the men and women were to be separated. Since our family was the only one with children, we were allowed to stay at the school with my mother and the rest of the women, while the men were all taken to the prison facilities.

The Japanese commandant of the camp turned out to be the same officer who had visited us earlier. Almost all of the women were acquainted with him from his storekeeper days and were content to know that someone they knew was in charge. But there were a few who had difficulty dealing with the fact that this man was to have control over their lives in the foreseeable future. Several women rose in opposition when they learned that their husbands would be separated from them. As commandant of the camp, he soon impressed the women as a fair man who governed with a stern hand. Because of the mutual respect and understanding that developed between them, the women began to view him as a friend rather than as an adversary.

Knowing that we were going to be incarcerated for longer than the promised two weeks, the commandant from the first day had encouraged ways to put energy to good use to prevent the women from becoming bored. He suggested that we establish a committee, select room captains and volunteers, think of things to do, be occupied and make up chores for everybody. The days were quiet for the most part, but during my time there I received an education in ways that I would not have had under normal circumstances.

My mother was already assigned the job of food distributor of our daily catered meals from the jailhouse. The meals were delivered by two prisoners who carried the large uncovered containers on a pole between them over a distance of two to three miles. On one occasion, while my mother was distributing the vegetable soup as part of our meal, she noticed something that looked like a stalk floating close to the surface. Thinking nothing of it at first, she continued filling the bowls. Towards the end, she became highly suspicious and realized that what she had thought to be a stalk might be something else. She immediately stopped the women from taking their bowls off the table until she had cleared up the mystery of the floating object. She scooped to the bottom of the container and to everyone's disgust, she fished up a boiled rodent. Needless to say, the vegetable soup was taken off the menu that day.

My aunt, elected as camp gardener, anticipated problems in the months to come, because the women assigned to her team did not even know the basics of gardening, let alone how to hold or use a hoe. She also had to take into consideration the extreme heat in which the women would have to work in the field. In addition, the prospect of having to expose her workers later on to the nasty, smelly process of fertilizing with the contents of septic tanks made her even less enthusiastic about her newly acquired responsibility.

Nevertheless, she accepted the assignment gracefully and carried it out to the end, enthusiastically and effectively, simply because she loved gardening so much. The commandant even nicknamed her "Little Woman." He made it a priority, out of high regard for her courage to handle such a big responsibility, to make very sure that she and her team were especially well looked after and cared for. In return, he expected the same courtesy from them plus a regular harvest of the vegetables he favored once the garden was producing.

On one occasion, a group of castaways who had survived after their ship was torpedoed off the coast in the Strait of Malacca was welcomed into the camp. The group included two teenagers who arrived with their mother, the ship captain's wife, her 80-year-old blind mother, and a medical team consisting of two physicians and nurses. All had been in the water for 45 hours prior to their rescue.

The physicians and nurses were immediately placed on hospital duty outside the camp. They were taken on a two-mile walk to work daily and returned by nightfall. One of the nurses, a Scottish native, ministered to an injury I incurred when I slipped climbing a barbed wire fence, catching my foot on a rusty barb.

Then one day, several of us witnessed one particularly brutal incident. A man was killed, execution style, by the *Kempeitai*. It happened right before our eyes. The corpse was left in place where passersby could view it. This exhibition, we were told later, was to impress upon the public that the Japanese were in power and to demonstrate the consequences of non-cooperation. This murder was a horrible shock to the camp population and the main topic of conversation for weeks afterward.

Camp life was filled with a variety of happenings. After a day's work, the women would usually gather in front of the building to enjoy the cool evening air before retiring. Exchanging life stories was their way of getting acquainted with fellow prisoners. It was a therapeutically well founded practice for many. On one such evening, a Japanese officer crossed the street. He was coming from the house of the commandant to invite everyone to a party already in full swing. As some of the women shied away, to my dismay, a handful of others accepted the invitation.

Shortly thereafter, the same officer returned to meet with the owner of an accordion engraved with the name *la Fontaine*. The instrument was traced to me by way of one of the women at the party. The officer asked me to come along with him at the invitation of the commandant. My mother tried to detain me but realized that it would do her no good to object. She had to let me go.

The party was fun, at first. It felt good to have my accordion strapped around my shoulders once again and to play to my heart's content. I regretted not knowing any Japanese songs, but since my performance was ordered to liven up the party, I had no choice but to play from memory the Dutch songs I had practiced over the last few months. I also paid careful attention to the variety of songs sung by the guests and tried to find the notes on my keyboard. Soon, I was able to improvise my way through a few Japanese tunes.

For me, the party was a break from the monotony. But never having attended this kind of a party before, I was surprised when at one point during the evening, my attention was drawn to the behavior of the women. They were showing signs of having had too much to drink and began to engage in activities which I was unable to comprehend. Their attitude filled my mind with questions. They seemed to be a bit too submissive to the amorous advances of the Japanese officers accompanying them. I knew that some of these women were married, so why were they behaving this way?

Observing the situation through the eyes of a young child, I became uncomfortable and embarrassed. Was this the way grown-ups acted at a party? I concluded that this could not be the case since we had had numerous parties at home, and I could not recall any of my parents' friends engaging in such behavior. I could only conclude that this was something for which I had not been prepared. As a matter of fact, at one point during the evening, I had the distinct feeling that I was not supposed to be at this party.

For days, I wondered whether I should tell my mother about what I had seen and how all of this was confusing me. She had noticed my uneasiness and suspected that there was something on my mind that was weighing heavily, but decided not to approach me until I would come to talk to her. But when I started to lose my appetite and withdraw from crowds altogether, she decided to have a talk with me.

When I told her of what had happened the evening of the party, she became outraged, primarily because she felt responsible for being the cause of my confusion. I was under the impression that she felt very guilty and powerless to undo the harm. In fact, during our talk, I had the distinct feeling that she wanted to let me know that she had failed as a mother by not having told me about life and the world of grown-ups in particular, to prepare me for the things that had occurred. The long and frank mother-daughter talk which ensued was supposed to clear up doubts and prepare me for future encounters, but it did not do so. At this time, I remembered the words of our parish priest as he attempted to convince me of the necessity for the disguise: "Grown-up women know the rules of the games that are being played. Innocent little girls like you do not, and they only get hurt because of it!" The meaning of these words became very clear at that moment.

A few weeks later, a second party was organized, and the same group of women attended. The commandant invited me in the presence of my mother, complimenting me on my ability to liven up the party and entertain his guests. He also expressed his amazement about the ease with which I picked up the songs and how everyone readily joined in. "Your son is the life of the party," he said. Then he promised to pick me up for the ride to the restaurant and return me home safely afterwards. My mother had no choice but to let me go. Both of us thought the talk we had would have been enough to make the next confrontation easier, but we were wrong.

The second party was worse than the first. It was held in a downtown restaurant known for its solicitation by ladies of leisure. This, combined with the presence of the women prisoners, escalated into a very demeaning situation. I was again disappointed in my fellow prisoners, and further confused about their actions. My mother had told me that no one could be held responsible for anyone else's actions, but despite this warning, I was still ashamed of what these women were doing. Did they have no pride? The advice my mother had given me was to ignore the entire situation and concentrate on what I was doing. I was not to judge how these women chose to live their lives. But I could not help but think of the men in their lives. I was constantly distracted by the unsettling atmosphere around me.

I watched the party going from bad to worse. The guests, in particular the camp women, were taking turns occupying the available private booths with their respective partners. As far as I could see there was no trace of shame or hesitation present. Having watched the situation for a while, I was suddenly overcome by the seediness of it all.

The next thing I knew, I was walking the streets without a guard. When I realized where I was and what I was doing, it was too late to return to the restaurant. So, I continued walking towards the camp, which was only 15 minutes away, feeling justified for having left the scene. This party was not the place for a 13-year-old.

My absence must have been noticed almost instantly, as moments later, a small car approached me. Screaming and yelling confirmed that the culprit—the runaway, meaning me—had been apprehended. I was picked up, pushed into the vehicle, and officially returned to my mother's care.

The next morning, the commandant came to apologize to my

mother and to ask me for an explanation of my behavior the night before. Upon hearing my views on adult parties, he was impressed by my honesty and innocence and spoke to me as though I were his son. To make up for all that had transpired, he invited my family, including my aunt, as he had learned that the "Little Woman" was related to my mother, to his quarters for dinner that evening. Before he left, he solemnly promised my mother that as long as he was commandant of this camp and responsible for the well-being of the prisoners, he would never again invite me to parties.

My mother expressed appreciation for his concern and accepted his dinner invitation. It was that evening after dinner that my mother came to see her portrait on the wall in the commandant's study. She was understandably embarrassed by the sight and blushed even more when he whispered to her why her picture was in his possession and how he got it.

Two other less pleasant incidents occurred at around the same time. One of the young Eurasian nurses was almost raped by one of the guards. Fortunately, an eyewitness identified the guard, who was immediately reported and never seen again. We never learned whether the guard was punished for the attack or simply dismissed.

The second incident concerned a woman who was under medical treatment and became mentally disoriented and violent due to her confinement. Her condition worsened, and it became necessary to take her away and place her under protective care. During one of her wild outbursts, she climbed a chair, fell off, and struck her head on the edge of her bed. She broke her neck and died instantly, thus becoming our first casualty of the war.

Things were not always serious in the camp, however. At one point, a monkey owned by the *Kempeitai* broke loose, finding its way to our camp. He somehow landed on the beams of one of the two outdoor lavatory and bath facilities, which was at the time occupied by one of the women. She had just soaped herself and was covered with suds when the playful young ape appeared overhead, terrifying her. The animal, however, was having the time of his life during this liberty. He began jumping up and down on the beam, swaying his long arms to and fro, pulling the woman's clothes off the hook and throwing them around. His loud screams caused the woman a lot of anxiety. Finally, the primate was captured and the woman rescued from her predicament—badly shaken and trembling, but unharmed.

After having been locked up for eight months, my family and a few others received the good news that we were to be reunited with our men. At the same time, the commandant informed us that we would not be allowed to return to the home we left behind. We were to find housing in the *kampong* (Indonesian village) and adjust to living among the natives, a people of comparatively primitive culture.

Having nothing better to look forward to, this type of degrading existence was very difficult for my parents. Unfortunately, it was our only option if we were to be together. My mother prepared us for a simple, primitive lifestyle, one with which we were unfamiliar. She emphasized how important it was for us to be together and to make the best of what we were offered, no matter what the circumstances or conditions under which we had to live. She stressed that we should be grateful for this opportunity and never dwell on what could have been. "Being given back to be a family, in wartime, should make up for living among natives in a shack in the woods, no matter how humiliating." These were her words.

In the meantime, my father was once again responsible for providing for his family. A *Kempeitai* officer came to the house to check on us and to assist my father in finding employment. Noticing my presence, he informed my father that I might be old enough to assist in family support and suggested that he would take up the matter with the former camp commandant, who knew us personally. "He might be able to come up with something for your son to do," he suggested.

In the process of finding a job and in talking to several people, my father was told that young boys were hired to work in Japanese households as houseboys. It was a known fact that these boys were often abused and exposed to drugs. My father was shocked to hear about it. It was clear in his mind that he did not want me to wander into such a place and prepared himself for the return visit of the *Kempeitai* officer. However, before my father could say anything when he stood face to face with the officer, good news was presented. There was a job awaiting me at the Office of Finance. I was expected to start immediately.

This was a unique and challenging position for me. My Japanese employers only spoke their own language, while my Indonesian boss did not speak a word of Japanese. Fortunately, at the same time that I started my job, an announcement was circulated about a soon-to-be-available course in the Japanese language. I could not wait for it to start!

I was one of the first to enroll in this course, the youngest student in class, and completed the course a year later. Having had to be armed with a drawing pad, making use of hand movements or facial expressions to communicate, I became more self-sufficient and could allow myself to do away with these aids. I was not aware of the benefits of mastering the Japanese language at the time, however.

Our standard of living was certainly not what we were accustomed to before the war. But thanks to my mother's strength and constant reminders to be appreciative, we lived a moderately happy life. During this time, she would often refer to the shack we lived in as paradise, which simply expressed her inner feeling of being a family once again. Sadly, paradise did not last long for her. She died a few months later.

Exactly one week after my mother's death, my father and all the other men were picked up once again to be interned. My aunt was now sole caretaker of the three of us, and I became the breadwinner for our family at the age of 13.

Without an adult male in the household, we were vulnerable and an easy target when a manhunt was conducted for an escaped murderer. Our house was evidently placed under surveillance and my aunt was suspected of harboring this fugitive. The search parties for this murderer in the middle of the night were usually accompanied by shouting and unfounded accusations. Nothing suggesting that we had harbored the man was ever found. After the last house invasion, my aunt and I seriously considered taking in a male friend for protection but decided against the idea in view of my identity. We finally decided to find a new place in a more protective neighborhood.

Shortly after the move, my brother and a friend were offered jobs as houseboys. Although we were aware of the unsafe conditions for houseboys, we agreed to allow my brother and his friend to accept the position because they would be working together and not be alone. Not long after that, I was invited to the house to meet my brother's employer, who had heard that I spoke Japanese. Flattered and with no reason to suspect that his intentions were other than honorable, I accepted the invitation. My aunt, on the other hand, had some concern but never mentioned anything to me, afraid that she might offend me with her opinion.

The evening started casually enough to feel comfortable. Conversing in Japanese was quite a challenge and even mentally tiresome. But with some assistance, I was able to communicate rather well. I had fun in the process, and my host seemed to appreciate my efforts. As the evening progressed, he brought out a few family pictures and invited me into his room to see more. Although I felt uneasy about this at first, my innocence prevailed, and I could see no harm in following him. We were both males, as far as he knew, so what could happen between two of the same sex?

As promised, my host showed me a few more pictures of his family at their home in Japan. What I did not realize was that when we entered the room, he quietly locked the door behind him. Excusing himself, he disappeared behind a room divider. A few moments later he returned, exposing himself to me and expressing homosexual desires. As he grabbed me, he pulled me up and pushed me onto the bed. My reflexes immediately took over, and I kicked him in the groin. He fell to the floor. He must have hit his head against something hard to lose consciousness, because he didn't move after that.

In sheer panic I ran for the door, finding it locked. I noticed that there were two windows in the room, one of which was barred. The man was still on the floor and not moving! I opened the second window, jumped out into the pitch darkness of the night, and ran all the way home. I never reported the incident because it would jeopardize my identity. If I had reported him, the officer would most likely have been executed.

In the meantime, I worked hard on my Japanese course and devoted every available moment to it. I felt that in the short time that I had started the study, I had made progress in communicating with my bosses and was very proud of myself.

Six months later, I noticed that the school where we were interned before was abandoned overnight. Unable to find out what happened to the prisoners, I became uneasy about our fate. I suspected that our freedom was soon to end as well, and so it did, two weeks later.

On my last day at work I received two envelopes. One contained my paycheck plus an additional amount collected by everyone in the office. "Pocket money!" I was told. Another envelope contained a letter of recommendation signed by my three bosses. This letter and my certificates for the course in Japanese became my two most important assets. Unknown to me then, they were the key to a secure future for the duration of the war.

A week later, all the families were transported by bus to Palembang through the dense Sumatran jungle. Before departure, we were instructed to keep the windows closed during daylight travel. They were allowed to be opened after nightfall and remain so until the next morning. We assumed that this was a precaution to prevent the outside world from knowing about us, the special cargo. After days of riding and suffering in a closed bus, having to hide behind wooden shutters, experiencing agonizing, sweltering heat during the three-day trip, we finally reached our destination, the town of Palembang.

We were welcomed and reunited with our old friends from the Jambi camp. The new camp was large and housed approximately 700 women and children of many nationalities.

Upon arrival, my certificates and the letter of recommendation I had received from my bosses were removed from my luggage without my knowledge. Then, when an officer addressed me in Japanese during *tenko* (roll call) a few days later, inviting me to come to the commandant's office, I became suspicious as to how he could have known that I spoke his language. It was then that I realized that my papers were missing and concluded that the invitation had something to do with my qualifications as a clerk and my proficiency in the language. The Dutch interpreter, whose daily duty it was to accompany the captain of the guard on his rounds, also seemed surprised. Although she said nothing, the expression on her face indicated that she felt threatened by this adolescent who was able to speak Japanese so fluently.

Later in the office, I learned the purpose of the call. The commandant wanted to become acquainted with the holder of the certificates and the letter of recommendation. Although he was informed about my age by the captain of the guard, and was prepared to meet with the 13-year-old boy, he still showed surprise when we came face to face. He admitted that he had been seeking someone with my credentials to fill a position in the office, but he never thought to be presented with such a young person. The interview went well. I had the feeling that I had been accepted for whatever the commandant had in mind. What it was he had in mind was not known to me at that time.

A few days later, the Dutch interpreter and I were given a language proficiency test. I passed it with ease and confidence. Because of my multilingual ability and experience as an administrative aide, I qualified to become the camp's new interpreter and clerk. As a clerk, I was to set up a filing system for every prisoner whose name appeared on handwritten lists. Because of the assignment, I was allowed to have my daily meals at the officers' mess, where two Dutch ladies were running the household. I was given a key to the back door of the camp for easy exit and the freedom to come and go whenever I pleased. Although I was lucky to be living an easy life which included virtually unlimited freedom, good food, and relatively good working conditions, in reality, my daily existence was one of loneliness. This aspect of my life was known only to my aunt.

It was in this camp that I found myself in a peculiar work setting. I, as a teenager, was expected to work side by side with mothers, grand-mothers, and nuns under the direction of Mother Superior. Because I was acting as liaison between the commandant and the prisoners, it was important to me to have a good working relationship with com-mittee members.

I was unable to accomplish my goal until I had a talk with Mother Superior about my position as interpreter and the attitude of the mem-bership. Clearly qualified through the language test, I had earned my rightful place in camp management despite my young age. I also argued that the commandant would never have assigned me the job if he had not thought me to be the right person for it. Mother could not deny any of what I had presented her with. Finally she agreed with me and acknowledged that it was not a question of age or who would be respon-sible for whom. It was the willingness to work together for the cause of the prisoners that was important.

It took some convincing to make the committee members accept me for what I was and what I stood for. At one point, after our rela-tionship had evolved into a positive one, I felt I owed Mother Supe-rior the truth about my identity and decided to confide in her. She was surprised and impressed that I trusted her with my secret. My only request of her was that she not tell anyone else unless she felt it was absolutely essential. She readily agreed. And from then on, she became my ally to support me in any way she could and was readily available whenever I needed assistance.

Shortly thereafter, I started my English lessons. I wanted Eng-lish to be included in my repertoire of languages, as it was the only language used in camp that I had not mastered adequately. My tutor was a nun of an order involved in education. She was a strict but fair teacher who helped me accomplish my goal in a few short months of hard work.

In my position as camp interpreter, I was usually the first to be con-tacted at any sign of trouble. In one case, it concerned a middle-aged Dutch woman who was reported to be smuggling items which were clandestinely delivered behind the barracks by her former servant. I was informed of the smuggling when one of the Japanese officers approached me and questioned me about the situation. After truthfully telling him

I knew nothing of the smuggling, I felt that I should warn the woman of his suspicions before she found herself in unwanted trouble. This officer, nicknamed by the women as "the Snake," was known to sneak around dressed in dark clothing, and wait to prey on women doing something illegal or inappropriate.

With the help of my aunt, I got in contact with the woman in question and warned her that she was being watched. My warnings were apparently ignored. The woman was caught. Although I was merely the one to relay the intended punishment to her, it made me feel like the punisher. Several times, I fought unsuccessfully for a penalty less severe than what the officer proposed, but he was determined to give her what—according to him—she deserved.

More extreme was the punishment received by a young English Eurasian woman who had sex with a guard and became pregnant. The young woman was interrogated about the affair and asked to name the guard involved. Mother Superior and I tried to make her see the dangers of withholding the information, but still she refused to divulge the name of her lover. After confrontation with the entire crew of guards as a last resort to find the male involved, a lot of hair-pulling, finger pointing, and harsh words occurred. It was finally determined which of the guards had been involved with her. The guard was immediately taken away and was never seen again. The young woman was taken away that same afternoon. Months later, after having given birth, she was returned and reunited with her mother. She was told by authorities that her baby had died. Whether or not that was true, nobody knew, not even her.

There were times when I needed to detach myself from unpleasantries around me. And the only thing that I could do to accomplish that was my work. It became my life. I was proud of what I was doing, and I felt good making a contribution to my fellow prisoners' well-being. I fought for what I felt would benefit all of us and constantly looked for ways to overcome obstacles in my path. The darkest moments in my young life were precipitated by the occasional arrival of death notices from the men's camp. The policy was that the woman in question was not to be told about the loss of her loved one until the commandant was ready and had time to make the announcement. The trouble was that I never knew how much time would lapse between receiving the message and notifying the widow. In the meantime, to watch the woman conducting herself, oblivious to what had transpired, was quite painful for me. I felt terrible not to be able to prepare and console her for the upcoming bad news. To deal with these feelings and emotions, I rationalized that I owed it to myself to be stronger and less personally involved in order to measure up to my job responsibilities without falling apart.

After my first experience as the bearer of bad tidings, I distinctly remembered the look given to me by the woman as I relayed the message to her. It was as though she was disappointed that I had not prepared her for the news. Little did she know that I was dealing with similar feelings. I had been tempted numerous times to brace her for her sorrow but could not, due to the existing policy of confidentiality.

In another instance of this type, I was the recipient of more than disappointed looks. I was attacked, scratched, and hit by one of three women called in simultaneously for the official announcement of the deaths of their husbands and son. The attacker later apologized, but her actions made me well aware that this part of the job could be physically hazardous as well as emotionally painful and lonely. At 14, I was carrying a very heavy load with no shoulder to cry on.

The word soon spread throughout the camp that I had access to this type of information, and women began coming to me to inquire about their loved ones in the men's camp. Even nuns approached me, asking about clergymen. I tried to make all of them understand that I could not divulge any information and pleaded that they not put me in such a position. My hands were tied.

About the same time, I found out that I was able to read some written Japanese words by deciphering some of the intricate characters. Combining them with other less fancy lettering, I was able to make some sense of what I was reading. But fearful of being caught by the commandant, I could not devote as much time to this endeavor as I would have liked.

Approximately a year later, the Palembang camp was closed, and the occupants were moved to the town of Mentok on the island of Bangka. The two-day crossing of the Strait of Bangka took place in a cargo ship. At first sight, this camp was larger and more spread out than the Palembang. It was also built at a higher elevation, and temperatures were very comfortable because of the prevailing sea breezes. Less comforting was the knowledge that the camp was built on a Chinese graveyard. This fact was confirmed by the hollow sound in front of the kitchen, as if there were a chamber below the surface, whenever fire wood was chopped. According to Indonesian superstition, the community was cursed and would pay dearly for trespassing on sacred grounds. Earlier groups of internees had already started to feel the ill effects of the curse in the form of deteriorating health. But little attention was paid to what was happening because only a few among the women were superstitious. And there was not much that could be done to remedy the situation anyway.

Barely a week after our arrival, I was shocked by the news that I was to go to the men's camp. Panic overcame me. The worst thoughts came to mind: maintaining my identity would land me in the men's camp, while revealing my secret could mean execution. What was I to do?

Luckily for me, the order had nothing to do with my gender, and I was in no danger. I was expected to go to the men's camp simply to fill in for a Japanese office worker who was in charge of administrative matters of the men's population. The officer had to undergo surgery and the reason of the call for me was simply to revamp the filing system in his absence, as I had done in our camp.

At the mansion, I was accommodated in a converted storage room separated from the main building, where the commandant and his staff were housed. My room was big enough to contain a bed, a small desk and a chair. It had a window overlooking the courtyard and three airholes on the opposite side, a few feet off the ground.

While I was residing at the mansion, I managed, with permission of the commandant, to provide my father with small packages of fruits and other food. He was already in the routine of delivering bags of fruit to my aunt and brothers on days that he made rounds in the women's camp. This service was supposedly my pay for clerical services rendered. My family and I were certainly very appreciative of this privilege.

I stayed at the mansion for almost seven weeks, during which time I completed the upgrade of the card system for the men's camp. I had had a wonderful time, but as all good things, it came to an end. Upon returning to the women's camp, I found that health conditions had further deteriorated, almost to epidemic proportion. I was surprised to hear that the camp was receiving an abundance of nutritious food products. Fresh fruits, vegetables, dairy products, and ray and other fish were delivered on a daily basis. At the same time, I was informed that there was absolutely no medication available for treatment of the prevailing diseases and neither was there any medical assistance, such as lab testing for proper diagnosis.

The patients suffered from headaches, joint pains, rashes, and diarrhea in conjunction with elevated temperatures, unconsciousness, and skin irritability. This, combined with malnutrition and other illnesses, such as dysentery and beriberi, caused most women to become weaker by the day, physically and mentally. It was scary to see some of the sick just lying there, staring into empty space, waiting for their bodies to give out.

I immediately plunged back into my responsibilities, working long and hard to obtain the necessary medication and anything else necessary to ease the suffering of my fellow prisoners and their children. But the suffering had already gone too far. The situation became utterly hopeless, as recurring fever weakened the patients even more. They became lifeless victims seeing death as their only chance for relief from hunger and disease. They had lost all hope. The conditions demanded immediate emergency action. Indeed, within a few short weeks, the camp was ordered to be abandoned. The population was to be transported back to the mainland of Sumatra.

The boat trip took merely a day and a half. Upon arrival, we were put on buses for the trip to Lubuklinggau, hidden once again behind wood-paneled windows during the day. The difference was that the temperature was much milder on this trip and easier to take because we were traveling through the mountains. The air was much cooler and clean.

Belalau, the new camp, was an abandoned rubber plantation. The housing was adequate, and the food seemed to be better. This camp provided us with a lifestyle which we had not enjoyed in the previous camps. There was gradual improvement in the health situation, probably as a result of the clean mountain air and a more nutritious diet. The women's attitudes, too, began to improve. Slowly but surely, everyone seemed to be thriving again.

A week before the war officially ended, I had the distinct impression that something was brewing, but was unable to pinpoint what it might be. The mood among the officers in the office began to change. There was a kind of restlessness and more drinking than usual. And when they were drinking, singing about death and loss of loved ones was clearly audible. They were also much rowdier than usual and requested the company of women more frequently.

Then, one day, the answer to my question came when my eye was caught by a picture in the newspaper. The text said that the Japanese were losing the war! During that time frame, there was also a serious threat to liquidate the camp population, although there was never proof of such a plan. Fortunately, this threat was never carried out.

It was in Belalau in September 1945 that we were given the news of the end of the war. It was there, also, that I was finally able to unveil my secret. This took place not completely without sadness on my part. I knew that the commandant and his staff would feel betrayed and deceived by my charade, but I hoped they would understand the reason behind it.

After three and a half years under Japanese rule, we were free again; I celebrated this great moment by putting on an old dress and walking down the driveway towards the guardhouse. The buses were ready to go. It was the first organized bus trip into town. By being dressed as a girl, I felt justified in being called Rita again. The expressions on the faces of the guards in the guardhouse as I came into view were of complete disbelief. I walked up to them and apologized for what I, for my own safety, had felt forced to do.

Soon after that, the gates of both camps were opened for visitors. That was how we were reunited with my father. We found him in sickbay. We nourished him back to partial health, after which he was taken to a rehabilitation center in the mountains by our liberators. In the meantime, the rest of the prisoners were transported back to Palembang, where we were assigned houses. It was here that we were reunited with my father for a second time.

The years in captivity taught me many lessons. I looked life squarely in the eye, faced my shortcomings, and set personal goals because of what I have seen and experienced in those years. Above all, I have learned that nothing lasts forever and that freedom is a commodity not always appreciated until it is taken away. Camp life taught me how to fight for survival.

ABOUT THE CONTRIBUTOR

Rita la Fontaine–de Clercq Zubli was born in the former Dutch East Indies, where she lived and attended school. During World War II, under Japanese occupation, she and her family were confined to several camps.

In 1953 she married a Dutchman, with whom she and her baby returned to the Netherlands. A year later they had a second son. They lived in the Netherlands for four and one-half years and came to the United States in 1960. She was employed at the Smithsonian Astrophysical Observatory in Cambridge, Massachusetts, where she trained to become a technical typist.

She subsequently started her own business in 1963 and published a book entitled *A Guide to Technical Typing*. At this writing she is finishing a book in which she tells about her experiences when she was disguised as a boy during the Japanese occupation of the former Dutch East Indies.

GRETA KWIK

The Loss of My Father

Memories rip away protective scabs and expose wounds still festering after half a century. This is why I wanted to be included in this compilation of memoirs. Because it is time to face the past. We are supposed to learn from it, so what have I learned from what happened? I have learned that war is evil. That it is a great equalizer: the conquerors as well as the conquered suffer. That hellish times get the worst, but also the best, out of us. That every ethnic group has its bestial and its magnanimous individuals. That, in spite of their helpless exterior, some women are made of steel. That food must never be wasted.

Memories reel on like an old movie in sepia. Shivering with fear and delight as a child, leaning against my maid, incorporating stories about native gods and ghosts in the intimate yellow light of an oil lamp. Climbing on Dad's lap, pressing against his chest, listening to his deep laughter. With his arms tight around me, being so sure that nothing, nothing could harm me. I have never again felt that safe.

How could I have known that the sound of those early sirens changed forever this perfect existence? I must have thought the war was a game adults played and we kids were invited to join. My life was taking a turn, one of many to come. This one was for the worse.

Dad, Mom, my brother and I lived in Cepu, an oil center on the island of Java that was targeted by the Japanese in their urgent need for oil. My father worked for the Dutch Indies Railroads. When we heard the nerve-racking sirens, we ducked into the bomb shelter under the house. Somebody carried me in the night. During air raids we wore real pots and pans upside down on our heads in the bomb shelters at school. We fastened them with ribbons and had quite a laugh about it. Once we peeked out of the shelter and saw a formation of Japanese planes fly over and listened to their ominous droning.

We moved to Ambarawa on the slopes of the Ungaran in Central Java, where I had been born some nine years earlier. I assume we moved because the Japanese were not there as yet. They had already occupied the lower areas. Soon, however, they came to the little town up the mountain. My mother and I stood in the street to watch them. How innocent we were. Rows and rows of Japanese troops marched by. They had flapping neck pieces hanging from the back of their *kepis*, and bed-rolls, canteens, guns and other things on their backs. Someone carried the Japanese flag in front of the sweating men. They must have been some of the shock troops who had battled their way through the Philippines to get this far. Or had they been fighting in China, or in the Asian Peninsula, or in the Pacific? When my father was transferred to Semarang, the port city and capital of Central Java, we moved again.

If there was one event that had a crashing and lasting effect in my life, it was the loss of my father. One night I woke up to stare into a Japanese face. I must have screamed because my mother came instantly. There were Japs all over the house and yard. I saw my father in pajamas being escorted outside by Japanese and disappearing in their car. We were under house arrest for some time thereafter. A sentry was posted in front of the house. My mother cried for days. I hung on to her, wanting to know when Dad was coming back and being of no help at all.

Life went on as it always did. With no money coming in, Mom worked the black market. She was gone often. I was about ten, and I still wanted a doll. Everything we had was gone. Mom bought me one with a cloth body and a porcelain head with eyes that could close. It must have been much too expensive for us. I loved it to pieces. She also bought me a simple swimsuit, and I learned to swim in Semarang's public pool. I still swim like a fish, and often remember how it all began.

Rumors circulated that the Japs had set up bordellos and needed women. My mother cut my hair and put me in my brother's clothes. Anything Dutch was forbidden. We were not even allowed to speak Dutch in public. Since we carried only Dutch names, Mom invented Chinese names for us. So I became instantly a boy with a girl's name of "Mei Lan."

We found the only Dutch school still functioning in Semarang.

It was in a convent. We had to go to church and pray a couple of times a day. Before I finally took a long detour to avoid him, I had to pass a Japanese sentry daily on my way to school. I did not want him to guess where I was headed, so I hid my pencil stub and paper in my shirt. Since we had to bow to Japanese sentries wherever we came across one, I bowed to this one, wondering whether he would hear the paper rustle in my shirt and whether he knew that I really was a girl. With the disappearance of the nuns into concentration camps, my academic career was nipped in the bud.

One day, Mom had to stand for hours next to a sentry because she did not bow. Everybody had to bow; even those in cars and in pedicabs were ordered to step out and bow. Even women from the rural areas carrying vegetables and fruit to the market had to set down their baskets and bow, then reload the carefully balanced tower of baskets on their backs.

Mom thought that I could make money by selling food in the streets, so I did. When nobody bought anything in the merciless tropical heat, when the asphalt felt soft under my old slippers, I brought the heavy containers to my uncle who, pitying me, bought everything I still had left. My budding career in sales ended when my mother found out what I was doing.

Mom was summoned to the *Kempeitai*, the Japanese military police, whose name struck terror in everybody's heart. Somehow she was accused of listening to a forbidden radio transmission. All radios were fixed in such a way that we could not receive foreign transmissions. My mother gave us kids some money, packed our clothes, and instructed us to go to our uncle if she did not return at a certain time. Fortunately she did come home, but she never told us what happened at the *Kempeitai* headquarters. Mom must have gone through hell those years. She had to stay alive, take care of two children, literally face the enemy, and make far-reaching decisions, all by herself. Women the weaker sex?

The Japs forced children to attend a Japanese school. We went to the one on the corner of our street. In the morning we stood at attention in front of a Japanese. Behind him the Japanese flag fluttered from the top of a flagpole. We bowed and sang loudly the *Kimi ga yo*, the Japanese national anthem. The teachers were Japanese military men. I forgot what we learned in the classrooms.

There were Japs housed in our street. I used to squat down in the dusty road with native kids at night and spy on them through the dense hedge having a good time, eating, drinking, singing and clapping. They were sitting on the floor cross-legged around a long, low table, clad only in loincloths. One used to show off, cycling in circles without touching the handlebars in front of our house. Mom said that he was just a teenager, and that the Japs by then must be recruiting kids, since their men were being slaughtered as the Pacific war dragged on. I pitied this boy so far from home. I was afraid of the Japs. I always crossed the street and averted my eyes when I saw them coming my way, yet I could not hate them. I certainly had reason to.

Dad was in Jurnatan prison. There were nine in his group, all of whom were accused of sabotaging the railroads. I learned later that my father met with the other conspirators somewhere in the city. To protect my mother, he never told her where it was. We were allowed to bring him food daily. The women and children lined up early in the morning in front of the prison with its high, impenetrable walls. An Indonesian guard called us and we filed through the front door. Since he liked to shove us through the prison gate using the butt of his gun, nobody wanted to line up on his side. Inside prison, behind long working tables, native women inspected the food we brought by poking in it. What in the world were they looking for? Arms, secret letters? From prison I went to the central market to shop for the next day's food.

One day one of those women found my mom's grocery list in one of the food containers. The woman, who obviously could not read, took me to a small room and called a Japanese guard. I was terrified. I'd never leave prison! The women would have told my mother where I was, but would she be able to get me out? I explained to the interpreter what the list was and fortunately they let me go.

We knew that my father received the food we brought because a cellmate of his visited us and told us that Dad shared his food with him. We did not hear more, unfortunately, because at the sight of some Japs passing our house, the man ran out the back door, through the back yard, and simply jumped over the high wall with its top studded with glass shards to discourage burglars! What had they done to him in prison?

One of the wives, Mrs. W., and her children were called in by the *Kempeitai*. Her husband had to watch what the Japs did to his family because he did not confess. I understood that my father confessed because he was told that Mom and we kids would otherwise also be interrogated.

The hardest part was the time we could say good-bye to my father.

We were in Jurnatan prison—men, women and children—all crying and clinging to each other under the watchful eyes of the armed Japanese guards. Dissolved in tears I clung to my Dad. I had never seen him cry before. Neither he nor I wanted to let go of each other, but someone tore us apart.

The next morning we went to the railroad station where my father had been some kind of station master. An area was set aside by a ring of Japanese with bayonets drawn. My father's group arrived in a truck. The chained prisoners were unloaded, They frantically looked into the crowd searching for their wives and children. We waved and shouted. Then they disappeared onto the trains. I was sure my father recognized us. When the train left we all ran after it as if to stop it. I did not realize then that I was never to see my dad again.

I may still have the piece of paper on which Queen Wilhelmina of the Netherlands wrote that she was sorry about what happened. I never looked for it because everything still hurt. When we received it, much, much later, it finally dawned on me that my father was dead. I remember crying and banging my head against a wall in utter sorrow. I do not want to know how my dad died. Was he standing, blindfolded, and shot? Did he have to kneel, hands bound behind his back, and his head chopped off, to topple in a grave of his own digging? His last thoughts might have been for me, his little daughter that he adored. I just know that he faced death with courage.

I have waited for my father all my life. In the Netherlands I expected him to show up. Even here the thought has crossed my mind that perhaps he was still alive and would find me. For years I thought he was buried in a mass grave until I heard otherwise in 1989. I went to Indonesia in 1990 to visit his grave in Ancol to pay my respects. He must have died somewhere in the vicinity of that symbolic wooden cross. I thought that visit would enable me to finally let the episode rest. It did not. Whatever shields me from a painful past must be as thin as the film which forms over milk left uncovered. A little touch will tear it open and it hurts all over again. For most of the past 50 years, I have shed a tear every January 29, his execution date. He died in 1945, seven months before liberation. The memory whizzes by, growing in strength, thundering by, and slowly losing its power, and I am all right again for the rest of the year. There must be millions of people who lead normal productive lives but carry a dark painful secret.

After the Japanese occupation ended, I still passed the prison daily on my way to the market. Somebody had killed the Indonesian guard.

The bloated corpse was barring the wide open prison gates. The stench was indescribable. I held my nose as long as I could. The second day someone had stripped the corpse of its uniform. The third day the dogs had their turn, and soon the skeleton bleached in the merciless sun and fell apart. Justice was done!

In 1945 the Japanese promised the Indonesians independence. The atom bombs on Hiroshima and Nagasaki changed the picture. Expecting the Dutch to return to power, Indonesian nationalists armed by the Japanese were prepared to fight for the realization of the Japanese promise. On August 17, 1945, two days after the Japanese capitulation, Sukarno and Hatta proclaimed Indonesia independent. The Allies arranged with the Japanese that the latter would continue to maintain law and order until the arrival of the Allied troops. Overnight the Japanese enemies had become friends. Indonesia fell under the Southeast Asia Command, under Admiral Mountbatten, and the British were appointed to take over from the Japanese. British troops—together with Japanese troops, until they were rounded up and returned to Japan—became our protectors against the Indonesian nationalists who by then were ready to kill anybody with white skin. The Indonesians fought the Japanese, the British, and also the Dutch when the latter came back to "reclaim their colonies." This oversimplification is an attempt to make those violent, turbulent, overlapping times understandable.

Rumors circulated that Semarang would be leveled by the liberating Brits and that it would be wise to dig a bomb shelter. So we dug an elongated hole in the back yard, just deep enough to be able to huddle in it. Unfortunately it filled with rainwater and the only ones who used it were our ducks.

One day when I was on my knees cleaning the bathroom floor, I heard the gnashing of boots behind me. My heart nearly stopped when I saw a Jap. I called Mom. In sign language he told us that we should leave because the area would be a battlefield. So we did. My mother was loaded down. My brother and I carried homemade rucksacks stuffed full. We and our dogs walked all the way to my grandmother's house. I fell once in the dusty hot streets and could not get up by myself because of the heavy rucksack. We were still in the wrong place at the wrong time, because we were hardly installed in Grandma's house when a local war broke out. There was a school at the end of the street that was occupied by Indonesian troops. British planes machine-gunned the school. Each time we heard a plane approach we dove under Grandma's bed and Mom threw herself over us. There were only minutes in between the low-flying planes. Thundering over, they darkened our window. The next morning, while collecting empty shell casings, I saw an Indonesian officer on a motorbike go by. A shot rang out. He zigzagged and fell across the street on the sidewalk. Nobody dared to help him.

My brother and I had quite a number of adventures in and around that house in Citarum Laan. When the Indonesian revolution began, we heard shooting in the native sector just behind the high stone walls surrounding our back yard. We climbed a tree to see what was going on when shots were fired at us. My brother just let go of the tree and tumbled down on top of me, and we both landed hard in the yard.

I don't remember whether it was before or after the trip to my grandma's house, but back home we had another war going. On both sides of Citarum Laan were schools, one occupied by Japanese, the other by Indonesians. It seemed that every corner in the city of Semarang had a school occupied by one side of the warring parties. And we certainly lived between them most of the time. The adversaries were shelling each other, both advancing and retreating. We and our neighbors made holes in the hedges and escaped to the far end of the street. Someone fashioned a white flag and thus we could cross the street without being shot in order to collect ourselves in some house designated for refugees. Unfortunately I lost one of our dogs. Without telling my mother I slipped all the way back home where I found him whimpering with fear of all the noise and destruction. Dodging shells, fallen telephone poles, and electrical wires, I dragged the dog back to the refugee house, crossing the street without a white flag. My mother, worried sick about me, gave me a good thrashing.

We had our doors barricaded. The front yard had been shelled, and the low stone patio walls were leveled. Soldiers, of which side we knew not, crawled outside in the yard. We heard an Indonesian soldier cry for water, for help, and for his mother. Mom, being a mother, carefully opened the window and lowered some water. That was a courageous and foolish thing to do, because anyone and anything that moved after curfew was shot.

We were very poor then. We could not even buy rice at times. We could not afford a maid and thus I had to function as one. I used to cook some mush of taro, or corn, or some other substitute for rice and hide part of it to feed the dogs. Our rabbit population fortunately increased at a precipitous rate, and we had some meat to eat. I also had to get our chickens slaughtered by a man in a native village who did that for a pittance. It was never easy to watch the way he went about it. I never thought I could eat my own pets, but my hunger must have been stronger than my aversion.

There was no law and order. Native bands used to roam the streets looking for white people or anybody else they did not like. We then huddled and listened to their shouting and the hollow clangs their sharpened bamboo sticks made when hitting a metal pole, and we relaxed only after they had passed the house.

When the Dutch women's camp in Semarang was open for a short while, Mom and I visited Mrs. V., whose husband had also worked for the railroad. We took her daughter home with us in order to feed her. Even though food outside camp was lousy as to both quality and quantity by then, it was apparently still better than the swill in camp. Mom planned to keep the little girl for a couple of days, but that night the native guerrilla fighters chose to be active again and we brought the girl back to her camp next morning in a hurry. It would not do for a little blonde girl to be found by Indonesians outside the protective walls of the camps, nor would it do for families who harbored Dutch people.

I remember the speeches of Sukarno, the president-elect of the nascent Republic of Indonesia. A loudspeaker was fastened in a tree at almost every streetcorner, and everybody had to listen to his various addresses which could last hours. I once was fixing my bicycle, together with a native repairman. On our haunches in the shade of tamarind trees on a streetcorner, we both had to endure another one of his rousing orations.

I learned later that Semarang was one of the roughest spots during the Indonesian struggle for independence. The images that remain strongest in my mind are of a canal stopped up by a heap of corpses, hands tied in the back, heads missing, and of a young white male disemboweled by Indonesian rebels with sharpened bamboo sticks, the universal and readily available folk weapon, while the crowd cheered on. All over the city the smell of rotting flesh hung, the air saturated with the thick stench of death.

Young Indonesian men were thrown into a war without adequate training or arms, such as our playmates from across the street. One day they climbed into a truck with other young natives and waved at us. Sometime later I saw their mother crying because both of her sons had died fighting for their country's independence. Again I stood at a mother's side and did not know how to comfort her. How many had to die for the right to self-government?

The British army unloaded huge Sikhs with flashing black eyes and turbans, tall British-Indian soldiers with a tuft of hair on their otherwise bald heads, and Asian-looking Gurkhas. Even then safety was illusory. A British-Indian soldier came to the house one day when Mom was not in. He motioned for me to come with him. I told my brother that I would be across the street with friends and fled. From my friend's house I saw the soldier put my brother against a wall and point his gun at him. My brother did not betray me. Another time when the British-Indian military were looking for women, I hid in a chicken coop in the back yard of an empty house nearby. Mom, my brother and I had invented a special tune to whistle when there was danger and another one when it was safe. I stayed in the smelly coop until I heard the safe signal.

By then Mom received some kind of compensation from the Dutch government, so she hired a maid and I could go to school. I went to another Catholic school, only because it was close to home. I kept being promoted to higher classes. This was because I used to help my brother with his homework. He had returned to school much earlier than I.

When the Dutch returned to Semarang and set up schools, I entered the Dutch HBS (secondary level school.) I was introduced to Western history, cultures and languages on a grand scale. This short period, before the Dutch schools closed again, was a breather. I participated in athletics and cheered for our soccer team, helped organize a school play, made lasting friends, and went to the movies for the first time. The seats were infested with vermin.

I discovered boys, and they discovered me. Apparently, during those miserable yet exciting years, I had almost imperceptibly grown into a young woman.

All the while the revolutionary war was still raging in parts of the city and around it. One day, arriving on the school grounds, I noticed the Dutch flag fluttering at half mast. One of my classmates, the son of a Dutch officer, had been murdered. An Indonesian sniper must have mistaken my classmate, who always wore the khaki of his father's uniforms, for his dad, and shot him when the family was gathered around the dinner table. I looked at my friend's pale face at his funeral. A fly buzzed around a small black hole in the middle of his forehead.

A school trip could illustrate how dangerous it still was, especially in the countryside. A group from our school went to the majestic eighth century Buddhist stupa, the Borobudur, located in Central Java. I had to beg my mother to let me go. We went under military escort!

On August 17, 1945, the Dutch red, white, and blue was lowered and the Indonesian red and white was hoisted. I did not realize then that a new nation, a new republic, was just born, and I was there! After the Pacific war the world has never been the same again. Colony after colony gained independence. Those Japs had shown that an Asian nation could take on the supposedly invincible white colonizers.

Soon we had to either opt for Indonesian citizenship, become an alien in the land of our birth, or leave. Being of Chinese ancestry, we could also go to China, which was no choice at all. Having been associated with the European-educated section of the population before the war, my mother opted to go to the Netherlands. The circumstances were such that we really could not have stayed, even if we had wanted to. The Indonesian army simply installed a family in the rear part of our house. One day a few soldiers sat in our part of the house and wanted me to serve them something to drink. I thought my mother would have a heart attack when she came home at that moment and saw what was happening.

Within a short time after that incident we were on our way to the Netherlands. Relatives advised us to stay, but fortunately my mom's independent spirit won out. How did she manage the paperwork, money, and other practical obstacles? My admiration for my mother still has no end.

I don't remember how we got to Jakarta to board the *Sorrento*, the Italian ship which brought us to the Netherlands. It felt odd to have white people serve me on board. It was hot and crowded in the refugee quarters below. We got clothes from the Red Cross. In the Suez Canal we yelled "Wrong way!" to military personnel who hung over the railing of an Asia-bound ship. While still in Asia at the mouth of the Suez canal, we steamed in between Africa and the Middle East for some time, to burst into Europe at the other end of the canal. I was just 17. And my life took yet another turn.

ABOUT THE CONTRIBUTOR

Born in 1933 in Ambarawa, Central Java, Greta Kwik left Indonesia in 1950 for the Netherlands, where she finished school. She has also lived in Paris and Brussels to improve her French. Kwik emigrated to the United States in 1961 and presently lives in Los Angeles, California. She has been a waitress, student, legal secretary, model, salesperson, college instructor, columnist, and author.

Kwik obtained a doctorate in anthropology from Syracuse University. She chose the Eurasians of Indonesia residing in Southern California as her dissertation topic. A popularized version of her dissertation appeared under the title *The Indos in Southern California.*

Kwik loves Indonesia and the Netherlands, but America is her country of choice. "I knew I was home the first time I set foot on U.S. soil."

GERDA DIKMAN-
VAN DEN BROEK

Innocence Denied

In the beginning, we were not affected too much by the war in the mountain region of Pacet, East Java, where we lived in the early forties. After the Dutch surrender, our fathers were all taken away in the Resident's red car, and we children were literally left out in the street with our mothers. Fortunately, this did not last too long. Many families of different nationalities (Dutch, French, Belgian, German, and Indonesian) soon moved in with each other. Possessions of those who were already interned were taken over immediately by those who were still free.

My mother and I spent a peaceful three months in the beautiful estate of French architect Monsieur Estourgie, who himself with his family lived in Surabaya, East Java, in his other villa. The villa in Pacet was built on a rock outcropping and had terraced gardens with large rose bushes and statues similar to those at the palace in Versailles. There were also orchards with a variety of European fruit trees like apple and plum, grapevines, and a vegetable garden with many European vegetables.

It was really fun living there; the house was so much larger and nicer than ours. For me the main curiosity was the bidet; now you didn't even have to wash your behind by hand after doing your job! In the Indies, customarily a water-filled bottle was used for this purpose, as many who were born and raised there will remember.

This chapter was submitted in Dutch and translated by Jan Krancher.

Every now and then, planes would swoop low overhead and many wild rumors were going around, scaring the women. Then one day we heard an unusual humming sound of engines, coming from the distance. It definitely did not sound like the Resident's car. As it turned out, the Japanese invasion had begun.

My mother immediately took charge of the situation; she sent everybody into the surrounding jungle and ordered me to hide in the barn behind a pile of old newspapers. Even though she was sacred stiff herself, she nevertheless confronted the approaching Japanese soldiers.

From my hiding place I could hear the sound of boots coming up the stone walkway towards the house. The dog started barking, then it became awfully quiet. Since my mother was brave enough to face the enemy, why couldn't I? I was only nine years old then.

Walking towards the sound of their voices, I saw her sitting at the dining table with several high-ranking Japanese officers with numerous bars and stars on their uniforms. When my mother spotted me, she was surprised, and to have me go away, she called out, "Paper! Paper!"

Not realizing that in her excitement she was speaking English instead of Dutch, I thought she wanted some pepper. ("Paper" in English sounds like "pepper" in Dutch.) So when I placed a jar of pepper in front of her, she exclaimed nervously, "No, not pepper, I mean paper!"

"You did not say that!" I replied.

"But I spoke English to you!" she retorted.

"But you usually don't do that!" I came back.

"Gerda, please, get me some paper," she said again. Off I went, back to the barn, where I grabbed some old newspaper. Now she was completely exasperated and shouted, "Oh, no, not this kind of paper, Gerda! Get me writing paper, please!"

While this shouting match between us went on, I could not help but notice that the Japanese faces turned red. Soon they could not contain themselves any longer and they exploded into a roaring laughter. I made a childlike gesture in their direction, smiled sheepishly, and soon the ice was broken.

"The Colonel," as we came to know him throughout the war years, beckoned me and put a protective arm around me. He asked me what my name was and what kind of hobbies I had. After I told him, he declared that Gerda was too difficult to pronounce for him, so he would call me "Funny" instead.

"You know, you look like my little sister," he said.

With my hair cut in bangs, and particularly when I was dressed in my sailor uniform, I truly resembled a Japanese girl. From then on, I could do no wrong by him. When I told him that I loved to swim, he promised to fulfill that wish. Of course, I took this promise with a grain of salt, but to my surprise, within the hour, I was chauffeured to a villa nearby which had a swimming pool.

"For you," the Colonel said.

Then a large sign with all kinds of Japanese characters was posted at the entrance of the huge yard. We had no idea what the sign read. But when my mother pointed to it as soldiers began bothering us, they beat a fast retreat, bowing and apologizing profusely on the way out. It must have said something significant.

Every so often, the Colonel would inquire how we were getting along. We were frequently treated to dinners and lunches; he also bought me clothes, shoes, candy bars, and whatever else I desired. After I told him once that I had lost my piano during the move, he even had a concert piano delivered.

Against all rules, I did schoolwork and the Colonel himself would correct my paper and explain matters to me. I was even allowed to exchange letters with my father. During this time, many pictures and movies were taken of me. I had no fear whatsoever of the Japanese soldiers in those days. I now realize that not everybody was as fortunate as we were and that this story may differ from other war stories. Nevertheless, this was a true experience and should be told as it happened.

As the war progressed, especially towards the end, Emperor Hirohito and his military advisers must have became progressively more nervous. Suddenly, all people of Dutch descent had to be evacuated and were sent off to—of all places—dirty, hot and overcrowded Surabaya on the north coast of East Java. The Colonel himself escorted us and allowed my dog to come along.

In this town, my brother Hein, his friend and their girlfriends lived in a small two bedroom house on Kutei Street. My mother and I moved into their garage and stayed there for a short while. Hindsight shows me that we should have remained there; it was a good place to be. The place was relatively neat and clean, but my mother could not adapt to my brother's lifestyle, resulting in many conflicts and arguments. The transition from our life in the mountains, with a private swimming pool, abundant fruit trees and relatively good food, to living in this hot, dusty city with its many overcrowded houses, dirty-looking children and chicken feed as our food was just too much to take, even for my dog. "Queen" died within one week. Even now, while writing this story, I still get goosebumps when I think of the way she looked at me, so melancholy, when my mother took her away to the vet. It took me months to get over the loss of my playmate, and as a consequence of my grief I became ill myself.

Sick as I was, we moved again to a garage on Bout Street, where the food situation improved somewhat because there was a marketplace nearby. People were trading all kinds of items here, and my mother often sent me to buy fried bananas, fermented tapioca, sticky rice and other delicacies. I was too naïve to realize that all she wanted was to get rid of me so that she could be alone with my so-called "stepbrother," a guy the same age as my own brother.

Life went on and occasionally we were startled by air raid warnings. We would then crawl into a school storage room where we would be quiet for hours, playing Monopoly. These shelters were often well stocked with reading material and games, so we were never bored.

There were numerous fires, causing casualties, and many people were recruited to fight them and render first aid. Initially, I was assigned to the fire department. We had to haul water in buckets from several wells and form a bucket brigade to douse the fires. One day as I was performing this chore, a Japanese soldier motioned me to stop and summoned a boy who was standing nearby to take over. Later, at the administration office, I was told that, in their opinion, I was too small and too weak to carry those heavy buckets. Subsequently, I was given a different assignment. They gave me a khaki uniform with a red cross and "First Aid" embroidered on it, as well as a shoulder bag containing all kinds of bandages and medicine. I must admit that I really felt very grown up and important then!

It was unfortunate that my mother again became involved in an altercation, this time with a certain Mrs. S., who lived in the main building with her children. So we moved again to another garage on Kutei Street near my brother, his wife and their new baby boy. Hein was wounded in the so-called "flag incident." He had prematurely raised the Dutch flag downtown when the news came that Japan had capitulated. He was injured in the fracas that followed.

Not long thereafter we moved for the fifth time in six months, this time to Daendels Street. It seemed that we had come full circle with all our moving. I was taught by my mother how to make a charcoal fire, how to cook rice and how to set coffee and tea. She made me do all these chores so she could be alone with my "stepbrother." One day, when she was highly irritated with me and started to hit me, this "stepbrother" wanted to join in. I grabbed a pot of scalding hot soup and emptied it on him, then ran away as fast as I could to my brother's house. In the process, I had to go through territory held by Indonesian terrorists. Bullets were flying all around me, but fortunately I was not hurt.

Near my brother's home, I saw a Red Cross vehicle. In the skeleton that emerged, I barely recognized my father. I had a long conversation with him and he was definitely in bad shape. He had been mistreated by the Japanese in the various concentration camps he was in. He needed a lot of rest but he insisted that we have a family reunion.

Not long thereafter, all hell broke loose in our neighborhood. There were street battles, indiscriminate shootings and many other disturbances caused by Indonesian extremists. A week later, trucks with Indonesian soldiers stopped in front of the house and Dad was taken away in handcuffs. I ran after him with his tropical helmet in hand and put it on his balding head. Later that evening, when I thought I had the back porch all to myself, I cried and let out all my anger and hurt. Then, unexpectedly, from the darkness, a voice next to me asked, "Why are you crying, little girl?" It scared me half to death and I snapped back at the soldier, "What kind of question is that? The man with the helmet on is my father." I told the soldier that he was barely home a week after three and a half years in Japanese prison camps and that as a lawyer, he had always championed the Indonesian cause. "Why are you taking him now?" I asked.

"War, young lady, war!" the soldier replied.

Then I heard a voice I recognized. "What is going on, child?" this voice asked.

"Cheval!" I called out in surprise. It was the nickname of Sawal, one of our faithful Indonesian servants before the war.

"There is only one person in the world who would call me by that name. You must be the little Dijkman girl." (Sawal could not properly pronounce Dikman.) I asked him what they were going to do with my father and where they were taking him. He did not answer but he called out to the Indonesian soldiers nearby to hurry up and follow the truck. "We have to save that gentleman with the helmet; he is an honorable man," Cheval yelled, and off they went.

What actually happened to my father I learned from him years later. The trucks proceeded into the direction of Bubutan. After they arrived at this old prison, the Dutch men were pushed off the trucks and forced toward the gate through a gauntlet of soldiers wielding bayonets. My father had landed in the gravel on his knees and was crawling because he did not have the strength to get up. In this position, he escaped from being bayoneted, but he still received numerous blows to the body and head. Fortunately his helmet deflected many and he made it somehow through the gate.

Once inside, the real horror actually began. Those who survived the gauntlet were led to a bucket. Green, grey and blue eyeballs, amidst blood and gore, stared the next victim in the face. When it was Dad's turn to get his eyes plucked out, he was suddenly jerked away and somebody said, "This is our prisoner; we will deal with him."

This was music to my father's ears. It was Cheval who saved him. He pushed him to the rear section of the prison and told my dad to stay hidden behind the corpses of the tortured and killed prisoners. "Pretend you are dead, especially when more bodies are brought in," Cheval advised him. Dad remained at that location for a considerable time. Eventually, he was rescued by British-Indian troops, our Allied liberators and protectors.

In the meantime, our sector of the city had been turned into a protection camp with bamboo fencing built around it. For the first time in my young life, I found myself in a real internment camp. The adults did not concern themselves too much with me; all they could do was cry.

My brother Hein had escaped capture, also thanks to Cheval. During the Japanese occupation he had managed to stay outside camp because my mother had convinced the Japanese authorities that his father was a Javanese. He was much darker than I. Hein had stayed with us throughout, and I believe his presence may have been the reason why we were not bothered as much as others were.

In the early months of our internment, Cheval still brought us rice every day. Then, all of a sudden, we did not see him anymore. Just like the Colonel, he seemed to have vanished into thin air. Were they transferred, or did something bad happen to them? Who would know?

Our food situation soon became more precarious. Chickens and rabbits had already been butchered, but nobody dared to sacrifice the goat; she provided much-needed milk for the baby and young mother. So I decided to explore the surrounding area to find something edible. I did this when almost everybody was asleep and there were no guards around. Together with another girl, Irene Eduard, we picked fruit trees clean and "misappropriated" tapioca and other edible crops. With salt we found in a abandoned house, I then managed to make hearty soups.

It was about this time that British-Indian troops took over control of our camp from the Indonesians. I believe they were the Sikhs, members of a British-Indian tribe serving in the British army, and had long knives and wild eyes. They frightened us more than the Indonesians ever did! We also distanced ourselves from the Gurkhas, another tribe from Nepal that arrived later.

By this time, Allied planes had begun dropping pamphlets and also huge packages. We were elated. But one person died when one of these heavy loads landed on him. And in the meantime, fighting in the streets flared up again, with frequent machine gun fire, and bombings. Once more there was real war.

Out of free will and choice, I already parted company with my mother when Irene and I were transported to Malaysia on a British navy minesweeper. The three sets of clothing I wore on the morning of the departure and the many handkerchiefs I stuffed in my pocket proved handy. The latter were soon put to good use as diapers for Hein and Fien's baby. We now had a chance to eat bread with real butter for the first time after the war, and of course we gorged ourselves, making ourselves sick.

On board, Irene and I found a suitable hiding place behind one of the ship's big cannons. Exhausted, we bedded down, and soon we fell into a deep sleep. We only woke up when we were well into the open ocean where we felt relatively safe. The minesweeper proceeded very slowly to avoid the many floating mines. At some point we changed ships, and soon after, the minesweeper on which we had just been passengers ran into a mine on its return voyage. We saw our rescue vessel disappear in the waves.

Once again, I had passed through the eye of a needle. Sometimes I picture myself as one of those cartoon characters who always seem to manage to escape without a scratch. Throughout the years, it appeared as though there was some kind of protective power surrounding me—a guiding hand, you may call it. Or was it pure luck?

On that second ship there were many Dutch-Indonesian refugees who had terrible stories to tell, too horrible to recount. One baby died during the trip, and some time later, an old woman. Both were buried at sea in the traditional way. A baby girl was born, and she was given the ship's name, Ekma. This afforded her the privilege, as was customary, of getting free passage on any future voyage. I doubted if she would ever avail herself of this offer, however, because the ship was not exactly in tip-top shape.

Irene and I were among the first to set foot on shore and were transported by truck with many other kids my age. One of them played a harmonica as we entered Singapore, singing all kinds of songs which were popular at that time, such as "Lay That Pistol Down, Babe," and "Coming 'Round the Mountain." Our transit camp in Malaysia was called Sime Road and was located just outside town in the hills near a lake.

The Red Cross had assembled a team of doctors and nurses who turned us inside out, pumping us full of shots. We were deloused, defleaed and made to take a shower with disinfectant soap. We all received new clothes, sandals, towels, toothbrushes, and, of course, toothpaste. It was just great!

After we recuperated sufficiently, we went for walks in the countryside. One day I decided to take a swim across the lake—fully dressed—on a challenge from Malaysia's top swimmer. As it turned out, halfway towards the other side, I ended up saving him instead of his saving me. I had to actually drag him to the other shore.

There was a concert piano in the recreation hall of this refugee camp, and it was here that I made my debut as a boogie-woogie player. At age 13, I quickly matured into a teenager. With others my age I would hang out at a Roman Catholic chapel situated between the two camps. Romantically, we would sit down on beautifully shaped knolls, until we discovered that they were actually gravesites. Gone was any romantic sentiment from then on!

When I felt the urge to get educated, I enrolled myself in school. Using the prewar class assignment as a guide, I was supposed to be in the third grade. However, attendance in this class lasted only one day. Then I spent less than a week in the fourth, something like ten days in the fifth and about the same time in the sixth grade. I was certainly a precocious little girl.

There were no higher grades in Singapore at that time, so I remained in seventh grade for the duration of our stay. My only classmate in this particular grade was a Jewish girl called Flora. She had been secretly educated during the war by her mother, aunt and others. I think, however, that the Colonel had done a better job in teaching me than her family had in teaching her, because I did much better in the various exams we took.

Some time later, after returning to Jakarta, besides going to school in the daytime, I also started my "career" singing solo in nightclubs. After a while, the pressure became just too much to handle—I was exhausted all the time—so I decided to finally apply to become an evacuee, hoping to be reunited with my father in the Netherlands. In January 1947, I departed to my cold and strange "fatherland" on board the *Sibajak*.

On board the ship I took it upon myself to take care of two small orphaned boys, one Japanese boy called Bobby and one blonde two-year-old named Arend. Bobby in particular needed extra care; he was dirty, unkempt, and covered with eczema. Most passengers had no objection to my taking care of Arend, but about Bobby I heard all kinds of comments, such as, "Toss that Jap overboard!" They called me a "Japanese whore."

The only kind person who supported me in this endeavor was a certain Felix van den Broek, who was a KNIL soldier. He was also going to the Netherlands with his mother, brother and sister. He assisted me in taking care of Bobby until I handed him over to nuns in Rotterdam who were going to provide for him. I could not hold back my tears when he was led away, crying, "Mama." Both little boys called me by that name while on board.

Thus I found myself in my new "fatherland" in 1947. After several tumultuous years in the Indies and having been well educated in the Netherlands, I married the kind gentleman who assisted me on board ship.

ABOUT THE CONTRIBUTOR

Gerda Dikman was born on March 2, 1933, in Jakarta, West Java. Her father was Dutch and her mother Dutch-Indonesian. She attended elementary school in Mojokerto, East Java, but her schooling was interrupted by the Japanese occupation. She also attended a makeshift school in Singapore, and after the war she attended secondary school in Jakarta.

After repatriating to the Netherlands in 1947, she continued her higher education. She married Felix van den Broek in 1953. They have lived in Germany and the United States and currently make their home in Surinam. She teaches music at two local institutions and is chief piano instructor and a professor of music.

In her retirement, she frequently contributes articles on life in Surinam to the Dutch-Indonesian magazine *de INDO*.

J. Alexandra
Humphrey-Spier

Never to See the Land
of My Birth Again

In 1939 when we left the Netherlands and arrived in Probolinggo, a harbor town in East Java, I was 13. My sister Aletta was 10, and my brother Rico was 12. He attended school in the Hague. My father John Spier worked for the *Nederlands-Indische Handelsbank* (Netherlands-Indies Commerce Bank).

In May 1940 we received the bad news that Hitler had invaded the Netherlands. All communication stopped, so we no longer had contact with Rico. Then on December 8, 1941, the Japanese attacked Pearl Harbor. Since I happened to attend school in Surabaya, East Java, my parents immediately called me home. From then on, I attended the local MULO (more extended local instruction). We still were not very concerned about the war and its consequences.

On February 15, 1942, the British settlement of Singapore fell. On the 27th, the Battle of the Java Sea was fought, and the small Dutch fleet was virtually destroyed. Dad took us to Malang, East Java, where we eventually boarded with the wife of an army colonel and their little son.

One day the colonel came home to tell his wife that the war was over and that the Dutch had surrendered. He had to go back to his regiment where he expected to be taken prisoner. From then on, many women and children were left on their own. On March 1, 1942, the Japanese landed on Java. We were scared, not knowing what the invading forces might do to us. But even though Japanese soldiers swarmed all over Malang, as far as we knew, nobody was harmed. They took all the chickens, vegetables and fish they wanted. Some even offered to pay with their worthless Nippon money. When the situation settled down a bit, Dad managed to travel to Malang and take us home to Probolinggo.

We were learning to cope with being occupied. Our MULO was closed, and the building now served as army barracks for Japanese soldiers. After a few weeks the Japanese command ordered all Dutch government officials to gather at the club called the "Soos," short for *Societeit*. Anxious wives came along and soon found out that their men were being loaded on trucks. As it turned out, they were shipped off to prison camps. The women were allowed to pack a couple of suitcases with clothes and food, and the first contingent of civilian prisoners was off to one of the first camps in the town of Kesilir, East Java.

Before surrendering the bank offices, my father had removed as much money from the vault as he could without arousing suspicion. This money, hidden in a secret place, was used to support us and his four bank employees for the first two years of the occupation. He also managed to obtain a cache of guns and ammunition.

We expected that we might be caught in the middle if there were counterattacks by Allied troops. We were also concerned about the increasingly hostile Indonesian youth, the *pemudas*. They were being whipped up into a frenzy of animosity against the whites by their leader Sukarno, in cooperation with the Japanese.

The Japanese had everyone bring in their radios, but they did not confiscate them. The dial knobs were secured with a seal so that no one could tune in to outside newscasts, such as those from Australia or the BBC, but by simply opening the back panel, we could change channels using a pair of pliers. Dad listened to the newscasts every night. The news was not very encouraging. A curfew was imposed and a total blackout was in effect.

In July 1942, the Japanese started rounding up more and more civilians for imprisonment. Everyone who was more than half Dutch was told to report to a certain building with a suitcase packed with clothes and food. My dad qualified to be interned.

One of the newly appointed Japanese officials in Surabaya, through prior business dealings with the bank, knew my father quite well. Mom decided to try to get Dad out of camp. She traveled to Surabaya and managed to see him. The official granted my mother's wishes and to our great joy Dad came walking into the house a few days later.

Shortly after Dad's return, the Japanese confiscated our house. We temporarily moved into the empty house next door, but soon this too was commandeered by the Japanese, and we had to move into a smaller house. Min, our native butler, and Napsia, our cook, stood by us through thick and thin. Soon textiles were getting scarce and a black market sprang up. Indonesians started to offer good money for clothes, sheets, table clothes and other items. Dutch women dug into their trunks and linen closets.

Nobody had a job anymore. The Japanese took over banks and businesses. The schools were closed. However, Miss Borneman, who was our English teacher at the MULO, would invite small groups of children to her home. We pretended to be visiting, and she would teach us English, math, geography, and history. She kept this up until it became too risky as the *Kempeitai*, the Japanese military police, moved in across the street.

Soon all radios were confiscated, although my father still had access to a clandestine one. In September they took away our refrigerator too. But it did not matter much anyway since any bread or milk we still were able to get was consumed the same day.

A number of 15- to 17-year-old boys accused of conspiring against the Japanese had been taken prisoner by the *Kempeitai* and put in the local jail. Hygiene in jail was nonexistent. One of the boys contracted dysentery and eventually died. I remember how stunned we all were by this incident.

In December 1943 we were evicted again. This time we moved into a large old house, next door to Miss Borneman. Soon after this move, my father was taken prisoner by the *Kempeitai*. They had found out about the weapons cache and the clandestine radio.

With the help of a former neighbor, my mother contacted an Indonesian prison guard who, for a fee, would smuggle notes, cigarettes, and money to buy extra food into prison. In return, my mother would receive notes from my father, written on small scraps of paper. After reading them, she burned them immediately.

By now all people still outside camps, European and Dutch-Indonesian, were registered and had been issued an ID card. We had to carry this with us at all times. The card showed what nationality we were, and if Dutch-Indonesian, what percentage of Dutch blood we had. My mother claimed her French citizenship. According to French law, a French national would retain her citizenship even if married to someone of another nationality. France was not at war with Japan, and the French Vichy government was collaborating with the Germans, allies of the Japanese. Mom was, of course, actually a strong supporter of Charles De Gaulle, leader of the Free France Movement, but claiming French nationality was a way to stay out of camp. And as minors, Letta and I were in my mother's custody.

When the Japanese started the first women and children's camp in Malang, they cordoned off a section of town. The women were allowed to bring in as many belongings as they could carry. Later, they were relocated to other, less pleasant camps. Then they had to leave all they owned behind. These items were quickly confiscated by the Japanese.

In Probolinggo, more men and older boys were gradually taken prisoner or sent to internment camps. The clergy were also taken away this time. Food was getting scarcer. Just about everybody was recruited by the Japanese to plant rice in the irrigated paddies outside town. For several weeks we worked in these paddy fields under the direction of an Indonesian supervisor. We were shown how to plant the young rice plants, resembling sprouts of grass, in the mud. Actually, we had a good time doing this. After several weeks we had to come back to weed. Somehow, we never stayed around long enough to participate in the harvest.

It became difficult to find food such as meat, chicken, fish, or vegetables. We were still able to buy rice, coffee, tea and sugar, and we ate tofu and soybeans for protein. Min and Napsia still refused to leave, although my mother no longer could pay them. Min planted a vegetable garden for us in the back yard that yielded corn, yams, tomatoes, cucumbers and a kind of spinach. Every other afternoon he would dam up the open sewer, flooding the yard and thus watering and fertilizing the garden.

This was probably how I contracted a severe case of amoebic dysentery. The water must have contaminated some vegetables which were not properly washed or thoroughly cooked. There was no doctor left in town, and I needed shots of a special medicine to treat the disease. A Chinese dentist who lived next to the house occupied by the *Kempeitai* donated a few ampules of the medicine. Since the Japanese frowned on the Chinese helping the Dutch, he took a chance by coming over and personally administering the injections. I am sure I owe my life to that brave man.

April 29, 1944, was *Tenno Heika's* (the Japanese emperor's) birthday. It was a custom to give prisoners special privileges on that day.

We were informed that we could visit our men and bring them clothes and food. For days, we cooked, baked and prepared large portions of the best food we could scrounge up.

At the appointed time, the women and children were let into the back yard of a barracks-type building on the edge of town where we met our men. They were so skinny and their clothes so torn and dirty that we hardly recognized them. Initially, we were allowed to hand them clean clothing. Then the Japanese made them strip and change right in front of us. We were given permission to sit down in the grass under the shade trees and offer them our baskets of food. It was painful to see how they devoured the food. Some of them got awfully sick afterwards from eating too much and too fast. The visit was too short and was soon over.

One of the *Kempeitai* across the street got into the habit of visiting us every so often. We called him Little Pete. He was a short, muscular man with a shaven head and he was supposed to be the chief torturer and executioner in Probolinggo. We could hear him coming from afar. He would drag his heavy boots while his sword, dangling from his belt, scraped across the gravel.

He would clump up the steps and bang on the front door, which we always kept locked. Of course my mother had no choice but to let him in. She would invite him to sit down and he would smoke and converse in broken Malay. He would never accept anything to eat or drink. The first time Mom offered him a cup of tea, he gave us an evil grin, saying that surely we would try to poison him. Now there was a thought! We dreaded his visits and would moan and groan when we heard him approach. Little Pete told us that he had received his special training in Russia from the KGB, Russia's secret police. After the war, we learned that he had been lynched by a gang of angry Indonesians. The *Kempeitai* also terrorized the Indonesian population. Additionally, a large number of Indonesians had been sold out by their leader, Sukarno. They provided cheap forced labor for the Japanese who employed them throughout the archipelago.

Early one morning we went to visit Miss Borneman next door. We could get to her house through a gate in the wall dividing our backyards so no one across the street could see us. Miss Borneman, her mother, her niece and the three of us were sitting on her partly walled in front porch in the dark with bamboo blinds down, talking softly. Suddenly, from one of the *Kempeitai* houses that Little Pete shared with another man there came a loud lashing sound. It was as if something or someone was being beaten with a whip or bamboo lash. At the same time we heard a blood-curdling human howl, followed by the barking and howling of Little Pete's two large dogs. We sat speechless. It had completely unnerved us. The three of us shortly thereafter returned home the same way we came. The beating and howling occurred once more, coinciding with the next full moon. We never found out what actually occurred.

The days dragged on. I kept myself busy with reading, especially the English text which Miss Borneman loaned to me. I also did some drawing and painting, using bits of paper, water color and gouache paints.

Our clothes now were getting very threadbare. Letta, who had grown quite a lot in the last two years, had almost nothing left to wear. What she had was heavily patched and mended. By now most of our linens had been sold for cash to buy food. Luckily, Mom still had her old, foot-operated Singer sewing machine. She took a few of Dad's white drill pants and cotton shirts, ripped them apart, and sewed them together again to fit Letta. We used to make a "new" dress from two old ones.

One afternoon, an Indonesian policeman came to the door and told Mom that she had to appear before the local Japanese chief of police. They took off, and Letta and I sat on our front steps, anxiously waiting for Mom's return. Min and Napsia kept us company, refusing to go home, although it was already getting dark. After two or three hours, Mom finally came back, accompanied by the policeman. She told Min to give the man my father's British Raleigh bicycle. The chief of police offered to buy the bike at the going price. My mother was much relieved, because she thought that he had found out about her smuggling items into prison. Since no one refused the chief of police anything he wanted, the deal was soon consummated.

One hot afternoon in August 1944, Little Pete came over while Mom and I were in the bedroom getting dressed. I had just finished when we heard him banging on the door. I let him in. He was angry and growled at me, "Where is your mother? She is a bad woman. Go get her!" I told him that Mom was getting dressed and accompanied him to the sitting room. "Tell your mother to hurry up!" he yelled.

I was getting scared and ran into the bedroom. Mom had overheard our conversation and her face had turned ashen, her lips blue. She grabbed a small bottle from the medicine cabinet and swallowed a good mouthful. She saw the concerned expression on my face and whispered, "It's only Valarian, an herb to calm me down. Quick, go to Pete and keep him busy; talk to him till I'm dressed."

By now I was shaking. Mom had started to burn a few scraps of paper when I left the bedroom. Were they smuggled notes from prison? I went to sit with Little Pete, but I could not utter a word. He kept growling about my evil mother. Then he took a cigarette out of his pocket and told me to light it. With shaking hands, I managed to do so.

Finally Mom came, all dressed up and even made up with lipstick and rouge. Was this to hide her ashen color? Little Pete took Mom away. This time it was to the dreaded *Kempeitai*. Letta and I were sure we would never see our mother again. To everyone's surprise, after interrogating her, they let her go. They had indeed found out about the prison guard smuggling letters and money in and out of jail and about Mom paying him to assist her. The guard was badly beaten and jailed. We later heard that he died in prison. It was amazing that my mother got away.

In October 1944, Mom found out that my father and other prisoners had been relocated to a large prison in Malang. She decided to follow him there. With the help of an old friend, my mother found a place for us to move in. It was an annex to a house consisting of a small living room, bedroom, bath and WC. We packed only a few suitcases with whatever clothes we still had, some personal belongings, our mattresses, a couple of Indonesian hibachis, and a few pots, plates and cups. Mom sold the last of our furniture. There was a tearful farewell from Min and Napsia, who could not come along this time.

Our landlady was Mrs. Arnold, who lived in the main house with her small daughter. She had had the bright idea, when brassieres became a hard-to-find article of clothing, to make them herself and to sell them. It was such a success that she soon employed several women to meet the demand.

There were two women who sold all kinds of hand-crafted items. Everyone became very inventive and learned to do the most with the scarce resources we had. We no longer owned leather shoes. Consequently, one lady had an Indonesian clog maker adapt the Indonesian clog into a high-heeled platform sandal, complete with a wide canvas band across the toes. These bands were decorated with embroidery. I earned a few *rupiahs* (Indonesian money) by selling the embroidery and the paint work I did. Mom also made some money by embroidering bras. Embroidered bras were a hot item, often purchased by the mistresses of the Japanese occupying forces, military as well as civilian. Some women knitted handbags from coconut fiber twine, lined with a fine grass matting. Another lady made bowls out of old wax gramophone records, and I decorated these with flower designs using a box of stencil paints that my mother had found somewhere.

We found out later that my father's prison had small, overcrowded cells; the men had to sleep on concrete slabs without mattresses. Malang is a mountain town, and the nights were cold. The toilet was a hole over a sewer, which was crawling with roaches and rats. If a prison inmate broke any rule whatsoever, he was tortured and sometimes even beheaded.

After we had settled in somewhat, we started to make a few new friends. There were two sisters who lived close by and who gave us a few pieces of furniture for our "living room." We ran into the minister's wife from Probolinggo, her two daughters and son, a French hairdresser, and a few others.

As mentioned earlier, there was a scarcity of just about every commodity. My sister Letta did most of the waiting in line for rice, sugar, or watered-down milk. Once a week we were allotted a very small loaf of "bread." It tasted like sawdust and glue; the inside was all gray and gooey. Nevertheless, we toasted and ate it. Once in a great while we managed to buy a dozen eggs, which we conserved in a chalky, alkaline water solution.

There was an edible, leafy plant that was commonly used as a border in vegetable gardens. People started to eat it. From time to time we got hold of a few bean curd cakes. Once in a while, early in the morning, an Indonesian women would come by selling sweets made of yams, tapioca, sticky rice, coconut, and sesame seeds. Mom would buy us a few goodies for breakfast.

We were forced to join the air brigades and to learn first aid and how to put out fires. All of this was without the benefit of any equipment—even bandages or medicine—so these exercises were really pretty silly. We did a lot of marching and were taught to sing the Japanese national anthem, the *Kimi ga yo.*

All cars had long since been confiscated, and there was hardly any gasoline. We got around in ricksha-like vehicles based on bicycles. A seat in front held two people, and the driver in the rear pedaled to keep the contraption moving. Proper rubber bicycle tires were no longer available so these they had solid strips of hard rubber for tires, which made for a bumpy ride.

It was getting harder for people outside of the camps to make a living. But help was on the way. A Chinese businessman offered Mom sufficient money to support us. If I remember it correctly, she received a certain sum monthly until the end of the war. This was done very secretly, so neither the Japanese police nor the *Kempeitai* ever found out.

We tried to carry on with our lives as best we could. Through the underground grapevine we heard of more and more people dying in camps and prisons. There were two women who still had a clandestine radio, and from time to time they would pass on news about the war to a select few. But it seemed that our Allies were not always doing well, and progress was slow.

In April 1945, mother found out that my father had been moved again, this time to Ambarawa, a small mountain town in Central Java. *Tenno Heika*'s birthday was coming up again, and that meant that the prisoners would be allowed visitors. Mom was determined to make the journey and to see Dad in order to bring him food and medicine, if she could get any. To be able to travel, she needed a special permit from the chief of police in Malang. Mom managed to get her travel permit. We were allowed to stay in Ambarawa for about one month. Mom was able to obtain the name and address of a woman in Ambarawa, Mrs. van Lawick, who could provide us with room and board. We were very pleased.

We packed two small suitcases and a couple of bags so that we could carry our own luggage. Our Japanese neighbor, a civilian official, Takabatake-san, came over to give my mother vitamin B tablets. All the men in prison were suffering from beriberi, so Mom was grateful for the gift. Mom wore a lightweight coat and she sewed most of the money into the hem, carrying only enough to pay for the trip in her purse. I was sure she had been given extra money by our Chinese benefactor for this trip.

On the departure day we were at the railroad station very early to buy tickets and, we hoped, to board a train that same day. Trains were now few and far between and packed to capacity with people and baggage. We got on, but there were no seats for us so we had to stand. After an hour or two, we started to get very tired. After all, we were malnourished and our endurance was low. It was also very hot inside the compartment, because the train was shuttered and there was little air circulation.

After a few stops, a couple of Japanese soldiers entered and commandeered seats from the Indonesian passengers. Then they noticed us standing. We must have been the only European-looking women on the entire train. They ordered several people to give us their seats. I was surprised.

We thanked the soldiers for their help, since we were starting to feel faint from the heat, hunger, and thirst. Luckily, at the next station we were able to buy some food and drink from street vendors on the platform. Obviously, this was at our own risk. We could get sick, because flies were crawling all over their wares.

We stayed overnight in Yogyakarta with an old friend of my mother's. Early next morning, we boarded a train to Ambarawa. In Ambarawa we located Mrs. Van Lawick's residence in a native village. Narrow earth and cobblestone paths wound up and down the hillside leading to it. Canine and human excrement lay everywhere. The house was a typical village house with partially cemented walls, the remainder being made of bamboo and wood. There were hard earthen floors and a primitive toilet where you had to squat over a hole in the floor. Mrs. Van Lawick told us that farther down the path, two homes had recently been burned to the ground because the residents had died from bubonic plague. For a reasonable sum of money, Mrs. van Lawick provided us with a room and washed our clothes.

The three of us shared one large iron bed. The next morning my mother said she had not been able to sleep all night because she had been bothered by bedbugs. Letta and I had not felt a thing, but out of curiosity we looked underneath the mattress. Sure enough, there was a whole army of them, hiding and waiting to feast on our blood at night.

My mother started shopping for food to prepare for visiting day. In the main street, we saw two dead bodies, bloated and covered with flies. No one seemed to bother to remove them. We also saw carts coming from internment camps, each loaded with 10 or 12 crude wooden coffins, on their way to mass graves. People in camp were now dying by the dozen daily from hunger and disease.

For visiting day on April 29, Mom filled two baskets with the best food she could buy: fruit, tofu, cooked brown rice, chicken cooked in coconut milk, a few sweets, sugar and Takabatake-san's vitamins. We went early in the morning to Benteng prison, a little way out of town. Other visitors joined us. We followed a pleasant, wooded mountain path, shaded by tall trees, with flowers blooming and blue mountaintops in the far distance. Suddenly, we came upon the prison, a forbidding, grey, fortlike structure.

We were very apprehensive as to how this visit was going to come off. First, we were let in through the iron gates. Our food baskets, clearly labeled with the name of the prisoner, were thoroughly searched for contraband and taken away. Later we heard that much of the content was stolen before it reached the men, either by the guards or by other hungry prisoners.

Then the visitors, after identifying the person they wanted to see, were herded to another part of the prison buildings. We could see prisoners walking about. They were dressed in loose tops and knee-length pants made from gunny sack material and they were barefoot. All were skin and bones, tanned from sun exposure, heads shaven. Many were covered with tropical sores and suffering from scurvy. We stopped at a short distance from a small building. It had a front room with a window. One by one, a prisoner would appear in front of the window and his name would be announced. His visitor could then talk to him for a few minutes but only in Malay. No Dutch was allowed.

Finally my father showed up. Mom had told us not to cry and to act as cheerful as possible. For a few seconds, we were speechless with shock. I did not recognize him, with his head shaven, in his drab prison clothes, and swollen with beriberi. He had to be assisted to come to the window. I do not remember what I said. I must have uttered a few words of greeting and told him not to give up hope. Our time was soon over; we waved good-bye as two other fellow prisoners led him away. Terribly depressed, we all went back to Mrs. Van Lawick's. We were too much in shock to cry.

We were allowed to bring a food basket to the prison once a week, but there were no further visits. Through Mrs. Van Lawick, though, Mom had found a prison guard who was willing to smuggle letters. She received about three, but they had to be destroyed after reading. She told Letta and me that Pops did not think he would come out alive. He was very weak and ill with beriberi.

On May 28, 1945, my father died, a few months before the end of the war. When my mother heard the news, she sat down with us. We all cried when we heard of the terrible circumstances in which he had died, all alone. Mom could claim his body for burial outside the prison. Otherwise he would have been buried in a mass grave. With the help of Mrs. Van Lawick's friends, who knew the Indonesian priest in Ambarawa, my father was buried in the Catholic cemetery. Many years later, an Indonesian friend of mine visited Ambarawa and looked for this cemetery, but he could not find a trace of it.

Our permit was running out, so we had to leave Ambarawa. By now Mom had succumbed to all the stress and was feeling ill. We were all very depressed, and days went by in a blur. We went home by way of Semarang, Central Java. I do not remember much of the train ride, but we arrived in Surabaya on Uncle Pierre and Aunt Margot's doorsteps covered with head lice. Our hair was doused with kerosene, and we were marched to the bathroom for a cleansing bath. We stayed with them for about a week to recuperate. Then we went by train to Malang. The train was packed again as usual. There were no seats, and I stood next to a man covered with running sores with crusts of pus. I fainted but made it home, again crawling with lice.

The day after, August 9, 1945, our neighbor, Takabatake-san, told my mother with tears in his eyes that his wife and children in Nagasaki were all dead. The Americans had dropped a terrible bomb on the city, and it was totally destroyed. None of us had a clue at that time that this was the atom bomb, the bomb that also saved so many lives.

On August 15, Japan at long last capitulated. Takabatake-san told Mom that the war was finally over and that he was going home. He offered us the use of his house and all that was in it, but Mom politely declined the kind offer.

Malang was now deserted by the Japanese. The small European and Dutch-Indonesian community was hoping that we would soon see our Allied armies take over control of the city. We were in for a long wait. A swift takeover to free the people in prisons and camps was bungled by the Allies, resulting in the murder of many of these people by radical Indonesians. During this Bersiap period, preparatory to the declaration of Indonesian independence, the Indonesians were eager to fill the void and declare Indonesia's *merdeka* (freedom).

Quite a few people in the prisons and camps, no longer seeing the Japanese sentries at the gates, made their way out, and several of our friends came back to Malang. It was a time of great uncertainty and unrest. We were left to fend for ourselves. In September, my mother found an abandoned house. It was filthy, but it had a few pieces of furniture in it. We cleaned up the interior, and when the former bank manager and his son returned from camp, they moved in with us. More people started to move into abandoned houses to await further developments.

Sometime in October or November 1945, one of the more moderate Indonesian factions must have taken command. Barbed wire fences were erected again, marking off certain areas of town. All women and children went into these protection camps; the men and older boys once again found themselves in prison. The three of us shared a room in a house where several of our friends already had moved. We called our camp euphemistically "*De Wijk*" (neighborhood). This time every-one—Dutch, Dutch-Indonesian, and other nationalities—was interned. Some non–Dutch nationals were given a pass which allowed them to venture outside the fence. Being French, my mother obtained such a pass, and we used to go to the market. After the Japanese army had left so suddenly, more food became available.

Someone had donated an old baby carriage with a hollow bottom. We took it to the market and filled the bottom portion with extra food supplies, always placing our allotted purchases on top. The extras were shared with our friends who did not get permission to leave camp. The Indonesian authorities distributed food to the women in camp, but it was insufficient and of poor quality.

One day Letta went to the market alone, and when she returned through the gate, the sentry searched the buggy and discovered the hidden compartment, containing the extra food. He threatened to run her through with his bayonet. The buggy was confiscated. She came home badly shaken. Alas, this was the untimely end of our smuggling efforts.

By the end of 1945, negotiations had started between the Red Cross and the Indonesian authorities for an eventual evacuation of the Europeans. A Swiss gentleman in Malang, the representative of the Red Cross, started to organize matters. All non–Dutch Europeans were released from prison or camp. We also had to leave "*De Wijk*," and Mom was told to move into a certain house where we occupied a room over the garage. We could no longer visit with our friends in camp.

In February 1946, Mom met Monsieur Dupuis, a Frenchman who lived alone in a large house. He offered her a room in his house, and she accepted. All went well until our two Chinese friends invited the three of us to see *Gone with the Wind*, the first American movie to be shown since the Japanese occupation. Of course we gladly accepted his invitation. However, when the gentlemen delivered us home that evening, we found that Monsieur Dupuis had locked us out. He refused to answer our calls. For some mysterious reason, he was furious with Mom for having gone to the movie. He banned us from the house, but allowed us to live temporarily in his garage. Soon thereafter, we moved to another garage, closer to the former camp.

Because of the bad shape most internees were in upon their release and the fear of increased hostility, the Dutch government decided to repatriate as many of its citizens as possible from the Indies to the Netherlands. These included many who were born and raised in the colony and who had never been in the Netherlands before.

Final preparations for complete evacuation were now being made. We kept only the barest of necessities, like our mattresses, a hibachi, two pots, a few plates and cups, and some cutlery. However, the Indonesian authorities would not let the Allied troops come to Malang to evacuate us. The deal was that the new Indonesian army would put us on transport to the town of Surakarta, Central Java, which had a small airstrip. From there, British planes would fly us to Jakarta. The morning of June 20, 1946, we had to be at the gate with only what we could carry ourselves. Our motley group of women and children in our oft-mended clothes, worn suitcases, and bundles of goods was loaded onto trucks and driven to the train station. We took off with a few Indonesian soldiers to keep order and to protect us from possible attacks by hostile natives.

After arrival, we were taken to a place near the airstrip, where there were a few run-down, barracks-style buildings. Here we stayed until the planes arrived to fly us out. The building had no doors. Low bamboo cots ran along each wall. In the center of the building was some crude shelving on which we placed our luggage. Communal toilets were outside and there was a well where we could wash up. A soup kitchen had been set up where meager meals were served. We spent two days here before we could board a plane. There were only a few flights per day, and the planes were small. Only narrow benches were available. Two British soldiers kept an eye on us, while they themselves practically hung out the open door.

We finally landed in Jakarta, and were taken to a Red Cross camp. We were first registered to facilitate reunion of families, separated during the war. Subsequently, we were doused with DDT to delouse us and then were assigned a place in shared rooms. On our first day we were each issued a loaf of real white bread and real butter! We ate the whole thing in one sitting. We also got K-rations, those military cartons containing all sorts of goodies, like powdered milk, biscuits, soap, toothpaste, and even chocolate and cigarettes. Next we received clothing, one new cheap cotton dress and two used ones in excellent condition, a pair of saddle shoes, and some underwear.

Sukarno had declared the independence of Indonesia on August 17, 1945 and had appointed himself as president of the new Republic.

This action was at first not recognized by the Dutch government. After the Japanese surrender, the Allied forces occupied some of the larger cities, such as Jakarta and Surabaya. The British had sent a great number of their troops from India to Indonesia, and Jakarta was swarming with these majestic-looking Sikhs and fierce-looking Gurkhas.

After a few days in the Jakarta Red Cross camp, a Mr. Smith from the Netherlands-Indies Bank came to pick us up. He had a house and offered us a room until departure for the Netherlands. On August 5, he took the three of us to the *Harmonie*, the former Dutch club, to celebrate Princess Irene's birthday. We received improved food rations now and started to feel a bit better. Via the Red Cross, Mom finally received news that my brother Rico was safe and healthy.

On August 11, 1946, we boarded the *Boschfontein* with about 300 other women and children. Slowly the ship began to move away from shore. We all stood silently at the railing as Gershwin's "Rhapsody in Blue" was playing over the ship's loudspeakers. Slowly Java's coastline disappeared in the distance. I was never to see the land of my birth again. Now, whenever I hear "Rhapsody in Blue," it still makes me feel sad.

ABOUT THE CONTRIBUTOR

J. Alexandra Humphrey-Spier was born in 1926 in Jakarta. Her father was transferred frequently and they lived in Cirebon, Pasuruan, Surabaya, Pekalongan and Probolinggo. She was repatriated to the Netherlands in 1946 where she completed high school and business college after which she started her career as secretary.

She emigrated to Canada in 1955 and finally went to the United States in 1967. She currently lives in Oakland, California, and she has been retired since 1989.

AMANI J. FLIERS-HOEKE

The Missing Years

I don't ever remember being three, four or five.

There are no pictures of me between the ages of one and six. I have a few pictures showing me in my mother's arms, just a few weeks old, and some with my two older sisters. The last picture dates from 1940 when I was smiling—no, laughing—at the world and the camera. After that, I must have disappeared, because the next picture is from 1945. I am smiling again, but cautiously this time.

I was a happy, easy baby, my mother confessed. But did she know that later on I was frightened and scarred from being lost for five long years?

Looking at my baby pictures, I marvel about the fact that I do have some small mementos from before the war. My mother or someone else must have been brave to have saved them, for it was forbidden to keep photographs in the camps during the war. At least, I was told that.

I was told many other stories about the camp where my mother and my two older sisters must have been all those years when I seemed to have disappeared. Stories spin around in my head when I am quiet and alone. I wonder what is truth and what is fantasy. I actually don't care, because to me these lost years are lost. I can never get them back.

I had such skinny legs and a swollen belly, my aunt told me. Dysentery and sores all over my tiny body and a constant cough, my mother said. I don't remember, but they told me it was true. I even had to go to the camp hospital, or whatever that death house was called. More women and children never returned from there than did, I was told. My sisters looked the same or worse, but I do not remember them.

But what do I pull out of the cobwebs of my mind late at night? Sounds, smells, hunger pangs, sensations and shards of pictures still stick in my head. Is that why I always had headaches when I was growing up? I hear myself begging for only one grain of rice from the grown-ups. Or did I steal one from my sisters' bowl? I must have done something, because I still feel guilty, yet I don't really remember how or when it happened. I feel crawling sensations on my skin that irritate me to the point of repulsion when I see a stream of ants or other bugs, let alone the sight of cockroaches! Why do they stick to my skin and why do I want to kill them right away? Is it because we were covered with lice in the camps? Nowadays, there is nothing I like better than to take a shower and put on clean clothes, or swim and feel the cleansing water against my body. Why do I hate big shiny boots and the clicking sound they make when they touch? And I still have a dislike for barbed wire fences. And why do I still startle so quickly at the sound of loud noises?

But I do like to eat Japanese food, I like driving their cars, I have Japanese-American friends, I love Japanese art and their sense of culture. I laugh at Amy Hill, the Japanese-American comedienne. Am I weird or perverse? Or is it war that changes a human being so completely and allows us to have different standards? Why do I cry when I see small children from war-torn countries on television or in the movies? Their frightened eyes and skinny legs remind me of some child I used to know and somehow disappeared.

But wait. I *do* remember! I see a tiny girl sitting on a fence alongside a dirt road, waiting in a blazing hot afternoon for her mother to come back from kitchen duty in camp. In the distance a tired, skinny woman is approaching. She looks slightly lopsided. The girl waits patiently—or is she too exhausted to run towards her mother? She also sees a Japanese soldier on a bicycle coming. Then she panics! The soldier throws down his bike and starts hitting her mother hard in the face, first right, then left: he yells at her. She sinks to her knees. He keeps barking at her and as she stumbles to her feet, she bows three times and shouts the required salute in Japanese. The little girl walks towards her, frightened and confused, but she does not cry. The soldier wants to know why her mother is not working and why she did not bow to him before. Her mother explains in perfect Indonesian that she is just returning from kitchen duty and that she did not see him coming. By that time the girl has grabbed her mother's hand and the soldier, seeing that the child is frightened and harmless, kicks his bike with his big black boots and rides off on the hot and dusty road.

I told this story to my mother some ten years later. She did not remember. It must have been one of many such incidents for her and other women in the camps. I sadly let it rest.

Some 30 years later I told my own children this story. It was so utterly incomprehensible to them that I don't know if they will remember this really happened to their mother or grandmother so long ago. And maybe my grandchildren will never even know about Japanese concentration camps in some faraway tropical island called Java.

Yet I still don't remember ever being three, four or even five.

ABOUT THE CONTRIBUTOR

Amani J. Fliers was born on February 21, 1939, in Jakarta, Indonesia. She attended elementary schools in Palembang, Sumatra and Hilversum, the Netherlands. She continued her higher education in Amsterdam and worked as executive secretary at the Koninklijk Instituut voor de Tropen in Amsterdam.

She emigrated to the United States in 1960, settling in Los Angeles. She found employment as a medical secretary and later on she continued her education at Moorpark College and California State University, Northridge, earning a BA degree in psychology and a master of fine arts degree in painting and photography. She taught at Moorpark College, Pierce College and California Lutheran College, and is presently a professor of art and photography at Moorpark College.

She has curated many exhibits and been a guest lecturer at CalTech's YES program for three years. She has exhibited numerous award-winning paintings, photographs and computer artworks.

Presently she resides in Thousand Oaks, California, and has two children and two granddaughters.

Joyce F. Kater-Hoeke

Liberated, Yet Not Free

It was in March of 1945 that I had my tenth birthday. It was in a Japanese concentration camp called Lampersarie in Semarang, Central Java, in what is now called Indonesia. The Second World War in the Pacific would not end until five months later when the devastating atom bombs, developed and prepared in a remote mountain village in New Mexico, would force Japan to finally surrender. In the wake of this war, these beautiful islands and their people would be left in chaos and turmoil.

During these last five months, life in this concentration camp would go from bad to worse, leaving many women and children dead or very near death. I survived, but barely.

Of all my 60 birthdays, I remember this particular one the best, because of that bottomless hopelessness I felt so deeply that day. I stood by the scrawny little tree in the front yard of the stone house which we had to share with about 40 other women and children.

I still see myself standing there, intensely realizing what day it was, where and who I was—a young girl, her body growing more skeleton-like every day, wrecked with dysentery and tropical sores. The complete absence of schooling and medical care during these years had taken a heavy toll on the children. On every prisoner's mind was one question: "When, when will it all end?"

Every day was the same and yet a little worse than the day before. In the morning, there was the usual roll call, the forced exercises, and then the long wait for kitchen personnel to show up with their buckets of camp "food," consisting primarily of a gluelike porridge and some bread or a bowl of cooked rice in ever-decreasing amounts. The portions were made even smaller by putting marbles in the bottom of the measuring cup. This was an ingenious way to slowly starve us to death.

My still beautiful mother, my two younger sisters and I lived in the small garage of this house, together with seven other women. We slept on bedbug-infested mattresses on the floor. Numerous ticks were visible on the walls, but what was probably the worst of all were the lice we had in every fold of our clothing. The dirty feeling this gave me I will never forget.

The house had one bathroom with one overflowing toilet for all these people to use. Dysentery was everybody's disease and it was easily spread by lack of water and the deplorable sanitary conditions. The situation was the same in all the other houses. At night, we had to relieve ourselves in a large tin can in our garage.

How could life have changed so drastically for us in just a couple of years? For my family it started in April 1942 when Japanese soldiers came to our house and took my father away to a men's concentration camp. Not long thereafter my mother and her three daughters were sent to the Cihapit women's camp in Bandung, West Java. We were allowed to bring food, clothing, toys, etc., but upon arrival we found out that all we had was just one small room which we had to share with another woman and her teenage daughter. I can still visualize this woman endlessly writing all day on sheets of paper. "She is communicating with the spirits," my mother explained.

The first few months in this camp were like a great adventure for us kids. There were no schools and no doctors, and we had all day to play and run around. Food was not a problem yet, and many women could even cook some meals on a little charcoal stove outside the house. The use of electricity and radios was absolutely forbidden. One woman who dared to use an electric iron was burned with it "to teach her a lesson."

Gradually things started to deteriorate, especially towards the end of our stay here. Rumors were going around that women were being beaten as punishment for all kinds of real or imagined offenses.

One of the more pleasant memories I had of this period in my life was that of my mother and I walking in the early morning darkness to the church for my first communion. I was wearing a pretty white dress with blue embroidered flowers that my mother managed to make while in camp. Another memorable event was a Christmas celebration, complete with a small decorated tree, in another home.

Then one day we had to leave this camp. With just minimal clothing we had to travel in a boarded-up train two days and one night to the other end of Java. I clutched my little doll and wondered what was to come next. We did not know then that the camp we just left would be considered bearable in comparison with the next camp. But it was very comforting to be with my mother and sisters.

My thoughts went back to the last days in camp during this long train journey. We three girls went "treasure hunting" in the many deserted houses recently vacated by those who left before us. Many women had burned the possessions they were forced to leave behind, and thick smoke filled the air. When it was our turn, we left most of our things behind. I still have a small green beaded necklace I found somewhere which has become a reminder of those dark days.

The second camp was already filled to capacity, but the women had to make room for us new arrivals. This camp was worse. We were forced to do manual labor in the fields outside the camp, while the children had to keep the ditches inside clean, among other chores. On one occasion my mother returned deathly ill from eating a poisonous root found in the fields.

Then the rumors started. Japan had lost the war, but at that time we did not know of the atom bomb. Finally, the end of our internment came and we started receiving Red Cross packages filled with such treasures as corned beef, canned salmon, cheese and powdered milk. Because of the unsettled conditions outside the camp, we were advised to stay inside until further notice. We were liberated, yet not free. The mood was festive, yet mixed with uncertainty.

In the meantime, we started to trade clothing for food with the native population. They needed clothes and all we wanted was food, so over the bamboo fences chickens came flying, followed by bananas and coconuts and other things, in exchange for clothes, which we had stashed away until liberation day. It was a scene I'll never forget!

My aunt, who lived in Semarang but was not aware that her sister and nieces were held in a camp nearby, was notified that we were about to be released. There she was standing at the gate with a box full of edible goodies! We stayed at her home for about a week to recuperate. We were already getting sick from too much food too soon. As a precaution, she had to lock the kitchen door.

The Indonesian independence movement, stirred up during the Japanese occupation, was now picking up momentum, and the situation was getting very unsafe for us. My mother was advised to return to Bandung as soon as possible, so the four of us left again by train after this short stay at my aunt's house. During this trip, we had to endure taunting remarks from the native passengers on the train, but we made it safely back.

In Bandung we were reunited with our father. We never knew what had happened to him since he was arrested, and whether he had survived the camps or not. We were a complete family again. We three girls had to adjust to the fact that there were now again two parents in our life. Many families were incomplete or torn apart as a result of the war, so we were very fortunate. My father had been in the same camp as his father-in-law, but he had to give my mother the sad news of her father's death there.

It was a strange and dangerous year that followed. At night, the Indonesian freedom fighters were roaming around in the city, setting many houses on fire. Gunshots could be heard until dawn. During the day, we attended a makeshift school, but when it started to get dark, we had to retreat to better protected areas for our own safety.

Life for all of us had become completely different from that in the prewar era, and things would never be the same again. We had lost not only most of our possessions, our health, and a life in one of the most blessed places on earth, but also our innocence and the sense of being at home in the land where we were born and raised.

Now, half a century later, the longing to somehow reconnect the ties that still exist is always there in my heart. But that young girl from long ago, is now residing and doing well in her new homeland, the United States of America. Here, in the state of New Mexico, with a beauty all its own, she lives with her own family not too far from that same mountain village where the scientists produced those fateful bombs that ended the war in the Pacific and changed the world forever.

ABOUT THE CONTRIBUTOR

Born of Dutch-Indonesian parents in the capital of the former Dutch East Indies on March 5, 1935, Joyce Faye Kater-Hoeke spent a happy childhood with her two younger sisters in Indonesia until March 1942 when Japanese forces occupied and destroyed this part of Asia. A period of two and one-half years in Japanese concentration camps on Java followed, leaving a lasting effect on her and her loved ones.

She finished her schooling in Amsterdam, and after graduating in 1954, she worked as a secretary in various companies until her move to Washington, D.C., where she held a secretarial job at the Dutch embassy for five and one-half years.

She married Robert Kater in 1969, and she has two grown children. She has lived with her husband in Kirtland, New Mexico since 1979. She worked as a teacher's aide in the local grade school until her recent retirement. She devotes her time to creative hobbies including painting and ceramic decorations.

APPENDIX I

CHRONOLOGICAL SUMMARY OF EVENTS IN THE FORMER DUTCH EAST INDIES FROM DECEMBER 3, 1941, TO DECEMBER 31, 1942

December 3, 1941:   Mobilization of the Nederlandse Militaire Luchtvaart (Dutch Royal Air Force).

December 7, 1941:   The battle of Pearl Harbor.
                     The Dutch government declares war on Japan.

December 10, 1941:   Successful Japanese landing in the Philippines.
                     Loss of the British battleship *Repulse* and the *Prince of Wales* off east coast of Malaysia.

December 16, 1941:   Miri in British North Borneo (Serawak) occupied.

December 17, 1941:   Landing of Allied military forces (two-thirds Dutch and one-third Australian troops) on Portuguese island Timor near Dilli takes place without any resistance.

December 19, 1941:   Bombardment of Pontianak (Kalimantan) with extensive damage and 500 persons wounded or dead.

December 21, 1941:   Bombardment of airfield Singkawang II in West Borneo (now Kalimantan.)

December 23, 1941:   Second bombardment of airfield Singkawang II.

Source: Gedenkboek van de KNIL, *Amersfoort: N.V. Drukkerij G.J. van Ameron-gen & Co., 1961. Translated by Denis Dutrieux and used by permission of Verenig-ing Madjoe in Holland.*

December 24, 1941:   Kuching in British North Borneo (Serawak) occupied
                     by Japanese forces.
December 25, 1941:   Third bombardment of airfield Singkawang II.
December 27, 1941:   Occupation of the Tambelan Islands west of Kali-
                     mantan by Japanese forces.
December 29, 1941:   The 2nd battalion of the 15th Regiment Punjabi,
                     defenders of Miri and Kuching, falls back on
                     Singkawang II after suffering considerable losses.
December 31, 1941:   Japanese fighters machine gun the harbor and airfield
                     of Tarakan Island and surrounding area of Menado
                     off East Kalimantan (Sulawesi).
January 1, 1942:   Start of guerrilla activities in West Kalimantan.
January 3, 1942:   British General Sir Archibald P. Wavell is appointed
                     commander-in-chief of the American, British,
                     Dutch and Australian forces.
January 4, 1942:   Successful attack by eight Flying Fortresses from air-
                     field in Malang, East Java, on the Japanese fleet near
                     Davao (Mindanao), Philippines.
January 5, 1942:   Occupation of Brunei and the island of Labuan off
                     Sabah.
January 8, 1942:   Bombardment of Tarakan Island.
                     Repeat bombardment of Davao.
January 9, 1942:   Occupation of the island of Jolo, southwest of Min-
                     danao.
                     Repeat bombardment of Tarakan.
January 10, 1942:   General Wavell arrives in Java.
                     Bombardment of airfield near Balikpapan, Kalimantan.
January 11, 1942:   Landing in Menado (Sulawesi).
                     Landing of paratroopers in Menado.
                     Landings in Tarakan.
January 12, 1942:   Dutch troops capitulate in Tarakan after heavy fight-
                     ing.
                     Dutch troops in Menado move inland to wage guerilla
                     war.
                     Heavy bombardment of Ternate (Molucca).
January 13, 1942:   Bombardment of harbor of Balikpapan.
                     Heavy bombardment of airfield near Ambon.
January 15, 1942:   Bombardment of Balikpapan.
                     Bombardment of airfield near Ambon.
January 16, 1942:   Bombardment of Kendari II airfield near Medan, area
                     near Balikpapan and the harbor of Ambon.
January 17, 1942:   Bombardment of airfields in Pakanbaru (Sumatra),
                     Dilli (Timor) and Ambon.
January 18, 1942:   Airfield Singkawang II destroyed.
                     Bombing raid on Balikpapan.

	Arrival in Malaysia of four brigades of Dutch Corps Marachaussee from Aceh, north Sumatra, for guerrilla activities behind enemy lines.
January 19, 1942:	Bombardment of Sabang and Bandjarmasin.
January 20, 1942:	Military forces in Balikpapan receive an ultimatum from the Japanese commander of Tarakan. Military commander in Balikpapan orders destruction of the oil installation and manufacturing center.
	Bombardment of Medan and Bandjarmasin.
January 21, 1942:	Bombardment of Sabang and Belawan (Medan harbor), Sumatra.
January 22, 1942:	Second bombardment of Sabang and Belawan.
January 23, 1942:	Dutch bombers launch a successful air raid on transport fleet in Makassar Strait near Balikpapan.
	Bombardments of Samarinda and Manokwari (Irian Jaya).
January 24, 1942:	Landing and occupation of Balikpapan.
	Bombardment of airfield Samarinda II.
	Landing on eastern shore of southeast Sulawesi and conquest of airport Kendari II.
January 25, 1942:	Heavy bombardment of Ambon and airfield Samarinda II.
	Bombardment of airfield Namlea (Buru Island).
January 26, 1942:	Bombardment of Sabang, airfield Samarinda II and airfields near Ujung Padang (Sulawesi) and in Timor.
	Landing on west coast of Kalimantan.
January 27, 1942:	Bombardment of Padang harbor and airfields near Bandjarmasin and Namlea.
	Landing in West Kalimantan near Singkawang.
January 28, 1942:	Bombardment of Bangka, Belitung (off Sumatra's east coast), harbor of Padang and airports in Sulawesi.
January 29, 1942:	Bombardment of Sabang and Padang.
	Occupation of Pontianak, Kalimantan.
January 30, 1942:	Bombardment of Ambon, Sabang and airports in southeast Kalimantan and Timor.
January 31, 1942:	Superior Japanese troops land on the north and south coasts of the island of Ambon.
February 1, 1942:	City of Ambon occupied.
	Heavy bombardment of Palembang (Sumatra) and the airfields near Timor Kupang.
	Japanese advance to Bandjarmasin.
February 3, 1942:	Bombardment of Surabaya and the airfields near Malang and Madiun in East Java.
	The Japanese occupy Samarinda (Kalimantan).

February 4, 1942:   Bombardment of Timor Kupang.

February 5, 1942:   Bombardment of Ujung Padang and vicinity, Timor
                       Kupang, Surabaya, airfields Denpasar (Bali) and
                       near Palembang.

February 7, 1942:   Bombardment of the airfields near Palembang. A
                       considerable number of British airplanes are lost.
                       Bombardment of airfield near Bogor, West Java.
                       Bombardment of Surabaya, East Java.
                       Ambon falls into Japanese hands.

February 8, 1942:   Bombardment of airfield near Palembang.
                       Destruction of Bandjarmasin and nearby airfield.

February 9, 1942:   Landing of Japanese troops on the west coast of Celebes
                       near Ujung Padang.
                       Bombardments of airfields in the vicinity of Jakarta,
                       Pakanbaru (Sumatra) and Malang.
                       Japanese troops land on the north side of Singapore
                       Island.

February 11, 1942:   Oil installations in Pulusambu (south of Singapore,)
                       Pangkalanberandan and Pangkalansusu (Sumatra)
                       destroyed according to plans.

February 12, 1942:   Airfield Namlea occupied by Japanese forces.

February 13, 1942:   Bombardment of airfields in Timor and Sumatra.
                       Bandjarmasin occupied by enemy forces.

February 14, 1942:   Japanese paratroopers land in the vicinity of Palembang
                       but are driven off by Dutch troops.
                       Dutch forces leave the Riau Archipelago en route
                       to south Sumatra after execution of demolitions.

February 15, 1942:   Japanese forces land in the vicinity of Palembang.
                       Demolitions of Sungaigerong (Sumatra) emplace-
                       ments executed.
                       Fall of Singapore.

February 16, 1942:   Dutch airplanes partially destroy an oil emplacement
                       in Plaju, Sumatra.

February 17, 1942:   Heavy bombardment of Timor Kupang. Enemy trans-
                       port approaches Timor Kupang. Planned demoli-
                       tion is carried out.

February 18, 1942:   Heavy bombardment of Surabaya. Japanese forces land
                       on Bali. Den Pasar occupied.

February 19, 1942:   Heavy bombardment of airfields near Bogor and
                       Bandung, West Java.
                       Bombardment of airfields in Kalijati and near Malang.
                       Babo (Irian Jaya) occupied by Japanese forces.
                       Landing of Japanese paratroopers near Timor
                       Kupang.
                       Night landing of Japanese troops west of Timor Dilli.

February 21, 1942:   Timor Kupang occupied by enemy.
                      Bombardment of Surabaya, Malang, Madiun, and airfield Kalijati.
February 22, 1942:   Bombardment of airfields near Jakarta, Bogor, Yogyakarta and Malang.
February 23, 1942:   Bombardment of airfield near Malang.
February 24, 1942:   Bombardment of Tandjungpriok and Surabaya, airfields near Batavia (Jakarta) and Kalijati.
February 25, 1942:   Bangka occupied by Japanese forces.
February 27, 1942:   Bombardment of Tandjungpriok and airfield near Bogor.
                      Aircraft carrier *Langly* with 30 ready-to-use fighters on board sunk by the Japanese.
                      The Battle of the Java Sea lost.
February 28, 1942:   Bombardment of airfields near Surabaya.
March 1, 1942:   Landing of approximately seven Japanese divisions on Java in northwest Banten, near Eretan, west of Indramayu and in Kragan, east of Rembang.
                      Japanese take Subang and the airfield in Kalijati by surprise.
March 4, 1942:   Heavy bombardments in the mountain passes north of Bandung.
                      Tangerang (west of Jakarta), Leuwillang (west of Bogor), Cikampek, Blora, Cepoe and Bojonegoro occupied by Japanese.
                      Air raid on Cilacap, Central Java.
March 5, 1942:   Jakarta declared an open city and occupied by Japanese forces.
                      Heavy bombardment of Cilacap.
                      Bombardment of Bandung.
                      Surakarta occupied by the Japanese.
March 6, 1942:   Bombardment of Bandung and vicinity.
March 7, 1942:   State of affairs in Java very precarious.
                      Bandung threatened.
                      No Dutch air support available.
March 8, 1942:   Under threat of complete destruction of Bandung, Dutch forces decide to capitulate.
March 9, 1942:   Commander of the Dutch forces in central Sumatra decides to continue fighting in order to force prolonged stay of Japanese troops. The fighting in Timor and Central Sulawesi continues.
March 12, 1942:   Landing of Japanese troops on the east coast of Sumatra near Idi and south of Medan near Tandjungtiram.
                      Landing on Sabang.

March 13, 1942:	Medan occupied.
March 17, 1942:	Padang occupied.
March 19, 1942:	Takengon in Aceh (Sumatra) occupied.
March 27, 1942:	Guerrilla troops in central Celebes capitulate.
March 28, 1942:	Military commanders of central and north Sumatra decide to capitulate.
March 29, 1942:	Ternate occupied.
April 1, 1942:	Atambua (Timor) occupied.
April 12, 1942:	Manokwari (Irian Jaya) occupied. Dutch troops go inland and continue guerrilla activities until September 1944.
July 21, 1942:	Dutch and Australian troops reinforce the garrison at Marauke (Irian Jaya).
July 30, 1942:	Landing on Tanimbar Island, Australia.
December 10, 15, 18, 1942:	Evacuation of Allied guerrilla troops from Timor to Australia.
December 31, 1942:	Fighting continues in Irian Jaya.
	One of the Dutch posts was attacked by Papua tribes under direction of Japanese. The Dutch side suffered some losses.

Appendix II

FOREIGN TERMS AND ABBREVIATIONS

ABDA American, British, Dutch and Australian command in the South Pacific

Aceh the northern povince of Sumatra

Ambonese native of the Molucca Islands

AMS (Dutch) Algemene Middelbare School (general middle school)

anjing (Ind.) dog

aza (Jap.) group of city blocks

azacho (Jap.) leader

bagero (Jap.) you idiot!

bandrek (Ind.) hot, spicy extract of ginger root

bango (Jap.) command to start counting off (ichi, ni, san, etc.)

Belanda (Ind.) Dutch person

"benjo e ikimasu" (Jap.) "I am going to the toilet"

Bersiap period formative period of the Indonesian revolution; root is *siap*, meaning ready, or get ready

Bung Karno (Ind.) official nickname for Sukarno. Bung means brother.

bunuh (Ind.) to kill

Bushido code of Japanese conduct

Dai Nippon Japan

Gurkha soldier from Nepal in British service

HBS (Dutch) Hogere Burger School (secondary level school)

hancho (Jap.) district leader

hormat (–ing) (Ind.) pay(ing) hommage, bow(ing)

heiho (Jap.) auxiliary force

Indo person of Dutch-Indonesian ancestry, sometimes called Eurasian

ichi (Jap.) one

jagungan (Ind.) of or pertaining to corn

jahat (Ind.) bad or evil

Jannen (Dutch) troops consisting of pure Dutchmen, "Jan" being a popular first name

jasmi (Jap.) rest

Joyo Boyo Javanese prophet

kampong (Ind.) native village

kaneru (Jap.) stupid!

Kempeitai (Jap.) Japanese military police comparable to the Gestapo

kepis (Ind.) fish basket (referring to Japanese military head gear)

kere (Jap.) command to bow down

Kimi ga yo (Jap.) Japanese national anthem

KNIL (Dutch) Koninklijk Neder-

263

lands-Indisch Leger (Royal Netherlands Indies Army)

kiotske (Jap.)   attention!

konijn (Dutch)   rabbit

kongsi (Chin.)   self support group or cartel

kumicho (Jap.)   prisoners in charge of a tonari kumi

kura (Jap.)   hey you dog!

landstormer (Dutch)   reserve unit consisting of older men

Menadonese   inhabitant of north Sulawesi

Merdeka (Ind.)   free; liberated; freedom

MULO (Dutch)   Meer Uitgebreid Lager Onderwijs (more extended lower instruction)

nasi goreng (Ind.)   fried rice

NICA   Netherlands Indies Civil Administration

NIROM (Dutch)   Nederlands-Indische Radio Omroep Mij. (Netherlands Indies Radio Broadcast Co.)

ni (Jap.)   two

norre (Jap.)   at ease!

Opa (Dutch)   grandpa

pajol (Ind.)   native hoe

Pancasila (Ind.)   five guiding principles of the Indonesian Republic

pasar malam (Ind.)   night market

pap (Dutch)   porridge

peloppor (Ind.)   rebel

pemuda (Ind.)   politicized youth

pisang (Ind.)   banana

potverdomme (Dutch)   damn it!

potverdorie (Dutch)   darn it!

police action(s)   Dutch attempt to restore order in their colonial possessions after the war

Punjabi   soldier from India in British service

RAPWI   Recovery of Allied Prisoners of War and Internees

remusha (Ind.)   Indonesian auxiliary work force

runcing (Ind.)   sharpened bamboo spear

rupiah (Ind.)   Indonesian currency

SEAC   South East Asian Command

san (Jap.)   three

selamat tinggal (Ind.)   farewell

senzo awari (Jap.)   the war is over

Sikh   Indian in British-Indian service

sinjo (Ind.)   boy

Soos (Dutch)   Societeit club

stadwacht (Dutch)   city guard

taiso (Jap.)   calisthenics

tenko (Jap.)   roll call

Tenno Heika (Jap.)   Japanese emperor

Tojo, Hideki   Japan's wartime premier

tonari kumi (Jap.)   group of 20–30 prisoners

totok (Ind.)   pure Dutchman

TNI (Ind.)   Tentara National Indonesia (Indonesian Army)

APPENDIX III

MORTALITY STATISTICS OF CIVILIAN INTERNEES

The civilian internees were, on the whole, better treated by the Japanese than were the POWs. Civilians were interned because the Japanese were determined to wipe out all Western colonial influences. They felt threatened by the "enemy" Westerners walking about freely with antagonistic attitudes toward the occupying forces.

In total there were some 358 civilian internment centers scattered throughout the Dutch East Indies. A breakdown by islands follows.

Sumatra

Of the 93 camps that were at one time or another used, set up, established, or built in Sumatra, only nine camps existed at the time of liberation. At no time were civilian internees subjected to massive overseas transports, except the short-distance ones from Sumatra to Bangka. The mortality statistics are as follows:

Interned (by category)	Interned (by nationality)	Died
4,000 men	12,000 Dutch	1,100 Dutch
4,500 women	700 British	190 British
4,700 children	10 Americans	–
–	500 others	10 others
13,200 persons	13,210 persons	1,300 persons (appr. 10%)

The statistics in this appendix are adapted from Van Waterford, Prisoners of the Japanese in World War II: Statistical History, Personal Narratives and Memorials Concerning POWs in Camps and on Hellships, Civilian Internees, Asian Slave Laborers and Others Captured in the Pacific Theater *(Jefferson, N.C.: McFarland, 1994) and used by permission.*

Java

Java has always been the most densely populated island of the Indonesian archipelago, with regard to both the indigenous population and the Dutch people. With such a large number of civilians to intern—hundreds of thousands of Dutch and Eurasians—the Japanese faced a formidable task. By excluding most Eurasians from internment, the Japanese somewhat reduced the logistical problems of finding appropriate camps or housing.

Of the 114 camps that the Japanese established, set up, had built, or used in Java, only 30 remained at the time of liberation, August–October 1945. The mortality statistics are as follows:

Interned (by category)	Interned (by nationality)	Died
29,000 men	80,000 Dutch	–
25,000 women	700 British	–
29,000 children	100 Americans	–
–	1,800 others	–
83,000 persons (appr.)	82,600 persons	appr. 11,000 (13.2%)

Kalimantan

Of the 21 camps established on Kalimantan (formerly Borneo) at one time or another, only 3 were operative at the time of liberation. The mortality statistics are as follows:

Interned (by category)	Interned (by nationality)	Died
329 men	500 Dutch	–
330 women	225 British	–
120 children	10 Americans	–
–	35 others	–
779 persons	770 persons	60 (7.8%)

Except on the large islands of Sulawesi and Irian Jaya, by the end of 1942, there were virtually no "white" Allied civilians on the islands in the eastern part of the Dutch archipelago. All civilians were moved as quickly as possible to either Sulawesi or Java. The movement of these civilians from the smaller islands to the larger ones constituted the only massive overseas transport of civilian internees.

Sulawesi

Interned (by category)	Interned (by nationality)	Died
815 men	2,625 Dutch	–
1,120 women	240 others	–
935 children	– –	
2,870 persons	2,865 persons	182 (6.3%)

The Moluccas

Camp	Pop.	Died on islands	Died during transport	Total death	%
Amahei	1,012	47	247	294	29.0
Haruku	2,070	382			
Liang	1,037	125	1,331	1,838	59.1
Total	4,119	554	1,578	2,132	51.8

All other islands

On all other small islands, including those of the South Pacific, Bismarck Archipelago and Australian New Guinea, approximately 4,400 men, women and children were interned. Of that total, approximately 1,020 or 23.2 percent died or were killed. This was the highest percentage of any civilian internments.

APPENDIX IV
NEW VERSUS OLD INDONESIAN PLACENAMES

Spellings used in this book are the most accepted current forms. This appendix, showing current name or spelling in the left column and World War II–era form in the right, is provided as a reference to the name and spelling changes that have occurred since the time of the events described in the narratives.

Ancol	Antjol	Gresik	Griesse
Atambua	Aramboea	Gunungbohong	Goenoeng Bohong
Aceh	Atjeh	Indramayu	Indramajoe
Bangka	Banka	Irian Jaya	New Guinea
Banjubiru	Banjoe Biroe	Jambi	Djambi
Banjumas	Banjoemas	Jatinegara	Meester Cornelis,
Banten	Bantam		Djatinegara
Belitung	Billiton	Jombang	Djombang
Bendul	Bendoel	Jurnatan Prison	Djoernatan Prison
Benkulu	Benkoelen	Kalijajti	Kalidjati
Bogor	Buitenzorg	Kalimantan	Borneo
Buru	Boeroe	Kedungbadak	Kedoeng Badak
Candi	Tjandi	Keputran	Kepoetran
Cepu	Tjepoe	Kudus	Koedoes
Ciater Pass	Tjiater Pass	Lubuklinggau	Loeboek-Linggau
Cicalengka	Tjitjalengka	Madiun	Madioen
Cikadapateuh	Tjikadapateuh	Maguwo	Magoewo
Cikampek	Tjikampek	Makasura	Makasoera
Cilacap	Tjilatjap	Megamendung	Megamendoeng
Cilincing	Tjilintjing	Mentok	Muntok
Cimahi	Tjimahi	Mojokerto	Modjokerto
Cirebon	Cheribon	Mt. Muria	Mt. Moeria
Citarum	Tjitarum	Muntilan	Moentilan
Garut	Garoet	Pacet	Patjet

Pakanbaru	Pakan Baroe	Sukamiskin	Soekamiskin
Pangkalan-	Pangkalan	Sulawesi	Celebes
berandan	Bradan	Sumawono	Soemawono
Pangkalansusu	Pangkalan	Sungaigerong	Soengai Gerong
	Soesoe	Surabaya	Soerabaja
Pasuruan	Pasoeroean	Surakarta (Solo)	Soerakarta
Plaju	Pladjoe	Tambun	Tamboen
Pulusambu	Poeloe Samboe	Tanjung Oost	Tandjoeng Oost
Purwakarta	Poerwakarta	Tanjungpagar	Tandjong Pagar
Purwokerto	Poewokerto	Tanjungpriok	Tandjoeng Periuk
Purworedjo	Poerworedjo	Tasikmalaya	Tasikmalaja
Priangan	Preanger	Telukbayur	Emmahaven
Rawahseneng	Rawah Seneng	Temangung	Temangoeng
Seram	Ceram	Ujung Padang	Makassar
Serawak	British Borneo	Ungaran	Oengaran
Singkuwang	Singkawang	Yogyakarta	Jogjakarta,
Subang	Soebang	(Yogya)	Djogjakarta,
Sukabumi	Soekaboemi		Djogja

INDEX